Methods of Text and Discourse Analysis

Methods of Text and Discourse Analysis

Stefan Titscher, Michael Meyer, Ruth Wodak
and Eva Vetter

Translated by Bryan Jenner

Los Angeles | London | New Delhi
Singapore | Washington DC

First published 2000
Reprinted 2002, 2003, 2005, 2007, 2012

SAGE Publications Ltd
1 Oliver's Yard
55 City Road
London EC1Y 1SP

SAGE Publications Inc.
2455 Teller Road
Thousand Oaks, California 91320

SAGE Publications India Pvt Ltd
B 1/I 1, Mohan Cooperative Industrial Area
Mathura Road
New Delhi 110 044

SAGE Publications Asia-Pacific Pte Ltd
3 Church Street
#10-04 Samsung Hub
Singapore 049483

British Library Cataloguing in Publication data
A catalogue record for this book is available from the British Library

ISBN 978-0-7619-6482-7
ISBN 978-0-7619-6483-4 (pbk)

Typeset by M Rules
Printed in Great Britain by the MPG Books Group

CONTENTS

ACKNOWLEDGEMENTS

This book could not have been written without the help of many people and institutions. We extend our gratitude to them all.

In particular, we gratefully acknowledge three years of support from the Austrian Science Fund (FWF), who financed our research project 'Diplomacy and Language' (P09577). Without FWF support we could never have developed the ideas embodied in the book since it was in the course of this project, when we had to deal with various and extensive text corpora, that the idea of writing a book on methods of text analysis was born.

We also appreciate the support of the Austrian Federal Ministry of Science and Transport (BMWV) in financing the translation from German into English. This translation was done in a very professional, sensitive and effective way by Bryan Jenner. We gratefully acknowledge the collaboration with him.

The bibliometric investigation was undertaken with the help of Sybille Krausler. We are grateful for the support of the Social Science Information Unit (SOWIS) of the Library at the Vienna University of Economics and Business Administration, and in particular that of Bettina Schmeikal and Georg Fessler.

We appreciate the collaboration with Karl Berger, Thomas Gamperl and Gisela Hagmair. They wrote a German outline on objective hermeneutics which formed the basis of the corresponding chapter (Chapter 14) in this book and also undertook various pieces of analytical work using this method during our research project.

We value the helpful comments of our reviewer Michael Stubbs, which contributed to improving the quality of this book. In Julia Hall at Sage we found a very rare kind of supportive and encouraging publisher, and in Seth Edwards an editor who contributed very positively to the final result.

INTRODUCTION

This book is the result of interdisciplinary collaboration between linguists and sociologists or social scientists from other fields. It developed during the course of a research project on the theme of 'Language and Diplomacy' which was supported by the Austrian Science Fund (FWF). The factual results of this research undertaking are being published separately in individual studies. In retrospect it seems fairly typical of sociologically oriented text analysis that, in a project dedicated to the problem of expressing and conceptualizing on the linguistic level the approach of a professional group, a considerable part of the work was purely methodological in character. The territory is confusing, there is little agreement about its boundaries, and not all of the signposts are reliable. Survey maps of the area are unobtainable. For those who want to find a way through, little help is on hand. We endeavour here to provide an overview and hope that study of this orientation guide will not prevent the accumulation of personal experience.

The present publication is a methodological work: it presents methods of text analysis, describes their theoretical bases, and attempts to compare and contrast a total of 12 different methods in this field. We have restricted ourselves, in the main, to a critical presentation of methods and have avoided detailed examples of applications for the following reasons: (a) this book is primarily directed at students of the social sciences and intends to offer them material which provides a survey of the various (possible and practised) methods in the field of text analysis; (b) in our opinion, sample applications would require a more comprehensive description of practical procedures than is currently available; and finally, (c) there is a banal argument that a comparison of methods must presuppose that practical procedures can be so precisely described as to be replicable. This would require very detailed presentations with concrete examples. If we were to present all the selected methods in this way it would become a burden rather than an aid to the reader.

We hope that this book will provide a starting point for theoretically supported research into modes of procedure in empirical text analysis.

Interdisciplinary work can be profitable: it is also demanding. One possible effect for readers is that both linguists and sociologists, or other social scientists, seem to be constantly embroiled in matters that are self-evident to them but which sound alien to specialists from other disciplines. For this reason we assume that this book will be used selectively rather than read as a continuous integrated text. To facilitate such selective reading the following general guide-lines may be of use.

In Part 1 we present the foundations of our work. After giving an overview of social-scientific methods of text analysis, we deal with the question of what is to be understood by the term 'text' and how texts are identified: that is, what the possibilities for text selection are.

Part 2 brings together the discussion of 12 methods which have been used for text analysis. This collection provides an overview of both the more common and the less familiar procedures from various branches of the social sciences. The presentation gives readers the opportunity to select what is of interest to them. The annotated reading list in each chapter is provided in order to facilitate a deeper study of the method in question.

In Part 3 we first present the results of a bibliometric investigation, from which it may be seen how widely accepted or prominent the particular methods have become in scientific publications. The concluding section provides a comparison of the 12 methods.

A short Glossary explains a number of technical terms with the intention of making it easier for readers to cross disciplinary borders.

Methods and Texts

PART ONE

Methods and Texts

CHAPTER I

ON SOCIAL-SCIENTIFIC METHODS OF TEXT ANALYSIS

Before we embark on the critical and comparative presentation of individual methods (see Part 2), it seems both necessary and wise to clarify, from an inter-disciplinary viewpoint, certain basic concepts that relate to our theme of methods of text analysis. Even the simple question of what a text is permits no easy answer, but leads us immediately into the highly varied theoretical approaches of text linguistics and discourse analysis where even the concepts of *text* and *discourse* are used in a multiplicity of ways and where they are anchored in very different research traditions. A similar situation is found with the term *method*, and with our understanding of what social scientists actually do when they analyse texts: what procedures, rules and instruments do they use for this task? The two introductory chapters should be seen as a basis for all the expositions that follow; they are intended as an illustration of the interdisciplinary nature of our project.

Methods are not isolated in space, but are either explicitly or implicitly related to theoretical assumptions and structures. Quite often methods are applied without due reflection and without taking account of such theoretical roots. Our map of theories and methods aims to assist in a reflective approach by creating an awareness of the interconnection of traditions and the proximity or distance between the individual methods. It may be seen what theoretical preconditions are associated with the application of a particular method.

The final part of the book is devoted to a bibliometric comparison of methods, and a comparison of the frequencies of citation and reference in various literature databases. We are of course aware that this kind of comparison cannot pass judgement on the quality of a particular method. It merely reflects the extent of its diffusion within the 'scientific community': to what degree a method has gained acceptance, has been adopted and applied. Together with our comparison and the criteria to be discussed, the frequency of citation provides an additional perspective which may also be significant for the selection of a particular method.

1.1 WAYS OF ACCESSING DATA

The term 'method'[1] normally denotes research pathways: from the researcher's own standpoint or from point A (theoretical assumptions), another point B (observation) is reached by choosing a pathway which permits observations and facilitates the collection of experiences. If one proceeds systematically wrong turnings are avoidable. Methodical procedure can, like Ariadne's thread, guarantee the researcher a safe route back. By giving them experience along the way, methodical procedure may also assist those investigators who look over their shoulders and see their starting point differently, even deciding not to go back but to find other more interesting starting points. No matter how the investigative journey may turn out, methodical procedure will make it easier to record findings and to compile reports of experience.

In so-called empirical social research a distinction is made between elicitation and evaluation methods: between ways of collecting data (in the laboratory or by fieldwork) and procedures that have been developed for the analysis of collected data. Methodical procedures for the collection of data organize observation; evaluation methods regulate the transformation of data into information and further restrict the opportunities for inference and interpretation.[2] In the context of some empirical research, fieldwork implies those stages in a task that permit the collection of data *in situ*. In most cases this requires a direct discussion between the researchers and the carriers or representatives of the patterns and structures that are sought or being investigated.

Almost all of the methods that are brought together in this book may be ascribed to the area of social research[3] in so far as their results are obtained from tangible reality and this reality is acknowledged as a test case of their (theoretical) conclusions. None of these methods is a field-research method in the sense of observing actual behaviour of participants in a meeting which one wishes to analyse, since text analyses can begin only after the material has been collected. Although text analyses may precede fieldwork – if for instance answers from interviews are being analysed – they may also take place without this preparatory work, for example if generally accessible texts are being investigated and no special phase of field data collection is required.

The routes to be followed in empirical research will be decided initially by the general research questions – and these are, to a certain extent, determined by the theoretical approach one has decided to follow. If one believes it is vital to investigate attitudes, then questioning will seem more suitable than observation. If concrete non-verbal modes of behaviour are being examined, then observation is indispensable. If one wishes to study behaviour from some period of time in the past, one must make use of texts already elicited or documented in writing. If everyday behaviour is of primary interest, laboratory conditions are excluded. These simple examples should demonstrate that the initial framework is determined by the research questions to the extent that, while certain basic limitations derive from them, on the other hand they help in the selection of economic ways of clarifying the basic research problem. Not every mode of procedure is equally suited to handling every question. Data do not always need to be collected: use can often be made of materials that are already available.

Every piece of research begins with theoretical assumptions: 'The field worker cannot begin to describe any social event without some specification of his scientific theory, i.e. his theory of objects, his model of the actor, or the kind of social order presupposed' (Cicourel 1964: 51).

Using these models the research question can be clarified and from this can be derived a particular 'research strategy'. This term incorporates those decisions that need to be taken when planning a piece of research before the concrete stages of empirical work can be derived.[4]

First, at a fundamental level it depends on what the research aims to discover: (a) does one wish to explore and find explanations for the facts to be investigated; (b) are theoretical concepts or hypotheses to be tested; or (c) is it a matter of finding a description of a particular field or defined population?

Investigative processes (as referred to in (a) above) require **heuristic** or interpretative procedures, and have as their goal the clarification of ideas or concepts (consider the numerous investigations on the theme of 'politeness') and/or the development of theoretical assumptions (such as action-determining structures or historically and socially conditioned patterns of meaning). Such undertakings are often organized in the form of individual case studies. One example of this is the study by Bensman & Gerver (1973), in which deviant behaviour in a production department is investigated and interpreted, on the basis of observer participation, as an important element in the maintenance of the social system. Exploratory studies – in the traditional view[5] – are predominantly for the purpose of preparing research that tests hypotheses. If theoretical assumptions are to be tested (as suggested in point (b) above), then experimental or quasi-experimental research designs are required,[6] that is to say, research instruments which can be used to vary systematically independent variables in order to assess their possible influence on dependent variables (see in this connection Kleining's (1994) suggestions for experiments with texts). For the purpose of description (see point (c) above), it is, on the one hand, typical to use the types of study which in extreme cases may be conducted by counting distinctive features in a sampling and estimating procedure. Examples of this are public opinion surveys and – with reference to linguistic analysis – the assembly and evaluation of a 'Wendekorpus' ('corpus of change') to investigate the lexicon of the German language in the years 1989–90. On the other hand, description may have additional hidden aims and seek to describe the behaviour of actors in particular social fields. Such investigations do not aim to account for quantifiable distributions but rather to document spheres of existence, and sometimes also to go beyond description and explain the rules which determine them.

Secondly, at the level of the connection between the research process and the affected or possible consumers, one must enquire about the form of the contact between investigators and those who will provide the necessary data (responses, documents, etc.). The various possible positions in this respect may be located between the two extremes of greatest possible involvement and total withdrawal of the investigators. Typical of the first approach would be projects that feel obliged to use action-research, while the second approach is seen in non-reactive methods, experimental designs and all standardized procedures.

In connection with this, thirdly, some commitment must be made about the approach of the investigators. If they approach their field of research 'openly', this implies dispensing with standardized instruments or predetermined categories. It also implies a willingness to distance themselves from any prior understanding and thereby to change the mode of procedure in the course of the investigation. In contrast, the epistemological approach would require the setting up and testing of hypotheses, since procedural changes in the course of research can only lead to results that are difficult to verify.[7]

Fourthly and finally, under decisions concerning research strategy, there is the question whether the piece of research should provide a snapshot (generalizable over time) or whether it should investigate changes. The first type is considerably more frequent and implies data collection at a particular point in time or during a particular phase of the investigation. In the second case, the investigator must opt for one of the various types of sequential or 'panel' procedures[8] and either collect data on a number of occasions or analyse material from different periods.

The preliminary decisions outlined here narrow the spectrum of usable procedures but perhaps force a combination of particular modes of research. It may therefore seem necessary – or at least wise – to examine the content of texts first and then to enquire about their effect on recipients. Whatever the case, such questions should always be clarified before a decision is reached about the method which will actually be used in a particular project. An empirical method should be understood as a set of procedural rules which has available a set of principles governing how investigators should gather experiences and how they should organize their observations if they wish to proceed scientifically. Proceeding scientifically, in this respect, is understood as systematic, rule-governed work. Adhering to schematized modes of procedure makes it possible for investigators to remain uninvolved. It enables them to maintain the required distance from the phenomena (action-field, behavioural structures) that are being studied and, again despite appropriate sensitivity towards the field of research, to adopt the role of a neutral (as opposed to partisan) observer. Only in this way can scientists maintain their own 'meaning and relevance structures', which they use first to inform themselves about the object of study and to observe it, and then to interpret and classify.[9]

Among the methods of data collection most frequently used we find questioning, observation[10] or sociometry. The more highly elaborated a method is, the more differentiated are the various procedures with which data collection can be carried out. Distinctions can therefore be made between written/oral, individual/group questioning, participant or non-participant, and overt and covert observation. (Most of these procedures or fieldwork techniques may be applied in more standardized or less standardized variants.) Data for the analysis of group structures can be collected by means of sociometric questioning or with the help of a living sociogram. In objective hermeneutics (see Chapter 14), designated by its creator Oevermann et al. (1979) as a synthetic approach, there are also different procedures (such as sequential and detailed analysis, that is to say interpretative procedures) that can be applied according to the research goal.

Methods are therefore families of related procedures whose relationship is determined by one or more common features: by a common theoretical base (as in the case of objective hermeneutics), by their relationship to the object of study (sociometry is used in the analysis of group relations, content analysis for investigating the contents of communication), by their efficiency and limitations. For instance, observation techniques may also be used to approach non-verbal behaviour, but only behaviour that is currently observable or recorded on film. Questioning can be used to collect data on attitudes and intentions, 'internal' behaviour, or past activities. In many cases the individual methods make use of differently standardized procedures. Through a predetermined structuring of the collection process an attempt is made to minimize the interpersonal influences of those collecting the data: interviewers have predetermined questionnaires, observers have a standardized framework for classifying observations, content analysts use a system of categories to classify textual elements as uniformly as possible. In addition, highly structured modes of data collection have economic advantages in that they simplify the subsequent evaluation procedures. Whether standardized procedures can be used, however, depends to a considerable extent on prior knowledge, on the subject area and on the research goal. Any predetermination of categories presupposes knowledge of events that may possibly occur (for example, textual contents) or of reactions (such as answers to questions). The field of investigation and the subject area (such as daily rituals in spontaneously occurring face-to-face interactions[11]) can render pointless standardized modes of procedure. The development of a framework of answers, observations or categories requires clear theoretical assumptions. For this reason alone exploratory investigations (see above) have little or no structure.

For each of the procedures mentioned there is a range of more or less widely accepted *rules* that researchers are obliged to follow. If they do not follow the rules they may be accused of not operating 'cleanly'. In interviews, for example, the interviewees should not be over-questioned (in content or style of questions), the ordering of the questions should avoid 'halo effects', and so on. In sociometric questioning the questions selected should be positively formulated and not ask for negation, and so on. As a final example, in content analysis procedures the categories should be so clearly defined that different coders can achieve the same results. 'This means that the categories must be specifiable by a body of theory and by a set of **coding** rules which are invariant to the user's interpretation' (Cicourel 1964: 148, emphasis added). In the majority of the procedures described in this book, however, one will look in vain for concrete rules. If these are missing, one might suppose that very reliable results are not to be expected from such procedures, since the reliability (reproducibility or replicability of the findings) will decrease in inverse proportion to the text analyser's freedom of movement.[12]

Quite often there are particular *instruments* that belong to individual methods and their concrete procedures: written questioning is not possible without questionnaires and interviewers need at least guideline questions when they are conducting semi-standardized or unstandardized interviews. The results of observations are recorded in corresponding observational schemata or, in the case of covert participant observation, in subsequent reports. The rules to be followed within the framework of particular methods and procedures are (normally) learned in the context of research assignments during social science education. In universities *research techniques* are learned: that is, how to behave appropriately as an investigator in particular situations, how to construct and use research instruments. In this way, of course, a particular approach is acquired – a set of attitudes and observational frameworks that the training personnel regard as the appropriate research behaviour.

However, in order to implement particular procedures or develop and apply data collection instruments, a corresponding superstructure is needed: some theoretical approach to which researchers feel themselves to be committed and which, together with their common sense, influences their thinking. Using the selected approach, the main preliminary decisions are taken about possible routes that the researcher can, or wants to, follow to arrive at results. Traditional content analysis procedures, therefore, presuppose that the meaning which can be recovered from particular content corresponds to the meanings that the speakers or writers intended in their texts and to those that the receivers hear or read (see Chapter 5). These are preconditional assumptions, since a sender–receiver model is presumed to underlie communication.[13] It is postulated, moreover, that there exists a common set of meanings between participants. Only with these theoretical assumptions, however, can the investigator concentrate exclusively on analysing the manifest level of texts.

Figure 1.1 presents the stages in empirical research described above, from the theoretical approach down to rules or instruments, in the form of a hierarchical sequence.

This representation, of course, gives a simplified picture and in no way corresponds to the practices that regularly have to be employed in normal research. This is indicated by the dotted connecting lines: there are, for instance, research strategies that are not bound to particular methods and have no well-defined procedures, but which provide only concrete rules. As an example of this we

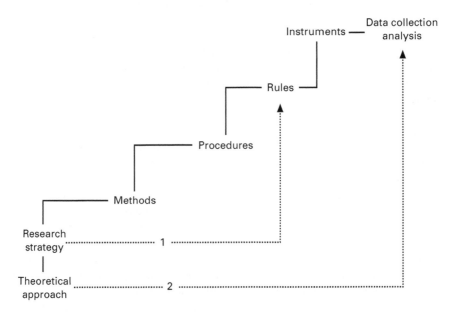

FIGURE 1.1   From the theory to the instruments of empirical research

may cite the coding rules of grounded theory (see Chapter 6). Membership categorization device analysis (cf. Chapter 8, 4.1) may be viewed as a theory-supported research method that pursues a limited set of questions and provides no concrete procedures and only a number of rules. The authors of distinction theory text analysis (presented in Chapter 13 of this book) stress that their approach depends on very precise theoretical assumptions and comprises clear analytical rules. In the different versions of distinction theory text *analysis* common theoretical assumptions can be identified, but the approach has no agreements as to method. Researchers involved in discourse analysis not only proceed in very different ways but even reject any binding methods (see dotted line 2). At the other end of a hypothetical continuum there are very refined instruments whose implementation is strictly rule-governed and procedures that are closely identified with a family of methods, requiring or presupposing a fixed research strategy. This does not mean, however, that they must be bound to a particular theoretical approach. There is no immediate link between questioning and any theoretical construct but at least interpretative approaches, for example, agree in most cases on the exclusion of standardized interviews.

There are, however, some instances where the given hierarchy is adhered to, such as SYMLOG (see Chapter 10). The following are the minimum pre-conditions for a stringent derivation of procedures from some method, the implementation of which may yield theoretically useful results: a limited or limitable set of questions, a fully developed theoretical basis, many years of empirical research in this area, and publication of the modes of procedure and the results, that is, some critical debate.

1.2 FOR WHAT PURPOSE?

A fundamental rule for any scientific work says that the manner in which the results were obtained must be verifiable. This requirement derives, in essence, from the postulate that scientific discovery is not merely self-discovery: research must be generalizable and transparent, and (where possible) capable of being replicated and repeated. The object of science is not experiences of individual events that cannot be shared by others; it aims to make meaningful comparisons and depends upon reproducible experiences. Every idea, discovery, observation or interpretation must therefore be recorded in such a way as to be reconstructable and verifiable by other investigators. The clearer the relationship between the selected theoretical approach, the research strategy, and the methods and procedures employed in a piece of research, the easier it will be for other researchers to reconstruct and even repeat an investigation and the conclusions derived from it. Because scientific investigations always have the intention of questioning knowledge that is thought to be fixed, such projects must themselves be particularly safeguarded.[14]

This last argument, however, may lead to the false assumption that the whole of the elaborate apparatus we sketched above is for the sole purpose of legitimizing or protecting research results. The requirement for a 'clean' procedure may be more thoroughly justified by means of the following four claims.

(a) Every purposeful observation presupposes a *decision about what one wishes to observe*. This assertion immediately distinguishes scientific investigations from chance discoveries. Ideas that someone has in bed, in the bath or on a bicycle[15] may lead to sensible research questions but need to be followed up by some desk-work: reading and thinking that lead to a more concrete formulation and delimitation of the research questions, the setting up of hypotheses, and so on. One may also say quite simply, however, that every observation (including, of course, every scientific observation) requires particular observational frameworks or categories. Scientists become accustomed to these in the course of their education and learn how to look at things and what to concentrate on when they are observing.

(b) A prerequisite of this is that the scientist has *some idea as to why it is sensible to investigate a particular phenomenon*, rather than some other phenomenon or in a different way. This focuses on the motivation for the research: traditionally a distinction is made between a commission, a theoretical interest and a social problem as possible starting points for a research project. But whatever the motivation that leads to a particular undertaking, if it is to be considered scientific, it must be based on previous investigations, must take account of results in this area and build on them, and distinguish itself from previous investigations on the chosen topic. The scientist's own assumptions require a foundation that is derived from previously published studies.

(c) *From this formulation of goals it must be possible to derive what procedures will be used to observe* what one wishes to investigate. Here the question arises what methods are most suitable and/or economical for the particular research question.

(d) The particular *procedure should make it possible to check what one wishes to observe* (that is, compare and distinguish). The decision concerning the procedure to be applied in the empirical investigation presupposes that phases (a) to (c) have been carried out. How else would one know the aspects according to which a text is to be coded, how the questions in an interview should be formulated, or what should be recorded during observation?

A simple example will serve to clarify these four steps: we may wish to examine the value orientations of young people. This decision is taken in step (a). In principle there are two routes that may be followed: questioning or the analysis of representative texts. Under (c) we decide on questioning; for economic reasons (extra-scientific criterion) this will be in written form. Let us assume that, in our example of the investigation of value orientation, we had decided under point (b) to use a concept that defines values as 'ideas of what is socially desirable'. We must now take account of this definition in our questionnaires (which we compile under point (d)). This may be more precisely viewed as an important step in the process of *operationalization*: the translation of the theoretical concept (in Clyde Kluckhohn's definition of values) into concrete modes of procedures. One of the questions that we put to the selected young people could therefore be: 'What division of housework between married couples is desirable, in your opinion?'. We will not consider, for the moment, what the concrete guidelines for responding might look like, neither will we consider under what part of our overall concept the question might be asked. Quite simply, this question is wrong. It is unsuitable because it does not follow the concept adopted under point (b). It asks about the ideas of individuals, not about what is socially desirable.[16] The investigation (or at any rate this question) would not be valid: it would not yield the data that we actually claim to be investigating.

In summary, the following may therefore be claimed:

> In order to be able to make particular observations, particular procedures are needed which, for their part, can only be justified with reference to particular theoretical approaches. Conversely this also means, however, that theoretical approaches whose adherents do not take the trouble to develop not only their own methodology of justification but also a methodology of observation, operationalization and hypothesis-formation, are still rooted in philosophy. They cannot engage in any research that could be of (direct) relevance to individual scientific disciplines. (Kreutz 1988: XXVIf.)

When a method is being selected, therefore, it must also be known what the theoretical research programme is. One must also refer to the method used if it is a matter of establishing whether the theoretical assumptions have been maintained or not and what other assumptions might replace them.

For many people this will appear to be too much like deductive, hypothesis-testing research, which – unlike hypothesis-generating research – it is often claimed yields nothing new. Here we are not speaking of a kind of research that follows a tradition of critical rationalism.[17] We are pleading, rather, for empirical studies to be planned (if one really wishes to undertake them) and, in that sense, to be conducted in an 'orderly' manner, so that explicit assumptions (not necessarily derived from major theories) form the starting point for all data-collection and that they can be transformed into transparent research operations. Innovations arise by combining or modifying elements of already existing theories. If one seeks to make new assumptions (discoveries) on the basis of observations, then that presupposes that there are assumptions.[18]

In general it is true to say that the quality of research results can be no better than the theoretical considerations that underlie the data collection and the methods derived from the theoretical approach. Theories define the framework for methods, methods determine conditions for concrete research operations. Admittedly the selection of a particular method does not determine everything and many decisions that need to be taken in the course of a research project still remain open.[19] For instance, the commitment to particular methods or procedures often fails to deal with a range of important questions: where or from whom should the data be collected and how? (For example, shall we use texts that we obtain in interviews or published self-descriptions? Do we include the news on the notice board and the graffiti in the toilets? Are texts sufficient for our purposes or should we also carry out observations?) Equally unde-cided is the matter of how the data collection is to be organized. (For example, do we generate our texts in group interviews or individual interviews? In what order shall we do the interviews?) The question of how the material is to be stored also remains open. (For example, will audio recordings be sufficient or do we need video recordings? What rules of transcription shall we apply?)

These brief remarks are intended to draw attention to the fact that the selec-tion of a mode of procedure can also lead to changes in the research questions: if one does not make use of videotapes, or if one conducts only text-generating interviews, then statements about non-verbal behaviour are ruled out. A further example would be that if one is investigating communication structures in a hos-pital, one might decide to analyse the linguistic texts that will be produced in interviews. The manner in which the interviewees are found and assembled has certain consequences, since conversations with a number of people only permit statements to be made about group communication if groups really have been interviewed. This consideration, of course, presupposes theoretical assumptions about groups and how they differ from interaction systems (= a number of people distinguished from others by their simultaneous presence). If the main focus is on interviews with teams (for example, nurses, doctors and other hos-pital staff who work together) an additional question can arise about whether, and by means of what communicative strategies, groups mark themselves off from the overall organization. But this requires another interviewing technique, since different questions can or should be put to groups, compared to individu-als who only come together in this formation because of an interview.

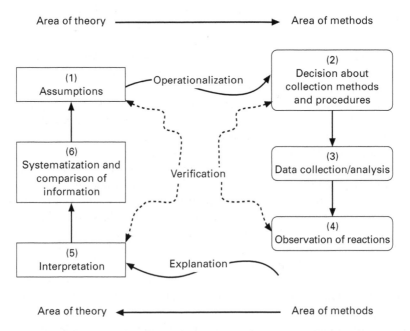

FIGURE 1.2   Theoretical and methodological research operations

In view of these considerations the presentation given above of the relationship between theoretical assumptions, concrete procedures, rules and instruments may be refined as shown in Figure 1.2. This representation follows the schema of Krohn & Küppers (1989: 58). In addition to what has been described so far, to ensure clarity: Hypotheses/assumptions (1) form the basis for any scientific investigation and have to be operationalized. This is done by means of the decision on empirical methods and procedures (2), through which researchers organize their observations and construct their views concerning the object of investigation. The reactive data collection, or (if there is no fieldwork) the analysis, produces effects (3) in those who are being observed and (also in non-reactive collection) in those who appear as investigating observers. These reactions (4) are characterized as data and interpreted (5) in the process of explanation. By means of systematization, categorization and comparison with other results the data become information (6), with the help of which the initial assumptions (1) can be corrected or supported. The interpretation of the data (5) permits verification of the assumptions (1), and these form the framework for the conclusions. The observation of reactions (4) gives indications about the results of the operationalization (2), the methods used, on the other hand, are the criterion for checking the results of the data collection (4).

The relationship between theoretical and methodological research operations sketched in Figure 1.2 should be imagined as a circle that is completed a number of times in the course of an empirical investigation. The following steps are performed: setting up of hypotheses, selection of method of data collection, collection and observation of reactions. Interpretation (5) of the first results (4) of an analysis of texts can lead to the conclusion that the hypotheses (1) need to be refined and that, using the same (or some additional) procedure, a supplementary analysis (3) needs to be carried out. This has implications for the systematization of the conclusions (6) and a reactive effect on the hypotheses (1).

The requirement to view this process as a circle goes against both the idea that research must operate 'from the bottom up', and the postulate that it should operate in the reverse direction – that is, select a one-way route from the theoretical assumptions to the data. It is a matter of moving between these two levels in a targeted way. Only the completeness of this process gives empirical research the right either to claim that it is finding assumptions that have hitherto not been proposed and that they are (under these particular research conditions) empirically appropriate or, alternatively, to question well-tested hypotheses in the light of new results.[20] The steps presented here should only be taken if researchers believe they can approach it without formulating any prior assumptions. (How can we know, in interpreting data, what they are looking at if they had no previous idea about it? How can they be surprised under such circumstances?) From the opposing perspective it might be asked how it is possible to make a discovery or increase one's problem-solving ability if one does not concern oneself with the ability to make connections, and if one does not consider previous studies – at the very latest before publishing one's own empirical work – and distance oneself from them. But at that stage it is already too late.

What, then, is the purpose? 'Methods have no other goal than to bring about a decision between what is true and what is untrue' (Luhmann 1990a: 415).[21] Is the claim true that women, more often than men, attribute their careers to accidents in a proportion which is beyond chance, whereas men attribute their success to their own achievements? This question can be decided if the appropriate investigation corresponds to the conditions outlined above.[22]

Is there a possibility that female investigators in this kind of research who rely, for instance, on the analysis given in published texts, come to different results than male investigators? This can, of course, also be investigated (but only if the studies are comparable, that is reproducible in their methodology).

The use of methods and procedures of empirical social research, however, should not serve the ultimate purpose of avoiding effects of this sort. Methods and procedures guide the observational process and therefore have the function of rendering the investigator's own observations observable: texts may be coded according to the basic rules of grounded theory, and memos are produced that record how each of the categories was arrived at. In a second phase this systematization is checked, which puts the investigator in a position of self-observation and of enquiring how he or she arrived at a particular categorization of certain sentence components. If there are no explicit indications, the ensuing check becomes a study in its own right, since the observational categories that the researcher wishes to use to observe the preceding observation must be developed after the event. Methods permit and 'require a shift of the process of observation to the level of a second order self-observation, to the level of observing one's own observations' (Luhmann 1990a: 413).

There is a shorter version of this: 'Methods are instructions for second order observation, the observation of the observers' (Luhmann 1990a: 579), which may be illustrated with an example. If one wishes to analyse a narrative text, the method of Greimas (see Chapter 9) is available for this. The starting point for this method is that one views the text to be investigated as the product of a narrator who is reporting events. The narrator is therefore a (first order) observer who is observed by other observers (the investigators who are examining the text). These (second order) observers, thanks to the work of Greimas (1983), can rely on concrete instructions, such as 'identify in the text those *actants* who determine the story, i.e. the *subject*, the *object*, the inhibiting power (*traitor*)', and so on.

In terms of the graphic representation given in Figure 1.2 (above), we have opted (in step 2) for Greimas's narrative semiotics; we are applying (step 3) his schema of six actants; and are able (step 4) to observe particular effects, to identify particular roles – in short, to collect data.

This not only sounds very extravagant, it is very extravagant. But science is carried out in order to augment the making of discoveries and to increase the complexity of science. Extravagance is time-consuming. And methods both need and provide time – as Luhmann (1990a) observes: for example, the period of time that is needed to translate and operationalize ideas ('attribution') and the theoretical concepts that lie behind them. In oral questioning, the thread of ideas that has already been developed has – as one of its purposes – the function of gaining the time needed for reflecting on the next question. Learning the underlying theoretical principles of objective hermeneutics and its instructions for concrete application demands time, as does the process of analysis. In the text analysis itself, however, these proposals and rules are helpful and supportive: they provide the framework that is indispensable for distancing oneself from the text.

Researchers can distance themselves, and develop detachment from their own assumptions and modes of procedure by giving themselves a chance for reflection, by taking a short break, by transferring their activities to some other level. The more researchers are involved in a topic, and the more they are (or become) affected by their own project, the more important this distancing becomes. Methods and theories, as has often been stressed, are also anchors that can prevent drifting and smooth the path from prejudice to sound judgement.

Chris Argyris (1995) offers an idea that draws attention to further hidden depths. He makes a distinction between 'espoused theories' and 'theories-in-use'. The former are familiar and can be articulated. They are those theory-components that have to do with content and method that investigators formulate and use in responding to questions about their project. Investigators often pursue the other type of theory ('theory-in-use') quite unconsciously at times when situations become threatening for them: when time is short, when results do not turn out as expected, when subjects do not react in the expected way, when data do not fit together, and so on. Changes creep in – almost unnoticed – in the mode of questioning, procedure, coding or interpretation. What is to be done? Nothing, if it goes unnoticed. How can one reduce the probability that other discrepancies will emerge? Only precise notes about the research process can make it possible to determine deviation or agreement between '(1) explicit or implicit design, (2) theory and methodology and (3) changing positions over time' (Cicourel 1964: 69).[23]

NOTES

1 See the criticism of this use of the term in Kriz & Lisch (1988: 176). These writers find 'model' a more appropriate term, since conventional methods actually depict information structures.

2 This equation of data collection and observation or evaluation and interpretation does not apply if the collection phase takes on a greater degree of significance, as, for example, with open interviews that are not recorded on tape or observations that leave the coders a great deal of freedom of movement.

3 Critical discourse analysis and functional pragmatics are exceptions. We are aware that this claim is by no means accepted by all linguists.

4 Another way of putting it is to call these decisions 'macro-questions'. See also the construction of five research directions given in Reichertz & Schröer (1994: 58f.), according to which, in our opinion, 'most empirical social science research work currently being conducted in Germany' can be classified.

  5 A more recent and comprehensive presentation of social–scientific research methods from the viewpoint of critical rationalism may be found in the manual by Bortz & Döring (1995).

  6 The basic significance of experiments derives from the following quotation from the physicist Ernst Mach (1968: 183): 'Humans collect experiences by observing changes in their environment. The changes that are most interesting and informative for them are, however, those that they may influence by their intervention and voluntary actions. In face of these humans do not need simply to remain passive but can rather adapt them to their needs. They also have the greatest economical, practical and intellectual importance. The value of an experiment is based on this.'

  7 With his description the current distinction between qualitative and quantitative research is formulated differently, since qualitative social research in no way implies dispensing with quantification or statistical analyses (see also Hopf 1979: 14f.).

  8 Sequential and panel investigations are intended to determine changes in the characteristics of the population studied over a defined time-scale. Such longitudinal studies presuppose at least the following: data is collected on three distinct occasions; the situations where data are collected are as similar as possible; and there is a constant set of variables. Panel investigations use the same sample on every occasion.

  9 This aspect is more precisely described in Cicourel (1964: 49ff.). The concepts in quotes refer to the theoretical basis of the ethnomethodologists – the phenomenological sociology of Alfred Schütz. See Chapter 8, Theoretical origins, for further discussion. Cf. also note 21.

 10 The term observation is used in at least three different ways: first – as here – as the designation of a particular method in which current action (social action in particular situations) is systematically observed and analysed. Secondly, the term is equated with methodically informed perception, irrespective of the method within which this is undertaken. (This use of the term opens a door to constructivist perspectives and emphasizes the role of scientists as observers (second order) who observe other observers (interviewees, members of discussion group being studied, etc.).) Thirdly, observation (e.g. Kleining 1994) is used as a characterization for all empirical modes of investigation that are conducted in a non-experimental fashion.

 11 The reader is directed to the works of Goffman: 'My perspective is situational, meaning here a concern for what one individual can be alive to at a particular moment, this often involving a few other particular individuals and not necessarily restricted to the mutually monitored arena of a face-to-face gathering. I assume that when individuals attend to any current situation, they face the question: "What is it that's going on here?"' (Goffman 1974: 8). With this observation, which he then classifies, Goffmann defines his programme of 'frame analysis'. A review of Goffman's method can be found in the article by Willems (1996).

 12 This topic is dealt with under the sub-heading 'Quality criteria' in the presentation of individual methods

 13 This matter is also dealt with under the sub-heading 'Quality criteria' in the presentation of individual methods.

 14 This is particularly true of research programmes that already convey their critical claim in their title, as, for example, in 'critical discourse analysis'. Safeguarding may be attempted by means of an immunization strategy. An

example of this is found in *Objective Hermeneutics*, which Oevermann described as a 'synthetic study' (see Reichertz 1994: 128, for discussion).

15   This is an allusion to the situations, referred to in Anglo-American research, where researchers have their best ideas: the three Bs of Bed, Bathroom, Bicycle.

16   This example is presented in more detail in Maag (1989).

17   This view is even found among ethnographers who, in general, can hardly be accused of obsessive application of method: 'Theory is a guide to practice; no study, ethnographic or otherwise, can be conducted without an underlying theory or model. Whether it is an explicit anthropological theory or an implicit personal model about how things work, the researcher's theoretical approach helps define the problem and how to tackle it' (Fetterman 1989: 15). On the matter of explicit/implicit theories, see note 23.

18   In linguistics the argument is frequently advanced against this view that empirical studies only serve the purpose of using results to illustrate theoretical assumptions. In such cases one cannot speak of empirical research: results have the status of elaborate analogies or inconclusive examples with no heuristic value. Tannen (1986) provides one example among many.

19   Here this approach is quite distinct from ideas from 'qualitative social research' which view methods as follows and quite understandably reject this self-constructed distortion: 'it names all the actions to be undertaken and describes them precisely. Methods are prescriptions for precise actions that can be written down, acquired even by distance-learning, and learned and applied by all adherents' (Reichertz 1994: 127).

20   See also Kelle's (1994: 351ff.) demands of methodology and methods of 'empirically well founded theory construction in qualitative social research', and the discussion of this topic in Meinefeld (1997), who examines Kelle's arguments.

21   In this quotation it should be noted that Luhmann uses the pair of antonyms *true* and *untrue* in a very specific sense, namely as observers' categories.

22   This example is, of course, greatly simplified but is nonetheless representative of questions that yield simple descriptions rather than contributions to theoretical work. The ability to make connections for theoretical work requires, among other things, the consideration of a broader context. In this respect, questions from questionnaire research display a certain similarity to the analysis of 'conversational fragments'.

23   This distinction between espoused theory and theory-in-use may also be used for a further explanation. If theoretical assumptions are rejected as a starting point for empirical research, the investigator is ignoring the distinction and proceeding solely on the basis of his/her own 'theories-in-use'. She or he will then, in all probability, have to present these subsequently as 'espoused theories'. Apart from this scientists have no choice but to distinguish their ideas appropriately, in their cognitive apparatus, from the everyday 'theories-in-use' that they wish to investigate. An attempt is made to achieve the essential distinction by means of theoretical categories and the implementation of methods. At the same time these two types of programme ought to facilitate the required approximation to the everyday categories being investigated.

CHAPTER 2

'What is a text?' This question has occupied text linguistics and discourse analysis since their beginnings,[2] although the two different scientific approaches are currently converging more and more. Both *text* and *discourse* are restricted, in everyday parlance, to written (texts) on the one hand and spoken (discourse) on the other, although this is contested to some extent in the scholarly literature (see Brünner & Graefen 1994a). Apart from this, texts are often considered to be longer pieces of writing. The word evokes the idea of a book, a letter, or a newspaper. The decisive contribution of linguistics in this respect has been to introduce, in the face of such popular opinions, a concept of text that is very broadly and generally accepted and which includes every type of communicative utterance (see below). Clear criteria ultimately decide whether or not something can be viewed as text or discourse (Fairclough 1992a: 3ff.). These criteria are linguistic in nature and relate, most of all, to the syntactic and semantic relations within a text (see sections 2.2 and 2.4 below). A text may equally be an inscription on a tombstone, a form, part of a conversation, or a newspaper article. On the one hand this indicates a very broad concept of communication that regards language and speech as forms of action and derives from Wittgenstein's 'language game' (Wittgenstein 1984: 250, Wodak 1996), while on the other hand it suggests a notion of 'sign', as used in modern semiotics (Kress 1993).[3] The concept of 'semiosis' (meaning-making) relates to any sign (including, for instance, a traffic sign) that according to social conventions is meaningful (Halliday 1978).[4]

In the final analysis, therefore, the answer to our opening question, 'what is a text?', is theory-dependent (see presentation of the individual methods in Part 2) and, as Gruber (1996: 31) claims, in view of its dependency on a particular context and situation, cannot be entirely unambiguous. Let us consider the following poems by Paul Celan (*Einmal*) and Christian Morgenstern (*Fisches Nachtgesang*):

> Einmal,
> Da hörte ich ihn,
> Da wusch er die Welt,
> Ungesehn, nachtlang, wirklich.
> Eins und Unendlich,

Vernichtet,
Ichten.
Licht war. Rettung

Paul Celan (1982) *Atemwende*, Frankfurt: Suhrkamp, 103

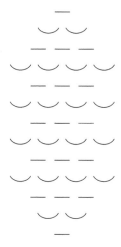

Christian Morgenstern (1975) *Galgenlieder*, Frankfurt: DTV, 27

It is only when we assume that we are dealing with poems that these are accept-able as texts; otherwise one might suppose that we are dealing with a typing exercise, in the case of Morgenstern, or, in the Celan example, with a random sequence of word-fragments.

One of the most widespread definitions of 'text' comes from de Beaugrande & Dressler (1981: 1ff.) They define a text as a 'communicative event' that must satisfy several conditions, namely the seven text criteria that we consider in detail below. According to this definition a traffic sign, a newspaper article, an argument and a novel are all texts that correspond to the differing rules of particular genres or text types. All the genres mentioned have particular lin-guistic features, fulfil particular functions and are bound to specific production and reception situations (Swales 1991). There are, therefore, text-internal as well as text-external conditions of meaning, which leads us ultimately to the dif-ficult question of how the extra-linguistic context may be defined and analysed (see below). The examples of the poems demonstrate that we cannot under-stand these two texts without clear contextual expectations. We bring different expectations, for example, to a political speech than to a news broadcast. The former follows, in part, classical patterns of rhetorical structure (Wodak et al. 1998), while the latter has equally precise conditions of content and form (Lutz & Wodak 1987). These implicit expectations are particularly evident when rules of genre are infringed – as, for example, when a news text is narratively formulated in dialect. Experimental subjects do not accept such texts as official information. They have more trust in news texts that 'sound official', even if they find them perhaps unintelligible (Wodak 1996: 110ff.).

2.2 THE SEVEN TEXT CRITERIA OF DE BEAUGRANDE AND DRESSLER

Here we shall first list the criteria that are invoked by Robert de Beaugrande and Wolfgang Dressler (1981) for the definition of texts. This taxonomy is widely adopted and accepted, and for this reason we wish to use it as the basis for our explanations. Later we shall examine each of the criteria in turn.

Cohesion concerns the components of the textual surface, that is the 'text-syntactic' connectedness. The linear sequence of linguistic elements in a text is in no way accidental, but obeys grammatical rules and dependencies. All the functions that are applied to create relationships between surface elements are categorized as cohesion. In what follows we shall present some of the means by which cohesion is achieved:

- *Recurrence* By means of the repetition of lexical elements, sentence components and other linguistic elements, text structures are formed.

- *Anaphora and Cataphora* Anaphora directs attention to what has previously been said or read (for example, through the use of pro-forms), cataphora points to what is to come through the use of deictic elements.

- *Ellipsis* This element of structure is normally unintelligible without the communicative situation and the shared world knowledge (presuppositions) of participants in a conversation. Textual abbreviations therefore depend particularly on elements of talk-constellations (the reliance on rhetorical devices within text linguistics is no accident since, apart from stylistics, from an historical point of view, rhetoric is one of the most important sources for a supra-sentential grammar).

- *Conjunctions* These signal relations or connections between events and situations. There are conjunctions (linking sentence structures of the same status), disjunctions (linking sentence structures with differing status), contra-junctions (linking sentence structures of the same status that seem to be irreconcilable, such as cause and unexpected effect) and subordinations (used where one sentence structure is dependent on another).

Coherence (or textual semantics) constitutes the meaning of a text. This often refers to elements that do not necessarily also require a linguistic realization. For example, some types of research assume cognitive structures in recipients that are actualized through a text and help to determine interpretations. Similarly, under certain circumstances elements of knowledge that are not expressed in a text may also be implied and may likewise influence reception (see Grice's concept of 'implicature' 1975, Kotthoff 1996, Lutz & Wodak 1987, Kintsch & van Dijk 1983). De Beaugrande & Dressler (1981) suggest that certain 'concepts' (meanings) are bound through 'relationship' and then realized in the textual surface.

For example, causality is a relationship: this affects the manner in which an event or situation may influence other events or situations; in 'Jack fell down and broke his crown' – *fall* is the cause of the event *break*. A text creates no sense in itself but only in connection with knowledge of the world and of the text. This implies that in the process of language acquisition certain ways of structuring both reality and texts also have to be acquired.[5] This already points to the central concept of intertextuality: every text relates both synchronically and diachronically to other texts, and this is the only way it achieves meaning.

Intentionality relates to the attitude and purpose of text producers. What do they want and intend with the text? Accordingly, talking in one's sleep would not count as a text, whereas a telephone directory would.

Acceptability is the mirror of intentionality. A text must be recognized as such by recipients in a particular situation. This criterion is of course related to conventionality, and does not mean that recipients can simply reject a text 'maliciously'. Acceptability therefore concerns the degree to which hearers and readers are prepared to expect a text that is useful or relevant. Here there can be enormous communicative conflicts. Either the text is not acceptable (unintelligible, incoherent, fragmentary, and so on), or hearers may question its acceptability even though the intentionality is clearly expressed. For example, in some narratives a listener may question a tiny detail that is totally irrelevant to the particular conversation.

Informativity refers to the quantity of new or expected information in a text. This addresses simultaneously not only the quantity but also the quality of what is offered: how is the new material structured and using what cohesive means?[6]

Situationality means that the talk-constellation and speech situation play an important role in text production (Wodak et al. 1989: 120). Only particular varieties or types of text, speech styles or forms of address are both situationally and culturally appropriate. This criterion already leads to the concept of 'discourse, since discourse is very generally defined as "text in context"' (see below).

Intertextuality has two types of meaning. On the one hand it suggests that a text always relates to preceding or simultaneously occurring discourse, and on the other hand it also implies that there are formal criteria that link texts to each other in particular genres or text varieties. In the terminology of text-planning such genres would be described as 'schemas' or 'frames' (Wodak 1986):

- Narrative text varieties (tales, stories, etc.) rely on temporal ordering principles.

- Argumentative text varieties (explanations, scientific articles, etc.) use contrastive devices.

- Descriptive text varieties employ predominantly local (that is, spatial or temporal) elements (as in descriptions, portrayals, etc.).

- Instructive text varieties (such as textbooks) are both argumentative and enumerative.

An additional important feature of all definitions of text is expressed in the seven text criteria: the first two criteria (cohesion and coherence) might be defined as text-internal, whereas the remaining criteria are text-external. In this way a first distinction may be made between traditional text linguistics and discourse analysis. In those approaches which are purely 'text linguistic' in orientation the investigation and modelling of cohesion and coherence are predominant, and all the text-external factors, in the sense of intervening variables, are in the background. In discourse analysis, however, it is precisely these external factors that play an essential role, and texts (that is, cohesion and coherence phenomena) are viewed as a manifestation and result of particular combinations of factors.[7] Modern approaches mostly emphasize the functional aspect (Renkema 1993, Dressler 1989).

2.3 LINGUISTIC TEXT ANALYSIS

Unlike de Beaugrande & Dressler (1981), we believe that these criteria concern different textual dimensions and should therefore not be considered to be of equal importance. We propose that cohesion and coherence should be characterized as constitutive of texts, that is to say, every text (or discourse) must satisfy these two criteria, independently of **cotext** and **context** (see below). In this sense *intentionality, informativity, acceptability* and *situationality* are independent of context. We proceed from a complex model of communication that is interactive and dialogic in character, rather than from the sender–hearer type of model used in traditional communication theory (Shannon & Weaver 1949). *Intertextuality* is directly related to this type of complex communication model in its assumption that every text is embedded in a context and is synchronically and diachronically related to many other texts (see Chapter 11). In this way one can, in one's own analysis, take the further step to a critical text or discourse theory: we are not satisfied merely to approach texts according to the linguistic dimensions of cohesion and coherence. On the contrary, we wish to include from the outset the differential relationship to the social, political or other context and to make this the basis of our interpretation.

A linguistic text analysis is therefore defined by its focus on cohesion and coherence, unlike other (sociological) methods of text analysis that select only a few instances of one of these two dimensions. Classical content analysis, therefore, restricts itself to the level of the lexicon (that is, to one dimension of semantics, see Chapter 5); distinction theory text analysis looks for counter-concepts. The focus is therefore on the semantic level. Syntax is used merely to support the selection of units of analysis (sentence **constituents**, see Chapter 13). A linguistic text analysis incorporates syntactic, semantic and pragmatic levels. Most of the sociological methods, on the other hand, are content with only one of these semiotic categories. The particular linguistic theory of grammar that is invoked to connect and specify individual instances of cohesion and coherence is entirely open and theory-dependent (see, for example, the account of functional pragmatics in Chapter 12, as opposed to Fairclough, in Chapter 11, 11.4.1). In what follows, after outlining the concepts of discourse and content, we shall point to a number of developments since de Beaugrande & Dressler (1981), although in the context of this introductory section we shall not be able to present a complete overview.

2.4 SOME REFLECTIONS ON THE TERM 'DISCOURSE'

Lastly, instead of gradually reducing the rather fluctuating meaning of the word 'discourse', I believe that I have in fact added to its meanings: treating it sometimes as the general domain of all statements, sometimes as an individualizable group of statements, and sometimes as a regulated practice that accounts for a certain number of statements; and have I not allowed this same word 'discourse', which should have served as a boundary around the term 'statement', to vary as I shifted my analysis or its point of application, as the statement itself faded from view? (Foucault 1972: 80)

Foucault is not the only one to have been confronted by the many meanings of 'discourse'. The notion of discourse, in both the popular and the philosophical use of the term, integrates a whole palette of different meanings that often seem to be contradictory or mutually exclusive. In this chapter we cannot embark on this multi-layered discussion. Instead we can only highlight a number of central modes of use of the term that are also found in the methods we shall discuss (see in Chapters 8(4.2), 11 and 12; see also van Dijk 1985a, 1985b, 1985c, 1990a, 1990b, Schiffrin 1994, Renkema 1993, Vass 1992). First of all we give a brief etymological sketch of the concept.

'Discourse' may be derived etymologically from the Latin *discurrere* (to run to and fro) or from the nominalization *discursus* ('running apart' in the transferred sense of 'indulging in something', or 'giving information about something') (Vass 1992: 7). Medieval Latin *discursus*, in addition to conversation, animated debate, and talkativeness, then also meant *orbit* and *traffic* (Vogt 1987b: 16). Thomas Aquinas (1225 or 1227–1274) was the first to use the term in philosophy. For him it meant something like intellectual reasoning. *Discursive*, 'by reasoning', is contrasted with *simplici intuitu*, 'by means of simple intuition'. Discursive means recognition through concepts and thinking in concepts (Eisler 1927: 286). This bi-polarity is also found in Hobbes, Leibniz and Kant who thought that human thought was quite generally discursive (Kant 1974: 109). Maas (1988) goes on to show that in all Western European languages the popular meaning has developed to refer to 'learned discussion' and then to 'dialogue'. Vass (1992: 9) enumerates the following meanings of 'discourse':

1 (general): speech, conversation, discussion;
2 discursive presentation of a train of thought by means of a series of statements;

3 series of statements or utterances, chain of statements;
4 form of a chain of statements/expressions; the manner in which they came about (archaeology): scientific, poetic, religious discourse;
5 rule-governed behaviour that leads to a chain or similarly interrelated system of statements (=forms of knowledge) (medicine, psychology, etc.) (for instance in the work of Michel Foucault);
6 language as something practised; spoken language (e.g. in the work of Paul Ricoeur);
7 language as a totality, the linguistic universe;
8 discussion and questioning of validity criteria with the aim of producing consensus among discourse participants (e.g. in the work of Jürgen Habermas).

Fairclough (1992a: 3ff.) lists several uses of the term, particularly as they occur in modern discourse analysis: 'samples of spoken dialogue, in contrast with written texts', 'spoken and written language', 'situational context of language use', 'interaction between reader/writer and text', 'notion of genre (for example, newspaper discourse)'. Often such different meanings are used without thinking, and it is frequently unclear whether they refer to a small sequence of text or a complete textual variety, or whether they embrace a very abstract phenomenon. We shall therefore attempt to define the concepts of discourse and discourse analysis very precisely in our own exposition.

First, we shall proceed from van Dijk's (1977) definition that sees discourse quite generally as text in context, and as evidence to be described empirically. Van Dijk points to one decisive aspect, namely that discourse should also be understood as action (see above). Apart from this, its self-contained nature and the act of communication are of central importance. This already leads to a fundamentally more difficult and complex question: how can we set about defining a discourse unit? Where does it begin and end? Is there any relationship between method and unit of investigation? Let us observe that, because of intertextuality, there can in principle be no objective beginning and no clear end, since every discourse is bound up with many others and can only be understood on the basis of others. The determination of the unit of investigation therefore depends on a subjective decision of the investigator and on the research questions that govern the investigation (Kress 1993).

In what follows we wish to emphasize above all else the action aspect. We therefore propose the following definition as a basis for subsequent development (Fairclough & Wodak 1997):

> Critical Discourse Analysis sees discourse – language in use in speech and writing – as a form of 'social practice'. Describing discourse as social practice implies a dialectical relationship between a particular discursive event and situation(s), institution(s) and social structure(s) which frame it: the discursive event is shaped by them, but it also shapes them. That is, discourse is socially constituted, as well as socially conditioned – it constitutes situations, objects of knowledge, and the social identities of and relationships between people and groups of people. It is constitutive both in the sense that it helps sustain and reproduce the social status quo, and in the sense that it contributes to transforming it (Wodak 1996: 15).

The idea of discourse as constitutive of reality is emphasized here. In addition it emerges clearly that questions of power and ideology are closely related to discourse: 'Since discourse is so socially consequential, it gives rise to important issues of power. Discursive practices may have major ideological effects – that is, they can help produce and reproduce unequal power relations . . . through the ways in which they represent things and position people' (ibid.). This introduces the notion of discourse used in critical discourse analysis (CDA) (see Chapter 11).

2.5 CONTEXT

Discourses occur, on the one hand, in macro-contexts, in organizations and institutions ('medical discourse' [Foucault 1993]), but on the other hand they occur at a particular time, in a particular place, with particular participants, and so on (that is, micro-context) (Wodak 1996). Therefore the complete individual discourse must be seen in the macro-context in order to capture the specific meaning of a particular textual or discourse sequence (Lalouschek et al. 1990). In addition there are patterns specific to particular textual varieties, since a political speech, for instance, follows rules that are different from those of a TV talk show or a biographical interview. These genre-specific elements must also be taken into consideration (Wodak et al. 1994: 36ff.). Socioculturally acquired values and norms, as well as psychic predispositions, are in a changing relationship with the process-governed, social production of discourse and can or must be included in the analysis. The inclusion of these factors that influence text production and comprehension goes beyond the limits of traditional investigations that are based on the analysis of content (Matouschek & Wodak 1995/6: 46ff.).[8]

Aaron Cicourel (1992: 295) distinguishes between two types of context: a *broad* and a *local* context. In this way he attempts to bring together the otherwise mutually exclusive starting-points of the ethnographic approach and conversation analysis, where the latter believes that the context is constantly being recreated exclusively through the discourse (Drew & Heritage 1992: 16ff., see Chapter 8). Conversation analysis is closely related to Gumperz's idea of 'contextualization cues' (Gumperz 1982: 162): 'any aspect of linguistic behavior – lexical, prosodic, phonological, and syntactic choices together with the use of particular codes, dialects or styles – may function as such, indicating those aspects of context which are relevant in interpreting what a speaker means'. There is some affinity between this concept and Goffman's 'frame' concept (Goffman 1974, 1981). In this sense the idea of 'frame' means the respective definitions of situation and action that individuals attribute to their communicative actions. This incorporates the subjective experience of individuals. We relate Cicourel's notion of the 'broad context' to the macro-level, and the 'local context' to the micro-level. The goal of sociological investigations is to bring together these two dimensions in all their complexity.

In specific analyses one can pursue the so-called 'discourse-sociolinguistic approach' (see Chapter 11). One the one hand a considerable amount of information is acquired through an ethnographic perspective, and on the other hand the discourse marks particular cases where the context is relevant. There remains a final problem, however: how can one decide how much contextual knowledge is necessary? Where does a context begin and end? This question becomes particularly acute in the analysis of allusions, where it is vital to include the world of the discourse and intterextuality as factors. Here we would associate ourselves with Cicourel, who says:

> A nagging issue undoubtedly remains for many readers is the familiar one that an infinite regress can occur whereby the observer presumably must describe 'everything' about a context. Such a demand is of course impossible to satisfy because no one could claim to have specified all of the local and larger sociocultural aspects of a context. Observers or analysts, like participants in speech events, must continually face practical circumstances that are an integral part of research of everyday living. (1992: 309)

Finally, the aspects of context that are to be included and excluded must be precisely argued and justified within the concrete analysis of a particular case. And these decisions should take into consideration the theoretical questions posed by the analysis.

2.6 FURTHER DISCUSSIONS ON THE CONCEPTS OF TEXT AND DISCOURSE

De Beaugrande & Dressler (1981) maintain that in the concrete case of a specific text all seven criteria must always apply (see above) if we are to be able to speak of a 'text'. This raises a number of problems because – as Renkema (1993) observes – criteria 3, 4 and 5 (that is, intentionality, acceptability, and informativity) are subjective and dependent on the particular observers. The sequence 'Shakespeare wrote more than 20 plays. Will you have dinner with me tonight?' (Renkema 1993: 36) is probably a 'non-text' for most recipients but might, in a particular situation, be totally acceptable (for instance, if someone has wagered a dinner on the basis that he or she knows roughly how many plays Shakespeare wrote). A consequence of this is that the criteria of de Beaugrande & Dressler (1981) do not admit of predictable and objectivizable distinctions between texts that can be determined in advance. In addition any utterance could ultimately be judged to be a text in a particular context.

Here expectations about genre must also be considered. Renkema (1993) does not deal with these but in Fairclough (1995a), for example, they do indeed play a role as 'orders of discourse'. A particular sequence of signs may therefore be entirely acceptable as a poem even if default expectations (that is, common sense) are infringed.

Van Dijk (1980: 41) sets up a definition of text similar to that of de

Beaugrande & Dressler (1981) which proceeds from the idea that 'only those sequences of sentences which have a macro-structure . . . can be designated as texts'. In simple terms, van Dijk understands 'macro-structure' as an underlying thematic and propositional framework that enables the text to hang together. Van Dijk goes on to introduce many limiting factors (basically similar to those of de Beaugrande & Dressler) which again permit any sequence of sentences, in particular cases, to be characterized as a text.

These problems are avoided in Halliday's purely functional definition of text (Halliday 1978). This assumes that social interaction should be seen as a central unit of investigation. In this way Halliday comes close to the 'critical text analysis' explained above. His approach is linguistically characterized by texts, by the speech situation and the linguistic system – that is to say, by factors that are inseparably bound up with one another. Therefore there can be no 'non-texts' in the sense of Beaugrande & Dressler. Halliday stresses 'the essential indeterminacy of the concept of a "text"'(1978: 136). A text, for him, is everything that is meaningful in a particular situation: 'By text, then, we understand a continuous process of semantic choice' (1978: 137) (see the concept of *semiosis*).

A further important sub-set of 'pure' text-linguistic approaches are the cognitive theories of text that have developed from (and partly as a contradiction of) the model of Kintsch & van Dijk (1983) since the late 1970s. In these, texts are viewed as more or less explicit epi-phenomena of cognitive processes (for example, the pursuance of the principles of causality). Context plays a subordinate role. Text analyses based on these cognitive theories of text also operate in a strictly experimental manner. Many of the models (with the exception of that of Kintsch & van Dijk 1983) can only be used for a very narrow set of specific textual varieties, namely reports and stories.

1 We are grateful to Helmut Gruber for some important suggestions in this chapter.

2 Cf. de Beaugrande (1996), van Dijk (1985a, 1985b, 1990a, 1990b), Wodak et al. (1989: 115ff.), Renkema (1993: 36ff.), Brünner & Graefen (1994a: 2), Wodak (1996: 12ff.), Jäger (1993: 138ff.), Shi-xu (1996: 12ff.). Text linguistics and discourse analysis have, in the course of their development, pursued very different goals: text linguistics concerned itself with the isolated text, while discourse analysis has dealt with the text in a context. Latterly, however, the two disciplines have converged more and more, and a clear distinction is often missing. However, many of the authors listed continue to make a clear distinction between text and discourse, as we shall show. This is particularly marked when the notion of discourse is related to the theoretical basis of Michel Foucault (Wodak 1996: 24ff., Jäger 1993: 172ff., Pennycook 1994, Fairclough 1992a: 56ff.) and implies a social construction. In empirical analysis, on the other hand, the two concepts are often used synonymously (cf. Vass 1992).

3 Jäger (1993) refers to Leontjew's speech activity theory that emphasizes a dimension of knowledge in addition to the action aspect. Ultimately the Wittgenstein tradition, that led to critical theory and to Habermas's notion of communication (cf. Wodak 1996: 28ff., Vass 1992), and the Soviet approach, come from different sources: the former from philosophy, the latter from psychology. Both stress the fundamental function of the (speech-)action and speaking as an activity or way of life.

4 Lemke (1995) and Kress & van Leeuwen (1996) give an excellent summary of the different approaches in modern semiotics that derive ultimately from C. Morris and Ch. S. Peirce. In the current context we shall have to dispense with further elaboration.

5 Textual and world knowledge have been modelled in a variety of ways. Some approaches simply relegate these to 'context', while others seek to construct models that do take account of elements of context (van Dijk 1977, Wodak 1996, Jäger 1993, Shi-xu 1996: 17ff.). The socio-psychological theories of text planning and textual comprehension (see Part 2, Chapter 11) seek to exemplify how, on the basis of empirical results, cognitive planning processes are decided upon and an operationalization of contextual factors is attempted (Wodak 1986, Lutz & Wodak 1987).

6 On this point cf. especially Sperber & Wilson 1986, Grice 1975, Kotthoff 1996.

7 Cf. the definitions of text and discourse used in functional pragmatics (Chapter 12), and in critical discourse analysis (Chapter 11).

8 Matouschek & Wodak (1995/6: 46ff.) stress, on the one hand, the difference from Content Analysis and, on the other hand, the similarity to Grounded Theory. Cf. also Kromrey's (1994: 170ff.) remarks.

CHAPTER 3

HOW TO OBTAIN MATERIAL FOR ANALYSIS – AN OVERVIEW

Those who wish to carry out empirical research must put four questions to themselves:

(a)   What research question am I trying to answer?
(b)   What analysis will provide a useful response to the question?
(c)   To conduct this analysis what data do I need and from whom?
(d)   What are the practical steps to obtain and record these data?

This inventory (from Burgoyne 1994: 195) may be used for purposes of orientation and organization in this chapter, which is concerned with suggestions as to how the third question may be answered. When the research question has been formulated and the research strategy established, it remains an open question as to how to obtain the material one wishes to analyse. In the first place researchers should have clearly in their minds the function of the text (corpus) in the context of the investigation, and the decisions about selection that have to be made. These factors relate directly to the question of what a text is and will be dealt with in 3.1 (below). The second section of this chapter (3.2) offers a compressed overview of the different techniques available for the selection of material for analysis. The fourth of the questions given above is presented and discussed in Part 2 of this book in relation to the individual methods and procedures.

3.1 WHAT DECISIONS HAVE TO BE MADE?

If one has more than a single text which one wishes to analyse for content, text-syntactic interconnectedness (cohesion), construction of meaning (coherence) and function, then the starting point is the same for all researchers. They are confronted with the question of what texts they should collect and which, of those collected, they should analyse. One relies then either (a) on the texts generated by the researcher to answer the research question, (b) on the collected material, or (c) on a combination of both. In the first case we are concerned with a reactive research design and in the second with a non-reactive procedure.

Investigations that are so arranged that the researcher, through his or her collection technique, excludes all influence on the data collected are still comparatively rare in the social sciences. Typical examples would be investigations that obtain their material from official statistics, secondary analyses or studies that use already available texts, rather than those collected for research purposes. Examples of the latter are published texts (newspaper articles, television broadcasts, and so on) or internal papers such as documents from organizations.[1] Even rarer are investigations in which the advantages of both procedures are combined together in a targeted way. This rarity is only understandable because of the demands involved, since the advantages are clear if material not influenced by the researcher is compared with data that arose in response to targeted questions.

The decision whether one should investigate texts stimulated by the researcher or pre-existing texts (or a combination of both types) is rarely the first decision to be taken. On the contrary, it depends quite essentially on the status of the research material. This means that the question of how texts are to be selected is first determined by whether the texts stand alone in the investigation or whether they represent something, and are seen as an expression of or for this.

Figure 3.1 distinguishes three fundamentally different functions that texts may have as research material. This differentiation refers to the different functions texts can have in the selection process: (1) Texts may themselves be the object of research. Such is the case when, from the researcher's viewpoint, there is nothing else 'behind' the text, that is, when the features of the text itself are of interest to the research; (2.1) Texts may be approached as utterances, as manifest components of communication, in order to be able to make some statement about the selected groups of people who produced the text. In this case the selected texts serve as an index in the analysis of phenomena for which individuals are seen as feature-bearers; (2.2) Texts may be approached as a manifest reflection of communication and constitute an aid or an indicator to make it possible to analyse the communication (or communicative situation) that is documented in this form. Each of these approaches depends on a different research question and requires quite different modes of text selection.

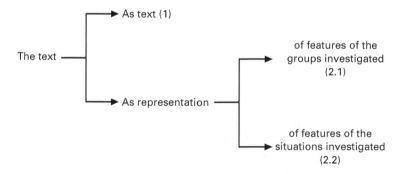

FIGURE 3.1   Functions of text material

The first type of material is the concern of all investigations that seek to draw conclusions exclusively about the texts themselves (see function 1) and that make no link to the extralinguistic reality.[2] Examples of this are found in investigations of the statistical structure of texts, immediate constituent analyses or descriptive grammatical studies. Here the samples that are selected for research are texts. In all such investigations the object of study has been relatively clearly defined. If the study is not restricted to a single text then a sample must be taken from the universe of available texts and the population can be relatively easily determined according to the research question. Since in these studies neither the situational context nor the text-generating actors are systematically considered, they do not belong in the field of social research. In what follows, therefore, we shall give no further attention to this branch of text analysis.

If texts are investigated as utterances of particular groups of people (as in 2.1), the selection must of course begin with the groups concerned – as data-collection units. The analysis of spoken (and transcribed) or written communicative extracts serves the purpose of investigating what has been formulated in the research question. If, for example, the researcher is interested in investigating the attribution style of diplomats – and examining it with a comparative group (such as television foreign correspondents) – a selection of diplomats (and foreign correspondents) must first be made. Then situations must be found where the question can be investigated and to which the researcher has access. This short sketch of the selection procedure already makes it clear that in studies of this type it is not texts that serve as the primary selection criterion (or collection units). This becomes even clearer in text analyses that are concerned with the evaluation of interviews or responses to open questions. In such cases the selection would have been made in advance by virtue of the choice of interviewee.

The third type (introduced in 2.2) implies that the texts used for analysis do not 'attach' to particular persons who represent something, but rather that the transcribed communication serves as a depiction of some situation or topic area indicated by the research question as an object of study. In this situation, the population must be defined specifically – that area about which the investigation seeks to draw some conclusion. Then a selection of meetings would have to be made, or situations would have to be identified (and a selection made), in which the themes that are the subject of the research are discussed. Now meetings are the units of collection and the recordings are the units of investigation.

Once it has been decided what role the text plays in the study, four further decisions have to be taken in order to arrive at material that can ultimately be analysed:

(a) *From what material do I make the selection?* The first stage in the selection process consists of identifying precisely that set of material from which the selection must be made for the concrete research task out of the basically incalculable set of spoken and written pieces of communication – that is from the universe of possible texts. In social research, however, we have to identify the groups or situations for the investigation of which texts are to be used. In this first stage – to use the language of sampling theory – it is a matter of identifying the population.

(b) *What do I select from this?* If the potential groups or situations have been identified and it has been discovered that these cannot be investigated in their population, there follows a second selection in which the sample is defined or the selection is made according to other criteria. For the definition of units of collection there is a range of possibilities, which will be further discussed below.

(c) *How much of this selection do I analyse?* Once the population has been defined and the selection made, the researchers can now proceed to define the texts for analysis – or to generate them if, for example, they are conducting interviews and transcribing the recordings. This newly created corpus of texts is often too large to be fully assessed. By means of further sampling, therefore, sections or locations within the collected material are selected for assessment. This problem does not arise if appropriate arrangements are made before the material is collected.

(d) *What are my units of analysis?* The smallest units used in the analyses may differ widely: syntagmatic locations, sentences, units of talk, themes or changes of theme, single words, signs and so on. Since in text analysis it is always relevant categories within a text that are analysed, the unit of analysis is that unit which seems, to an observer, to be relevant for the particular text as a unit to be investigated. For this there are three minimum requirements: units of analysis must (a) be theoretically justified, (b) be unambiguously defined, and (c) not overlap. For example, if one is investigating the relationship between 'critical life events' and 'emotional disturbances', not only must both concepts be precisely defined, but it must also be possible to decide for every relevant textual passage whether it is to be allocated to either or neither of the two concepts, and whether it is an indication for one (and for which one) of the theoretical constructs. (For further discussion of the unit of analysis, see Altmann 1996.)

These four decisions have two essential foundations: the chosen theoretical approach and the concrete question that guides the research. This is illustrated by three examples that differ as widely as possible (see Table 3.1). If one relates this framework to the differentiation of textual functions given above, the results are as follows.

Studies I and III are examples of the investigation of situations. Different though they may be, in the selection of their textual material, the authors both proceed from the question concerning which texts might portray the situations or episodes (social change, reports of dreams) they are investigating.

Study II investigates a particular group of people or the modes of behaviour and resistance strategies of a precisely defined group and therefore, as a first step, proceeds to the selection of individuals from this group. Then the decision is taken to conduct interviews, that is, the selected people will be used as text producers. Next the transcripts are scanned for themes, and these are finally analysed. This example (Study II) could, of course, be viewed differently if we

Table 3.1   The four selection decisions

4 selections	Example I	Example II	Example III
(1) From what material do I make the selection?	From newspapers: the *New York Times* and the *Los Angeles Times*	Pregnant women who take cocaine	From the tragedies of Aeschylos, Sophocles and Euripides
(2) What do I select from this?	The title pages for the years 1890 to1989	60 pregnant women who report taking cocaine	All text locations in which an actor describes a dream
(3) How much of this selection do I analyse?	A random sample (stratified multi-stage cluster sample) each of 10 sentences on 10 days of each year	The complete transcribed interviews	In every case the complete textual passage
(4) What are my units of analysis?	Selected words and word classes (e.g. 'ritual words', 'change words')	Themes that occur in the interviews	In every case the complete textual passage
Author:	Danielson & Lasorsa (1997)	Kearny et al. (1995)	Devereux (1976)
Research question:	What great social and political changes in American society are reflected in influential daily newspapers?	What mechanisms are being used by pregnant women to overcome this situation?	Are the dreams written by authors for actors in drama psychologically credible?
Function of the text:	'daily newspaper as a convenient repository of socially relevant symbols' (1997: 114)	Verbal utterances and an index for the use of . . . by . . .	Test of the psychoanalytic interpretability or authenticity of the dream character
Approach:	Content analysis	Grounded theory	Psychoanalytically oriented literary analysis

place the emphasis on the situation investigated and study this as an example of particularly difficult personal circumstances. (This resembles the investigation of the psychological aspects of difficult decisions, if one is studying people who are giving up smoking or who are confronted with the question of whether they should undergo a surgical operation.) The results are then seen as a phenomenon that is capable of generalization. The findings about a particular group in one situation or another are less important: the main factor is the value of the investigation as a contribution to the theoretical explanation of a complex situation. But this leads us on to the topic of case studies which will be discussed below (see 3.2.4).

Figure 3.2 depicts a summary of the decisions that have to be taken in order to proceed from the research question to the units of analysis and to be able to begin work on texts. The logic of this sequence in no way reflects the temporal succession that must be realized in all types of investigation. All of these decisions must, however, be made in the course of an empirical study. The individual 'modes of investigation' are distinguished here according to the viewpoint that governs the selection of the texts that form the material for their investigation.

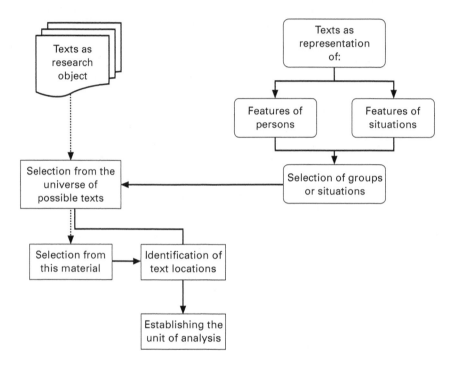

FIGURE 3.2   How does one find analysable material?

3.2 HOW CAN MATERIAL FOR ANALYSIS BE SELECTED?

The purpose of this section is to provide guidance as to how the question about the selection of material may be answered. What procedures are available for making a selection from the universe of possible texts? How can one then make a further selection from this material? What considerations must be borne in mind in identifying the passages for analysis?

To avoid possible disappointments, two restrictions need to be made: (a) the answers to these questions can be given only in a general way since they are closely bound up with the particular research question, and (b) establishing the unit of analysis is not dealt with. This is because that task is always dependent on the (theory-driven) decision about the method or mode of analysis to be used. These questions, therefore, can be handled only with reference to concrete examples or precise presentations of particular methods. We shall therefore compensate for the gaps in this section in the detailed discussion of individual methods in Part 2 of the book.

Figure 3.3 gives an overview of the most common among the different procedures that may be used in social research to select material. Later in this chapter these forms of selection will be outlined, but the individual types of sampling are described only in the Glossary. Here we focus on the significance of the different selection modes for text analyses. Statistical procedures are presented in a number of specialist textbooks, such as that of Sirkin (1995),[3] and sampling procedures are discussed in more detail by Sudman (1976) and Maisel & Persell (1996).

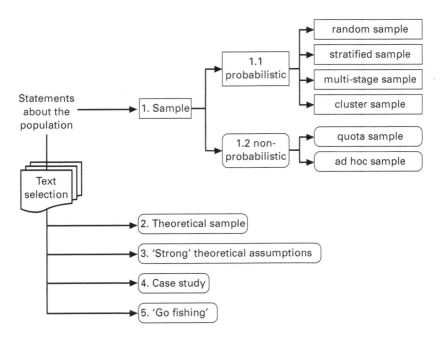

FIGURE 3.3   Modes of procedure in text selection

From Figure 3.3 it is clear that the possible ways of arriving at analysable material may be subdivided into two broad groups. All forms of selection given under **sample** (1) are strategies for collecting material for investigation which can be used to make predictions about a population. By definition they proceed on the basis that the decision about investigating by sample has already been taken. The second group comprises the four remaining procedures (2–5) shown in Figure 3.3. These procedures are denied the possibility of making predictions about the population if this has not been fully investigated. In addition (depending on the epistemological school or tradition), they are denied the chance of testing assumptions and hypotheses.

This distinction is reasonable in so far as it accords with at least two important viewpoints. First, many researchers (and therefore also journals) who rely on 'classical' criteria still assume that generalization can only be achieved through empirical research that is – in terms of sampling theory – watertight. The modes of selection in the first group correspond in essence to these criteria. Second, and apart from this methodological viewpoint, the distinction also draws a line between the functions, given at the beginning of this chapter, that texts may fulfil in social research. If one wishes to make generalized statements about groups (or individuals as bearers of particular features), one cannot avoid investigating a representative sample. If the texts to be investigated are supposed to represent particular situations then the researcher will use one of the other four procedures – and if necessary, the last, which we have called 'go fishing'.

3.2.1 Sample

The six selection procedures we have grouped under this superordinate concept have, at first sight, only one thing in common: they all contain the term 'sample' in their characterization. That is to say, they all require the drawing of samples from a population in order to make predictions about this population and to test the initial hypotheses on the basis of results. As may also be seen in Figure 3.3, these procedures are governed by two different principles.[4] First, under 1.1 we have listed those basic forms that use the principle of randomness:

- random sample;
- stratified sample;
- multi-stage sample;
- cluster sample.

It is a precondition of probability sampling that every element in the population has a known non-zero probability of selection. This condition is the best starting point for the representativity of a study. It is a concern of the probabilistic type of procedure that any subjective bias should be excluded by means of some external criterion, such as random numbers.

Second, the category 2.2 includes two modes of selection where the sampling is non-probabilistic:

- quota sample;
- ad hoc sample.

These non-probabilistic procedures attempt, in various differently accepted ways, to de-subjectivize the control of information selection. As simple selection guidelines they, of course, offer no advice on the matter of how the target population is to be defined.

All these types of sampling are normally associated with so-called 'quantitative' social research. In its strict form this is concerned first with the following basic assumption or justification: hypotheses are predictions that relate to a particular population. In other words, they claim no general validity but have a particular area of validity. Research hypotheses are tested on particular objects of investigation that are representative of the population in question. From this approach three assumptions emerge: (a) hypotheses can only be tested by those investigations that are either designed as censuses or that target a representative sample; (b) the question of how the target population (texts, groups, situations) is to be defined arises from the assumptions that drive the particular research; and (c) it is only possible to make statements about the particular population through controlled sampling (as opposed to arbitrary selection).

If one wishes to make statements about a particular population, data must be collected from all of those cases that relate to the research question. Since researchers rarely have or seek the opportunity to cover a population in its entirety, they must be satisfied with a reduced sub-section. Whether a census is possible depends in the first place on the research question and then on the possibility of access. If one seeks to examine changes in the style of a scholarly journal then one has a limited set (for example, fifteen years' issues of a particular journal) which can indeed be fully investigated. If it is a matter of dealing with typical verbal reactions to an election result that occur in conversations among regulars in a public house in a small village, it is relatively easy to organize this as a census. If one seeks to examine the ways in which doctors talk to patients in the out patients' department of a particular hospital, then one must be careful not to choose untypical times. (This requires particular assumptions, such as during an influenza epidemic the situation is different from that experienced in a normal holiday period.) Both examples – the pub and the hospital – may be used to make statements about the area investigated, for which one has complete data; but they cannot be used to make statements that generalize beyond the particular village or outpatients' department. The researcher will not be able to avoid sampling if, for example, a particular piece of research sets out to analyse the language of creative artists. A further example of an investigation focussing on samples is the analysis of the content of the *New York Times*' and the *Los Angeles Times*' title pages over the past 100 years (Danielson & Lasorsa 1997), which seeks to describe the symbolic representation of social change.[5]

In general it may be said that the more precisely the question is framed from a temporal and thematic point of view, and the more exactly the contents are defined, the easier it will be to make a census – assuming that one has access to the material. Of course generalizability falls with increasing precision. For example, an analysis of the latent sense of a promotional brochure from a particular company will permit conclusions to be drawn about that company (perhaps about its customer relations or its publicly presented self-image), but such a case provides no possibilities for more generalizable research results.

The logic of all sample-oriented investigations has the following features: empirical work begins with *identification of the population*. Which population is relevant is clear from the research question and the assumptions with which one starts. Then, from this population, a *sample* (as a reduced image of the population) is taken for *investigation*. The researchers select particular cases, and each case stands for a multiplicity of others and therefore represents a series of further cases. From the results of the analysis of this sample, *conclusions* are drawn about the population. The desired goal in this is clear: generalization. And this is, according to classical beliefs, only possible with conclusions that are guaranteed by means of probability theory (see 'inference', in Glossary). Such conclusions are only achieved with the modes of selection listed under 1.1 in Figure 3.3, that is probability samples.

In this strict sense all the selection procedures described below are also unscientific if the results based on them are generalized. Investigations conceived in this way yield no statements about populations. Here we are dealing with procedures that may be used for exploratory studies, they serve for hypothesis development or the clarification of concepts. Looked at in another way these modes of investigation are appropriate for ideas or where there is uncertainty. For that reason they are often relegated to the realm of pilot studies. Not all social scientists treat them as pre- or unscientific, apart from the last-named: 'go fishing' (see 3.2.5). How this is assessed depends on the answer given to a central question in this connection: can these procedures yield results that make possible some generalization?

Of course the answer will also depend upon how 'generalization' is defined.[6] In its usual form it is taken to mean *empirical* generalization: a conclusion from observations of a limited set of objects, applicable to the whole class to which the observed objects belong. Here we are dealing with an inductive conclusion that is actually not a conclusion at all but a hypothesis. Apart from this, however, there is also the theoretical or *analytical* generalization. This means that from the results of a study other theoretical assumptions may be made; for example, the findings of an investigation may count as more recent evidence and as an additional enrichment of (theoretical) assumptions that have already been set up, but which were not central to the study. This is one possibility of analytical generalization and it will be illustrated by means of another example: in a study of the linguistic behaviour of diplomats we established that this professional group, when making official statements, gave explanations more rarely than the control group (of foreign correspondents). We initially explained this by means of the assumption that diplomats, by virtue of their profession, are less able to commit themselves. A further analysis then showed that these first findings were not tenable, and that it could be shown that there was no difference between the two professional groups in respect of the frequency of explanations. We did establish, however, that foreign correspondents more frequently invoke persons and personal characteristics as explanations of particular political events. To put this very simply, a hypothesis from social psychological attribution research was again confirmed: the 'general attribution error', according to which external observers tend to attribute events to internal (personal) factors.

3.2.2 Theoretical sampling

This is the name given to a procedure in grounded theory (Glaser & Strauss 1967, Strauss & Corbin 1990) in which, after the analysis of collected cases, it is decided how the data material can be gradually extended.[7] It is a question, therefore, of a deliberate selection that can ensure that categories, topics or concepts considered to be central to the material can be represented sufficiently well (namely, fully or in as much detail) to facilitate the most precise possible analysis. For this, two types of procedure are recommended. First, an attempt is made to collect cases that correspond to the emerging hypotheses and, second, cases are collected that deviate, if possible, from the results so far obtained. In this process one principle of grounded theory is clearly expressed: the removal of the otherwise normal separation of the data-collection and analytical phases. The term 'theoretical sampling' allows one to presume a certain relationship between this type of material selection and traditional forms of sampling. This is not the case however. Since grounded theory seeks to make no statements about a population, it does not come up against the requirement that the material must be a typical sample of some population clearly definable in advance. There are researchers who follow this approach precisely in order to ensure the representativity of the concepts investigated (for example, theoretical terms such as conquest of pain, uncertainty, working routines) and to record the different variants of these concepts.[8] The starting point is the formulation of the research question. This is typically oriented towards a concrete problem (for example, what different organizational measures are there for dealing with drug addicts?) and not towards the search for possible ways of describing some population or the wish to test a hypothesis. From this research question it is decided where the phenomenon can be observed, using what events, what persons and what documents. The central criterion in the selection consists of the greatest possible variation in perspectives, so as to be able to investigate the research question using maximum contrasts or extreme cases. If this causes a narrowing of the field where the investigation is to be conducted, then a start is made with the collection of data which is then (on the basis of immediate analysis) gradually extended.

3.2.3 'Strong' theoretical assumptions

One possible way of steering the selection of material for investigation, without relying on considerations of sampling theory, is provided by 'strong' theoretical assumptions. By this we mean well-founded justifications which guide the selection of material without becoming involved in statistical aspects or questions of representativity. In essence, these modes of selection may occur in two forms: either the researchers determine why selection criteria are unnecessary in principle, or they invoke extra-textual theoretical considerations which they use to guide the selection.

One example of the first variant is provided by Oevermann's approach which is fully dealt with in Chapter 14. 'Objective hermeneutics' seeks to discover latent meaning structures using recordings of interactions. This method is used to analyse structures which have established themselves behind the backs of the actors and which cannot be directly influenced by them. The theoretical assumption is that these structures recur in every detail, that is in every unit of interaction. For this reason there is no need for deliberations about which texts or textual locations should be used in the analysis. An extract is selected at random[9] and the sole condition is that the selected 'scene' should be long enough for a consistent hypothesis about the system under investigation to be derived from it. In practice this could mean, for example, that out of a transcribed interview lasting 90 minutes perhaps eight lines are extracted and analysed.

For the second form of material selection, the reduction by extra-textual theoretical assumptions, we may refer to the 'talkogram' that Titscher and Meyer developed in the context of a study of the language of diplomats. Here we are concerned with a sociometrically oriented procedure (see Moreno 1953) which serves to capture quantitative indicators in the interactions displayed in discursive texts. In addition, as a first step the collected and transcribed episodes (in our case, meetings) are, as it were, 'measured' – that is, the numbers of words for individual speakers and contributions are determined. As a second step, references to persons absent or present, and content references to actual discourse contributions are noted and coded. In this way prominent speakers and contributions to the meetings can then be identified. Finally, on the basis of indicators that measure the density of active and passive references per speaker, 'talkograms' can be drawn for the particular meeting. These show the sociometric status (or 'prominence' of contributions) of individual speakers in the meeting.

The talkogram provides a sensible basis for data selection, particularly when texts are required to serve as a representation of features of the (social interaction) situation. An interaction, it is assumed, is always realized in texts if reference is made to other actors. In this way texts may, for example, concentrate on those textual locations where these kinds of reference are found. Alternatively one may focus on those contributions to which particularly frequent reference is made, since these have apparently shown themselves to be especially 'connectable' and can therefore tell us more about the structure of the interaction system than other contributions. As a further option, however, texts may be selected – on the basis of this quantitative talkogram analysis – for contrastive study. For instance, a study might be made of particularly prominent or non-prominent contributions.

The two examples represent alternative ways of overcoming the problem of reducing an enormous quantity of text to a manageable size for analysis. This is important if the investigator is interested in qualitative types of analysis which cannot be performed by computer programs. For example, with the help of the talkogram we were able, in a substantiated way, to reduce a text quantity of 295 contributions with a total of 81,036 words to 6 contributions and 8,045 words.

The term 'case studies' refers to a research strategy rather than a method. This strategy consists of studying a particular phenomenon using one or more objects of investigation in its real context.[10] Case studies are particularly appropriate if the context is unusually rich or complex. A context may be described as complex if a study has more variables than collection units. An investigator conducting a case study is not bound to a particular method; it is rather more typical that case studies are rarely satisfied with a single method of data collection. An explanation for this is that an attempt to analyse a particular case comprehensively (in its context) almost always needs to involve different levels, and these require different methods of data collection.

Case studies aim to analyse a phenomenon very precisely and every unit of investigation as an entity in itself. They also seek to investigate in a very detailed way – as if under a microscope – the relations between variables, using the case in question. Case studies may be implemented in the exploratory phase to provide insight into the research object. They may be used to test hypotheses or for later reinforcement of quantifying studies.

In case studies the units of investigation are not drawn from a defined population. The selection criterion for cases is their particular typology – their membership of the class of problems that are of interest. In that sense this type of investigation pursues quite different goals from those pursued by a study based on representativity, and is an alternative to the drawing of samples. This is the basis of the objections that are raised about the comparability, representativity and generalizability of the results of such studies.[11]

In contrast to what the term perhaps suggests, case studies are normally very expensive since they seek a complete description, a precise understanding and a full explanation of a complex case. From this characterization it may be seen that case studies may be conceived in very different ways and that the concentration on a single case does not mean that only a single 'object' is investigated. In an extreme case there may be a hundred. Even when a large number of individual cases are included in a study of this sort, each individual case study has the status of an independent investigation.

Every kind of case study, as Yin (1984: 29) claims, must take account of five factors in its design:

- the research question;

- the theoretical assumptions;

- the unit(s) of analysis;

- the logical relation between assumptions and data; and

- the criteria for the interpretation of the results.

Particular importance is attached to the third point (already mentioned in several places): the unit of analysis or the 'case' of the case study. What is to be defined as a unit of analysis depends essentially on the precise formulation of the research question. As a further subordinate criterion it must be added that the choice of the unit of investigation is dependent on existing literature or on other investigations which the researcher wishes to use comparatively. Normally a distinction is made between 'single-case studies' and 'multiple-case studies'. In the following characterization of the two forms of investigation the emphasis is on the single-case study, since in this the particular features of the strategy may more readily be presented.

Single-case studies are carried out if one wishes to describe, document and/or analyse a particular extreme or hitherto uninvestigable case (description); and/or one is attempting to use this case to set up hypotheses (exploration); and/or one wishes to use this single-case study to investigate the explanatory power of competing theories. The questions 'how?' and 'why?' are the most typical initial questions in case studies. It is a matter of approaching or apprehending the investigated object in its population, to understand how it 'works'. Many things can constitute a 'case' – an individual, a group, a class of persons, a family or an organization, a community, a particular event, or a class of events, that represent something particular.

The single-case study is oriented towards maintaining the singularity of the social object investigated (Goode & Hatt 1952).[12] It therefore differs from all procedures in which the single-case becomes an item of data that does not reappear as a unit in the assessment. This is because it is always concerned with describing and elaborating the uniqueness of the complex case of which it is typical.

Single-case studies are subject to a great risk. Since they necessarily require a very intensive involvement of the researchers with their case, researchers may easily become subject to the illusion that they know everything (or more than is necessary) about 'their' research object. This false security is best countered by a painstaking methodology (see Chapter 1, section 1 for discussion) and a very detailed research plan. Here Yin (1993) gives appropriate guidance.

From the four different possible functions of single-case studies we may derive their possible uses (see von Aleman & Ortlieb 1975: 162ff. for discussion):

(a) *Illustration*: quite often one finds in social science publications general claims (that is generalizations) which may be illustrated by material from a single case. Such cases then illustrate what is being claimed, but they cannot prove it.

(b) *Hypothesis development*: this is the principal function normally ascribed to single-case studies. Either this procedure takes on an important role (as exploration) in the preliminary study or else single-case studies already carried out (by others) are subjected to a secondary analysis in order to arrive at one's own research hypothesis.

(c) *Testing of hypotheses*: if one holds the view that even one deviant case is sufficient to refute regularity set up as a social law, then an assumption may be tested by means of a 'deviant case analysis'. One should therefore take a proven hypothesis, look for a case where it should apply, and investigate this in detail. If the assumption does not prove to be true then it is refuted, but if the results of the single case match the hypothesis, it continues to be valid. To be able, in the context of a single-case study, to test a hypothesis that underlies the investigation, random sampling is necessary. In case studies this is not done by sampling a number of objects, but by sampling different episodes (that are necessarily remote in time from each other) within the single case. If the case consists of a single person (as in biographical studies), then different behaviour samples need to be taken: for example reactions on the part of the person investigated to different professional situations. If the case is an organization then the samples to be investigated may consist of different competitive situations and the firm's reaction to these). The precise definition of the samples is of course dependent on the research question that underlies the case study. But it is always necessary to define a 'baseline', to describe a norm, and to be able to distinguish from those situations where the effect of an independent variable can and should be investigated. In the specialist methodological literature there are accounts of experimental designs which have been developed for this purpose. A further example is provided by studies where a special case is extracted from the population studied (perhaps by questionnaire) and investigated in greater detail to check the conclusions that were drawn from the statistical analysis.

(d) *Prediction*: it is rather contentious whether one can derive predictions from a single case. But it is done, for example, in all job interviews and tests: from the previous history of a person decisions are made about behaviour patterns that might be expected in particular situations.

Multiple-case studies refers to a form of investigation in the context of which several case studies are carried out. Every case is in itself a complete study. Such multiple-case studies are not designed to achieve representativity of results by an increase in the number of cases. Researchers who use this kind of design are interested in theoretical rather than statistical generalizations.

On the number of cases involved, in general, it may be said that if two cases are included the investigation becomes a comparison. If many cases are included in the study then it is directed towards the elaboration of a system of classification or it serves as a replication. In replication studies it is possible to make predictions from one case for the next case and either assume a similar outcome or predict different results in the subsequent case(s). From this brief description it is already clear that case studies of this type require a very well-developed theoretical framework.

The case study strategy has been described here rather extensively because in our opinion it constitutes the alternative to strictly sampling-oriented methods of data selection.[13] Whatever the case, and this should be clear from this exposition, case studies are not an undertaking that one can embark on in a carefree manner and one is not liberated from all precise methodological procedures: 'the typical atheoretic statement "Let's collect information about everything" does not work, and the investigator without descriptive theory will soon encounter enormous problems in limiting the scope of the study' (Yin 1993: 21). This requirement differs from the final mode of procedure to be handled here.

The expression 'go fishing' here designates a procedure in which researchers attempt to arrive at their data more or less at random, or at least with no precise plan. This data set is then assessed without answering (or being able to answer) the question of how typical the collected cases are, what they are typical of, or what the spectrum of differences reveal. We have chosen the term 'go fishing' because this form of data collection is comparable to casting a net: if one knows the fishing grounds then one will catch something. When the net is pulled in the catch can be examined. In addition, approaches such as the 'self-selected sample' and the 'convenience or haphazard sample' (Maisel & Persell 1996: 4) can be regarded as 'going fishing'.

The procedure has at least two major disadvantages: unfortunately, in the social sciences, it is not always easy or even possible to distinguish unambiguously between an old boot and an edible fish. Here the statement of Silverman (1993: 82) seems apposite: 'Social life, unlike foreign films, does not come with subtitles attached.' The second objection is that in any case it remains unclear what the data represent.

An example of this procedure is to be found in the approach of Brown & Kreps (1993: 53) where 'organizational stories are collected and subjected to a narrative analysis'. They advise the investigator only 'to gather relevant organizational stories from individuals representing different areas and levels of the organization, as well as from members of the organization's relevant environment'. Where does this lead? 'These stories enable the researcher to identify and examine different problems confronting the organization.' It is uncontested that this procedure may yield interesting results. The only question is whether these results are of interest to the investigator or to the members of the organization, and whether 'interest' is the same as 'relevant to the research'. The difficulties begin with the fact that there are no criteria for the identification of 'relevant' stories, and they end with the fact that it remains unclear which problems of the organization are being addressed here. If one wished to proceed in a precise manner, one ought to take a sample from the organizational stories and analyse that. Here a totally unsystematic selection is made from persons in the organization (as carriers of the stories) and from the 'relevant' environment.

Werner & Bernard (1994) begin their study with the assertion: 'for many cultural anthropologists, the term "ethnographic sampling" is an oxymoron'. At the end they advance four recommendations about what should be borne in mind in this kind of sampling. They arrive at these on the basis of an analysis of which collection of stories underlie the work of Kluckhohn (1944). This study comes under the heading 'go fishing' precisely because the authors arrive at the following assertion about Kluckhohn's choice of interview subjects: 'he interviewed those he could'. It therefore emerges, in the opinion of Werner & Bernard, that the study – informative though it may be – admits of no statistically based generalizations. Furthermore it remains unclear what is to be regarded as typical of the investigated system ('Navajo witchcraft').

Further examples of this kind of 'wild data collection' are provided by investigations where texts are lifted, sampled and then analysed more or less haphazardly from a huge corpus, irrespective of why it was set up. One illustration of this is to be found in Keppler's (1994) conversation analysis study of table talk in families. The report on the database (1994: 33) begins with the claim that 'this investigation is based on a rich corpus of *tape recordings*. In detail, we are concerned in the recordings [. . .] with *table conversations* from families and groups living together with a total duration of more than 100 hours' (italics in original). We are told nothing about the selection of the families: there are no details about the corpus in question (which derived from a different research project). 'This material was partially transcribed in the named project and referred to for the analysis of individual communicative genres' (1994: 34). How the selection came about is not explained. The presentation of the database ends with the statement (1994: 44): 'We cannot explain all of this here sufficiently and exhaustively. Moreover, it is not necessary to do so. For it is [. . .] a matter of using significant examples to arrive at informative interpretations that can be confirmed, differentiated and extended through further examples.' The problem is always the same: if there is a mention of 'significant' examples or 'typical' stories, it is always unclear in this mode of operation how the researcher defined the 'typical' about which the statements are ultimately made. Studies of this kind are exclusively inductive and therefore lead to bold generalizations. And since research must aim at generalization, these investigations cannot restrict themselves to the interpretation of revealing examples but also formulate 'certain hypothetical consequences for the mode of cohesion in modern families' (Keppler 1994: 269).

In what circumstances is it appropriate and reasonable to 'go fishing'? The first condition is that one should be aware that one is casting a net that may be either narrow- or wide-meshed. This implies, to relate this image to Hempel's (1952: 36) claims, that it consists of knots and connecting lines that may be formed by concepts and assumptions. The investigator therefore catches what these concepts are capable of catching. The label 'relevant' (cf. Brown & Kreps 1993, above) is too vague and provides too wide-meshed a net. The second condition for adopting this kind of procedure is that the investigator should be aware of the limited value of the results achieved with this kind of data collection. From this it follows that this form of collection is a reasonable, and perhaps the only possible, way of narrowing a field of investigation in order to make a preliminary study. This can then lead to assumptions which await further testing or lead directly to a follow-up study. In the latter case the researcher proceeds in such a way that material is first collected and assessed with very few prior assumptions. The collection of material is complete when nothing further is discovered, when information on the matters of interest dries up, and when both patterns (or repetitions) and differences (or differing types) begin to appear. Then one has data and interpretations that will facilitate a more detailed investigation. Werner & Bernard (1994) show how important it is to chart the material collection precisely and to document it in the form of tables. Only in this way is it possible for the investigator to gain an overview of the material and communicate it to other researchers, to remain aware of the limits of the study and to retain at least partial control of any subjective bias.

The procedure does have one big advantage: one is spared the development of an elaborate research plan. Of course, this advantage normally catches up with the investigator and, in the course of the analysis, turns into the disadvantage that one does not know how to assess the texts. The question of which assessment procedure or method is suitable, if one has no precise initial questions and no systematically gathered material, can hardly be given a satisfactory or – from the researcher's viewpoint – helpful answer. In the final assessment, what is fitting for this kind of study is the **metaphor** often used for the characterization of statistical investigations: 'a jungle of data, a desert of concepts'.

THEY THINK THEY'VE CRACKED THE GENERALISATION PROBLEM JUST BECAUSE EVERYTHING CAN TURN UP IN A BOWL OF ALPHABET SOUP

NOTES

1 Certain principles for the design of investigations that rely on the analysis of internal documents from organizations are described in Forster (1994). The question of the kind of reality that is displayed in documents is discussed in Atkinson & Coffey (1997).
2 Here the term 'text' is used in a different way from elsewhere in this book.
3 A more detailed treatment would have to consider the more specialized procedures. Here we refer to a single study, which deals with a topic that is important in the present context and that will be discussed below: generalization. The article by Cook (1993) describes 'quasi-sampling' as a way of being able to make causal connections, i.e. to generalize.
4 Brief definitions of the types of sampling listed here are given in the Glossary.
5 This study is shown in Table 3.1.
6 A fuller discussion of this topic is in the article by Firestone (1993).
7 The approach is presented in more detail below (see Part 2, Chapter 2).

8   An example is given in Table 3.1 above, from the study by Kearny et al. 1995.

9   One exception is the investigation of a newly arising interaction system, such as for instance a first contact: 'We are aware, therefore, that in a trivial sense in the analysis of interactions with no previous history, the true beginning – the opening sequence in Schegloff's terms – must also form the beginning of the interaction scene to be analysed' (Oevermann et al. 1979: 434).

10 This cannot be taken for granted since context is by no means included in all research. One need only think of questionnaire studies or laboratory experiments.

11 This research strategy has a long tradition in psychology and sociology. Here are two examples from contemporary social research, which are dealt with in more detail elsewhere in this book: one of the specific characteristics of grounded theory is to proceed from a single case as a discrete unit of investigation. A further example consists of studies within the framework of 'objective hermeneutics', which investigates familiar interaction sequences. From this, Oevermann develops a description and an analysis of the relational structure of a particular family in its 'objective' population, i.e. the structure that exists independently of the motifs and features of individual family members. The use of case studies in a special area of research, organization research, is described in an article by Hartley (1994).

12 This 'entirety' is always an intellectual construct. In the classical study of Goode & Hatt (1952) four criteria are set up with the help of which one may attempt to analyse a case in its entirety: (a) breadth of information (through extensive data and material collection); (b) abstraction (ignore the single-case and analyse links to the environment; (c) set up indices and types (to discover to what class of phenomena the single-case belongs, and what versions of reality it is typical of; (d) record the temporal dimension (single-case studies reveal their significance when they not only make statements fixed in time but when they record and analyse temporal changes).

13 For this reason we must again refer to additional literature: the articles by Tellis (1997a, 1997b) give a good overview. We also suggest Hakim's (1992) book because with the help of these readings case studies may be evaluated in comparison with other research strategies.

CHAPTER 4

___

MAP OF METHODS AND THEORIES

M ethods are in a factual relationship with theories and in a social relationship with scientific networks. They depend on theoretical
foundations, that is to say, on explanatory patterns for a specific field, and
normally develop within the boundaries of a particular discipline. Figure 4.1
provides a general overview of the 12 methods of text analysis which we have
selected and shows the relationship between methods and theories.

Figure 4.1 should be read in the following way:

- The methods of text analysis discussed in this book are in the shaded rec-
tangles.

- The different geometric shapes symbolize theory types of different degrees
of abstraction: (a) philosophical and epistemological approaches (for example, Phenomenology, Hermeneutics, General Semiotics); (b) social theories
(for example, Foucault, Cultural Anthropology, Critical Theory, Field
Theory; (c) linguistic theories (for example, Functional Systemic Linguistics,
Speech Act Theory, Prague School, Structural Linguistics); and (d) communication concepts (for example, von Luhmann, Bühler, Shannon & Weaver).
The allocation of particular approaches to these types was often problematic and in a number of cases could have been done differently.

- The linking arrows between theories and methods indicate that the particular theory is an important reference for the development of the
method, and is often quoted in the literature concerning that method.
The thickness of the arrows or lines is an indicator of the strength of the
bond between theory and method. Unbroken lines indicate the adoption of
theoretical concepts and the absence of distancing from particular parts of
the theory. Lines composed of dashes or dots indicate a weaker relationship, or some distancing from parts of the theory. To take one example:
the line between Speech Act Theory and Hymes's Ethnography of
Communication consists of dashes because Hymes does indeed build on
the notion of the Speech Act (see Hymes 1962: 24, for example), but ultimately he analyses 'Speech Events' and replaces the category 'Speaker's
Intentions' with the 'Ethnographic Context' (ibid.: 21) – that is, with cultural patterns.

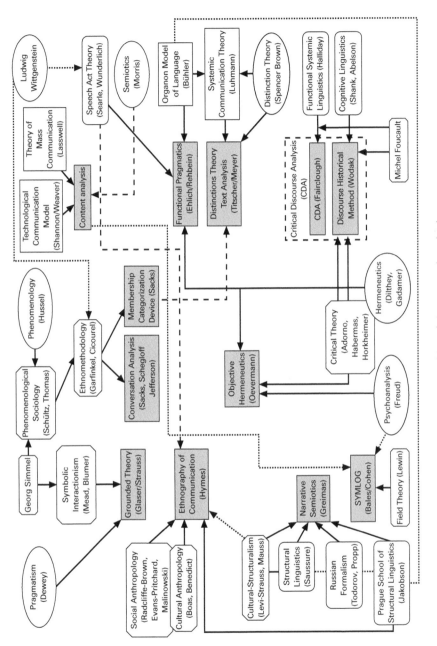

FIGURE 4.1 Map of theories and methods

The overview of relationships between theories and methods of text analysis that is given in Figure 4.1 will not be further developed here, since we shall deal with this more fully in the presentations of the individual methods and their theoretical backgrounds.

Outline of Methods of Text Analysis

PART TWO

Outline of Methods of Text Analysis

CHAPTER 5

CONTENT ANALYSIS

Content analysis is the longest established method of text analysis among the set of empirical methods of social investigation (Holsti 1968, Silbermann 1974, Herkner 1974). It is for the present, however, somewhat difficult to proceed on the basis of a homogeneous understanding of method, in view of the rich and varied literature on 'content analysis'. Originally the term referred only to those methods that concentrate on directly and clearly quantifiable aspects of text content, and as a rule on absolute and relative frequencies of words per text or surface unit. Subsequently the concept was extended to include all those procedures which operate with (syntactic, semantic or pragmatic) categories, but which seek at least to quantify these categories by means of a frequency survey of classifications.

The establishment of 'qualitative content analyses' (Mayring 1988) has made it difficult to separate these from other methods of text analysis, particularly those oriented towards ethnographic methods or grounded theory. It has become clear 'that the range of procedures in content analysis is enormous, in terms of both analytical goals and the means or processes developed to pursue them' (Merten 1983: 46). If one were to accept this interpretation, one could describe as variants of content analysis all those methods of text analysis which somehow approach texts by means of categories, since it is no longer a matter only of the communicative content of texts but also of their (linguistic) form. In content analysis it is, therefore, more a question of a research strategy than of a single method of text analysis. We shall endeavour in what follows to present the fundamentals of classical, quantitative content analysis, and also to give a typology of content analysis procedures in the broader sense, with 'qualitative variants' as a further development.

5.1 THEORETICAL ORIGINS

The development of content analysis has, in essence, been influenced by the development of mass media and by international politics. If one discounts the early work in psychoanalysis (Freud's interpretation of dreams), then content analysis has grown in significance – particularly with the meteoric expansion of mass communication – in the first half of the twentieth century. Berelson

(1952), in his keynote work *Content Analysis in Communication Research*, argues that in the United States between 1921 and 1930 only 10 or 15 content analyses were carried out. The first noteworthy activity – brought about by the rapid development of the press, cinema and radio – was seen in the second half of the 1930s (Silbermann 1974: 254).

The theoretical basis of this first move towards analyses of content was Harold D. Lasswell's model of mass communication: Lasswell's formula 'who says what to whom and with what effect' determined the course of research in modern mass communication. Interest has consequently focussed communicator, receiver and communicative effect, where a clear causal interrelation is assumed. To investigate this interrelation the communicative content had to be quantified as precisely as possible. Lasswell succeeded in establishing the method by emphasizing above all the political value of content analysis. (For work on war propaganda see Smith et al. 1946.)

The development of content analysis was marked quite essentially by three conferences (see Merten 1983: 41ff.). In August 1941 the first conference on interdisciplinary mass communication research took place in Chicago, and – among others – Harold D. Lasswell, Bernhard Berelson and Paul Lazarsfeld took part. During this conference, not only was the term 'content analysis' coined for the new method but Lasswell, in a keynote address, set out the approach and the goals of content analysis: signs and statements are analysed to test their effect on the audience; the results are the frequencies of particular symbols, their intensity and the assessment of the senders. A second conference was organized by Charles E. Osgood at Allerton House (Monticello, Illinois) in 1955, during which qualitative and quantitative approaches were presented. New theories – such as Shannon and Weaver's (1949) 'information theory' – and refined analytical techniques (Osgood's 'contingency analysis' and 'evaluative assertion analysis' [Osgood et al. 1954, Osgood 1959]), together with Bales's (1950) 'Interaction Process Analysis' led to a situation where content analysis was understood as 'communication analysis' and its preoccupation with printed texts gradually diminished. In 1967 a third content analysis conference took place at Annenberg School in Philadelphia and here the scope of the method was discussed. From a theoretical viewpoint, previous analyses were criticized on the grounds that the results of content analysis must remain ambivalent as long as the investigator is not explicit about the selection procedure which is imposed by the context of some content and by the goals of the analysis (Krippendorff 1969: 70f.).

According to Merten (1983: 45) further discussion of content analysis has the following characteristics: the structure and selectivity of communication processes, the development of perceptible indicators and multivariate techniques of analysis, the improvement of systems of notation through inclusion of the non-verbal domain, and the improvement of data analysis through the development of dedicated electronic text analysis packages. 'The long overdue debate with linguistics, whose stock of experience of text classification and text analysis has hitherto been completely ignored by Content Analysis, is only slowly coming into existence' (Merten 1983: 45).

5.2 BASIC THEORETICAL ASSUMPTIONS

In the early days of content analysis research there was unquestionably a simple behaviourist-oriented stimulus-response model of communication which set up an asymmetrical relationship between sender, stimulus and recipient. Content was viewed as the result of a communication process structured in accordance with Lasswell's classic formula: 'Who says what in which channel to whom and with what effect' (Lasswell 1946: 37). 'It is no accident that we are concerned here with a model of mass communication, which views communication as the transportation of a container known as "content", which is transported by a communicator through some medium to a recipient' (Merten 1983: 56ff.).

Morris's (1938, 1946) semiotic works promoted the recognition that communication happens not on the basis of stimuli but on that of the meanings which are attributed to them and which cannot be accessed through the concrete form of a stimulus. Content analysis, on the other hand, was influenced more by the news transmission model of Shannon & Weaver (1949: 7), even though this was explicitly intended only for the syntactic level: an information source ('sender') conveys, via a transmitter, some news as a signal which goes to some receiver and is forwarded to its destination. During transmission there are a range of possible sources of interference. Schramm (1954) adapted this news transmission model as a general communication model and (mis)interpreted the syntactic decoding as semantic decoding of content (Merten 1983: 74). 'This simplification of the attribution of meaning and of the whole process of communication was simply taken over for the purposes of content analysis and may well have contributed significantly to the image of content analysis as an objectivisable mechanism for the analysis of signs' (Merten 1983: 74, with reference to Herkner 1974: 167, and Lisch & Kriz 1978: 32).

5.3 OBJECTIVES OF THE METHOD

The objectives which may be pursued by methods of content analysis may be understood with reference to the following list of quotations, arranged in chronological order:

> In content analysis we look upon statements and signs as raw materials to be summarized in order to bring out either (1) the impact of content upon audience, or (2) the influence of control upon content. (Lasswell 1941, quoted from Lasswell 1946: 90)

> Content Analysis is a research technique for the objective, systematic, and quantitative description of the manifest content of communication. (Berelson 1952: 18)

> Content Analysis is any research technique for making inferences by systematically and objectively identifying specified characteristics of messages. (Holsti 1968: 601)

The classification of symbolic material by scientifically trained observers who should judge, with the assistance of explicit classification and procedural rules, which parts of the textual material fall within the categories of the research schema, and are truly characteristic of the available content analyses. (Ritsert 1972: 17)

5.4 OUTLINE OF THE METHOD

5.4.1 The procedures, instruments and rules of classical Content Analysis

---

5.4.1.1 Sampling

It will be possible in only a very small number of cases to investigate all the material relevant to a particular problem. As an alternative to an ideal total treatment, samples may be used based on the probability method, and under certain circumstances quota samples (cf. Merten 1983: 280ff.). Holsti (1968: 653ff.) recommends a multi-stage process of selection: (a) selection of sender, (b) selection of documents, and (c) selection of a subset of the documents.

5.4.1.2 Units of analysis

The units of analysis are the smallest components of texts in which the occurrence and the characterization of variables (properties, categories) are examined. Since a text does not consist of 'natural units', these have to be defined at the syntactic or semantic level for every concrete investigation (Herkner 1974: 173): (a) syntactically defined units are, for example, sign (word), sentence, complete text, area and time; (b) semantically defined units are, for example, person, statement and unit of meaning.

Holsti (1968: 647f.) distinguishes between recording units and context units: (a) the recording unit is the smallest textual unit within which the occurrence of variables is examined; (b) the context unit is invoked to establish the characterization of variables, such as their positive or negative assessment.

5.4.1.3 Categories and coding

The core and the central tool of any content analysis is its system of categories: every unit of analysis must be coded, that is to say, allocated to one or more categories. Categories are understood as the more or less operational definitions of variables. Any definition of categories should be explicit, complete and adequate (Herkner 1974: 174). In the process of coding it is recommended that every category should also be illustrated with textual examples which are subsequently taken as given and which facilitate the allocation of further textual units. Programmes that relate units of analysis to codes (the so-called 'code-and-retrieve' programmes) can be helpful in this process (Weitzman & Miles 1995: 148ff.).

The system of categories – in contrast to ethnographically or GT-oriented analyses – should be established before coding is undertaken. If it becomes clear during the coding process, however, that a modified system of categories would be preferable – because some categories are missing or ambiguous, or are simply never used – then the entire textual material must be re-coded using the new categories.

In most cases categories are conceived as nominal scales: a unit of analysis either belongs or does not belong to this category. In principle, however, higher levels of scales are possible. The categories of a variable must fulfil the usual requirements: they must be mutually exclusive and complete (Herkner 1974: 175).

The system of categories, therefore, endeavours to operationalize the variables of the particular research question and thereby focuses on the research question or the hypotheses derived from it. Consequently, it is possible to set up both inductive schemata of categories, using some previous text interpretation (for example ethnographic or GT-oriented, cf. Chapters 6 and 7), and deductive schemata deriving from established theories. The desire for integrated systems of categories has often been expressed (see Herkner 1974: 175), but methods which use such standardized tools are not suited to all research questions. For particular areas there are well-established systems of categories, such as:

- for the analysis of interactions, Bales's (1950) interaction process analysis (IPA) and the SYMLOG method (*System for Multiple Level Observation of Groups*) of Bales and Cohen (1979);

- for the analysis of attitudes, the evaluative assertion analysis of Osgood et al. (1954); and

- for the analysis of achievement motivation, the method of McClelland et al. (1953).

Holsti (1968: 645), following Berelson (1952: 147ff.), formulates a list of types of category which may be used as the basis for the design of a system of categories:

- Subject, theme: what is it about?

- Direction: how is the theme dealt with?

- Norms: what is the basis for classification and evaluation?

- Values: what attitudes, goals and wishes are displayed?

- Means: what means are used to achieve the goals?

- Features: what features are used in the description of persons?

- Actors: who initiates particular actions and who carries them out?

- Authority: under what name are statements made?

- Origin: where did the communication come from?

- Goal: to whom is it directed?

- Place: where do the actions take place?

- Conflicts: what is the cause of any conflict? Who are the participants? How strong is the conflict?

- Outcome: is the end of the conflict happy, tragic or uncertain?

- Time: when does the action take place?

- Form or communication type: what channel of communication is used?

- Form of statement: what grammatical and syntactic forms can be discovered?

- Methods: what rhetorical or propaganda methods are employed?

This list shows great similarities to ethnographic question lists and shows that even classical content analysis does not confine itself purely to explicit communicative contents. Unlike ethnographic procedures (see Chapter 7) these questions are not answered directly by reference to a text, but form the basis for the development of a tool, that is a schema of categories.

5.4.1.4 Coding and reliability
When the schema of categories has been stated precisely, the coding process begins. Here the units of analysis are identified and allocated to categories. In order to ensure that a coder is using the same criteria for allocation of units of analysis and categories throughout the operation, and is not modifying the definitions of categories (intra-coder reliability), it is advisable that regular operational discussions are held (Herkner 1974: 176). To achieve an acceptable level of intra- and inter-coder reliability (agreement between different coders), there also need to be explicit definitions of the categories based on numerous examples and coder-training sessions, using material related to the text to be analysed. Inter-coder reliability can be assessed using a number of different measurements which indicate the relative proportion of units of analysis allocated to the same category by two different coders (cf. Herkner 1974: 177f., Lisch & Kriz 1978: 88ff., Merten 1983: 302ff.).

5.4.1.5 Analysis and evaluation
Frequencies and indices The simplest type of evaluation consists of counting the number of occurrences per category: here some relationship is assumed between frequency of content and meaning. The unconditional acceptance of this assumption was one of the principal causes of the disagreement between

Berelson (1952) and Kracauer (1952) who took a 'qualitative' standpoint. It is also customary to use different indices which correlate two separate measurements (Herkner 1974: 179f.). For purely syntactic indices this may be exemplified by the type-token ratio (quotient of the total of different words and the total word count) and the action quotient (quotient of the number of verbs and the number of adjectives). An example of a semantic index is provided by the discomfort-relief-quotient (total number of words indicating an unpleasant condition out of the total number of words indicating either a pleasant or an unpleasant condition).

Contingencies In contingency analysis it is not only the frequency which is investigated but also mutual dependency of variables. It is a question of whether the probability of a particular type of phenomenon (for example two themes) is more than randomly high or low.

More complex procedures Here grammatical and semantic aspects are examined for explicit rules. An example of this is evaluative assertion analysis (Osgood et al. 1954), where the attitude of a sender to particular persons or facts is investigated. This method comprises a standardized, scalar schema of categories and precise rules for coding and evaluation (for more detailed discussion see Herkner 1974: 181f., Merten 1983: 192ff.).

Additional multivariate analyses are available, based on the results of content analysis, and these are dependent on the scalar level of the variables. Evaluation must take account of problems of inference, both from the selected material to the total material, and also from the selected material to the senders, receivers or the communicative situation (cf. Merten 1983: 107ff., Herkner 1974: 183ff.).

5.4.1.6 A typology of content analysis procedures

Merten (1983: 115ff.), using the criteria 'analytical goals' and 'tools of analysis', attempts to provide a typology of content analysis procedures – where communicators, recipients and situational orientation belong to analytical goals, and semiotic levels (confusingly) belong to methods of analysis (Merten 1983: 101ff.).

- At the syntactic level we find analysis of such features as letters, syllables, words or sentences and their structures, in so far as these are purely formal.

- At the syntactic-semantic level it is a question of the influence of syntactic structures on meaning-formation.

- At the semantic level the meanings of words, sentences and so on are analysed.

- At the syntactic-pragmatic level there is an attempt to justify a relationship between syntax and textual effect.

- The semantic-pragmatic analysis seeks to relate this effect to particular meaning-bearing words or sentences.

- Finally, the purely pragmatic analysis looks for the truly pragmatic structures which govern the reception of the text (for example rhetorical structures).

Herkner (1974: 165), following Holsti (1968), classifies content analysis procedures according to the following features: purpose of investigation, semiotic level, type of comparison and research question (using Lasswell's formula). If one tries to combine these two taxonomies, the content analysis procedures found in the relevant literature may be classified on the basis of semiotic levels and research questions (see Figure 5.1).

5.4.2 Qualitative content analysis

In the 1950s a controversy was already developing about research strategies in content analysis. Berelson (1952) was the first to put together the methods and goals of quantitative content analysis which had been developed up to that time, and these concentrated on assessment on the basis of frequency analyses. Kracauer (1952) reacted critically to this quantitative orientation because it neglected the particular quality of texts – their meaning content. Kracauer felt that particular attention had to be paid to the reconstruction of contexts. 'Patterns' or 'wholes' in texts could be demonstrated, not by counting and measuring their manifest contents, but by showing the different possibilities of interpretation of 'multiple connotations'. For Kracauer, categories are also of central importance: 'What counts alone in quantitative analysis is the selection and rational organization of such categories as condense substantive meanings of the given text, with a view to testing pertinent assumptions and hypotheses' (Kracauer 1952: 637f.). He preferred, however, to construct these categories with reference to latent contents and the reconstruction of context, and to take account of the meaning of particular instances. Nevertheless, Kracauer's suggestions represent rather a shift of emphasis than an independent method. (Also see Ritsert 1972: 14ff. for discussion of the controversy between qualitative and quantitative content analysis.)

More recently Mayring's (1988) qualitative content analysis has achieved popularity (see, for example, Lamnek 1989: 202ff., Mayring 1991) although its independence, compared to the classical model, has been questioned (Lamnek 1989: 213). Mayring has developed a sequential model and proposes, as far as goals are concerned, three distinct analytical procedures which may be carried out either independently or in combination, depending upon the particular research question:

1 The *summary* attempts to reduce the material in such a way as to preserve the essential content and by abstraction to create a manageable corpus which still reflects the original material (Mayring 1988: 53). For this the text is (a) paraphrased, (b) generalized or abstracted, and (c) reduced.
2 *Explication* involves explaining, clarifying and annotating the material (Mayring 1988: 68). As a first step (a) a lexico-grammatical definition is

Semiotic levels	Object	Examples of procedure	Research question						
			Who?	What?	How?	To whom?	Why?	What situation?	What effect?
Syntactic	Syntactic characteristics of message	• Author analysis (style analysis)	○		○				
		• Personality structure analysis	○		○		○		
Syntactic-semantic	Syntax and meaning-creation	• Word class analysis	○		○				
		• Syntactic complexity analysis	○		○			○	
Semantic	Meanings of words, sentences	• Theme analysis	○	○					
		• Contingency analysis	○	○				○	
		• Field of meaning analysis	○	○			○		
Syntactic-pragmatic	Syntax and effect of message	• Frequency readability analysis	○		○	○			○
		• Structural readability analysis	○		○	○			○
		• Impact analysis	○		○	○			○
Semantic-pragmatic	Meaning and effect of message	• Value analysis	○	○			○		
		• Attitude analysis (EAA)	○	○			○		
		• Motif analysis	○	○			○		
		• Personality structure analysis	○	○			○		○
		• Intelligibility analysis	○	○		○			
		• Objectivity analysis	○	○					
		• Semantic differential	○	○		○	○		○
		• Symbol analysis	○	○					
		• Reality analysis	○	○				○	
		• Interaction process analysis	○	○		○	○	○	○
		• Attribution analysis	○	○	○			○	○
Pragmatic	Effect of message	• Resonance analysis	○	○	○	○		○	○
		• Interview analysis	○	○	○	○	○		○

FIGURE 5.1 A typology of content analysis procedures

attempted, then (b) the material for explication is determined, and this is followed by (c) a narrow context analysis, and (d) a broad context analysis. The narrow context analysis incorporates the text (cotext) and this corresponds to the meaning of context used in conversation analysis (see Chapter 8), while the broad analysis includes additional information about the senders and the situation. (See also the distinctions between broad and local context, or macro- and micro-context in Chapter 2, 2.5.) Finally, (e) an explicatory paraphrase is made of the particular portion of text and (f) the explication is examined with reference to the total context.

3 *Structuring* corresponds more or less to the procedures used in classical context analysis and is also viewed by Mayring (1988: 75) as the most crucial technique of content analysis, the goal of which is 'to filter out a particular structure from the material'. Here the text can be structured according to content, form and scaling. The first stage (a) is the determination of the units of analysis, after which (b) the dimensions of the structuring are established on some theoretical basis and (c) the features of the system of categories are fixed. Subsequently (d) definitions are formulated and key examples, with rules for coding in separate categories, are agreed. (e) In the course of a first appraisal of the material the data locations are marked, and (f) in a second scrutiny these are processed and extracted. If necessary the system of categories is re-examined and revised, which necessitates a reappraisal of the material. (h) As a final stage the results are processed. (For further treatment of the process see Mayring 1988: 68.)

The central part of the process – structuring – is clearly derived from classical content analysis. Here, too, units of coding and evaluation are set up and arranged in a schema of categories.

The process of content analysis therefore consists of nine stages (Mayring 1988: 42ff.):

- determination of the material;

- analysis of the situation in which the text originated;

- the formal characterization of the material;

- determination of the direction of the analysis;

- theoretically informed differentiation of questions to be answered;

- selection of the analytical techniques (summary, explication, structuring);

- definition of the unit of analysis;

- analysis of the material (summary, explication, structuring);

- interpretation.

For 'classical' content analysis, Berelson's (1952) criteria of objectivity, systematicity and quantification are appropriate. The research strategy that is regularly pursued here is governed by the traditional criteria of validity and reliability, where the latter is a precondition for the former (and not vice versa). In particular, two specific problems of content analysis are discussed here: problems of inference and problems of reliability.

Problems of inference relate to the possibility of drawing conclusions, on the one hand, about the whole text on the basis of the text sample and, on the other hand, about the underlying (theoretical) constructs such as motives, attitudes, norms, etc., on the basis of the text. As a result, inference in content analysis confines itself only to specific features of external and internal validity: if the operationalization is valid, is there an (internal) fit between the constructs and indicators? If the process of measurement is successful, then is the sample (externally) representative of the totality?

In considering *problems of reliability* particular attention is paid to the trustworthiness of the coding. To what extent do different coders agree in the coding of the same text (inter-coder reliability)? How stable is the coding of the same coders (intra-coder reliability)? Particularly for the assessment of inter-coder reliability, a range of measures and indices has been developed which all attempt to express the number of identical codings in relation to the overall total of codings (for further discussion see Herkner 1974: 177f., Lisch & Kriz 1978: 88ff., Merten 1983: 302ff.). Herkner (1974: 178) recommends, for example, the reliability index π, which is calculated as follows:

$$(1) \quad \pi = \frac{P - P_e}{1 - P_e}$$

where

$$(2) \quad P_e = \sum_{l=1}^{k} P_{il}\, P_{jl}$$

P_e here represents the measure of agreement which could be expected on the basis of chance where P is the empirically established agreement and 1 is the maximum value of P. π is thus calculated as the quotient of the superiority of the actual agreement between coders over the chance value and the maximum possible superiority. The measure of purely chance agreement P_e is calculated in (2) as follows: the relative share P_{il} of coder i of the judgements in category 1 is multiplied by the relative share P_{jl} of coder j of the judgements in category 1. These probabilities are finally added up for all possible judgements k.

This index takes account of the empirical allocation of judgements to categories in a suitable form to measure chance agreement. It thus becomes possible not only to compare the empirically found and maximum possible agreements, but also to remove from both precisely this possibility of 'chance agreement'.

Krippendorff (1980: 158) formulates the following specific quality criteria for content analysis:

1 Validity:
   (a)   material-oriented – semantic validity, sample validity;
   (b)   result-oriented – correlative validity, prognostic validity;
   (c)   process-oriented – construct validity.
2 Reliability:
   (a)   stability;
   (b)   replicability;
   (c)   precision.

Semantic validity relates to the meaning reconstruction of the material, and is expressed in the appropriateness of the category definitions, the key examples and the rules for coders. Sample validity refers to the usual criteria for precise sampling. Correlative validity refers to the correlation with some external criterion (for example the results of other methods). Construct validity relates, for instance, to previous success with similar constructs, established models and theories, and representative interpretations. Stability refers to whether the same results are obtained in a renewed application of the analytical tool to the same text. Replicability is the extent to which the analysis achieves the same results under different circumstances, for instance with different coders. Finally, precision assumes stability and replicability and denotes the extent to which the analysis meets a particular functional standard (Mayring 1988: 96ff.).

Krippendorff (1980) suggests four possible sources of error that may lead to a lack of reliability: (a) Features of the units of evaluation – do the problem locations, where there is some disagreement about coding, differ systematically from other material? (b) Properties of individual categories – are instances of disagreement particularly common with particular categories? Do these categories have unclear definitions? (c) Differentiation of categories – are the distinctions between categories too fine? (d) Properties of the coders – if the lack of reliability cannot be attributed to (a) to (c), then the problem is usually with the coders and may perhaps be solved by more careful selection, more thorough training, shorter operating periods, etc.

5.6 PRECONDITIONS AND AREAS OF APPLICATION

Content analysis will always be used if communicative content is of greatest importance, if operational schemata of categories can be formulated in advance or if the analysis is concerned only with the lexicon of a text. If classical procedures are to be applied, there has to be a quite precisely formulated research question and, ideally, a set of interesting variables that can be encapsulated in the form of a hypothesis. There is an exception for those procedures which provide standardized schemata of categories and, thereby, also research goals.

Apart from the variants which confine themselves to simple word counts, content analyses are based on schemata of categories which must be predetermined in both quantitative and qualitative varieties.

The transcription requirements then depend on the variables under investigation. There is a tendency, however, for content analysis not to investigate non-verbal or para-verbal phenomena. Since inter-coder reliability is an essential criterion of quality for the results of text analysis, it is recommended that in the categorization process at least two independent coders should be involved in the coding of texts.

Whether and to what extent contextual information is required will depend upon the research strategy: in Berelson's classical (1952) methodology only the manifest textual content is of interest. The questions formulated by Holsti (1968: 645) as a basis for schemata of categories are indeed related to context but have to be answered only from textual content. It is difficult, however, to circumvent the influence of contextual knowledge on the researchers. Cotext plays a role in the sense that textual examples provide essential assistance in the coding process. In Mayring's (1988) explicatory procedure the analysis of both cotext and context is explicitly included.

For the processing of large quantities of text, computer programs are available. Depending on the unit of analysis a range of programs may be used: word counts and calculation of indices (for example Textpack), text retrievers (for example Wordcruncher), textbase managers (for example MAX), code and retrieve programs (for example WinMax, AQUAD) (see Weitzman & Miles 1995).

The catalogue of the different academic disciplines which use text analysis procedures covers the whole area of the social sciences and important areas of the humanities. As early as 1974 (163ff.), Herkner gave examples of applications in psychology, psychiatry, social psychology, sociology, communication studies, ethnology and literary studies. Examples of linguistic content analyses are to be found in Wodak (1981, 1984), and Wodak and Schulz (1986).

5.7 SIMILARITIES AND DIFFERENCES IN COMPARISON WITH OTHER METHODS

Ethnographic and grounded theory methods also work with categories that function as an analytical framework. Unlike these, however, the categorization processes of content analysis require that the categories be set up and operationalized in advance. Changes in the schema of categories during the coding process should only be made in exceptional circumstances. Ethnographic methods – and in particular grounded theory – postulate, in contrast, an inductive development of categories (concepts and indicators) on the basis of textual data. Moreover, these procedures often dispense with quantification and so the significance of individual categories is never operationalized by means of frequency of codings within these categories.

In addition, SYMLOG and also narrative semiotics may be classified as semantic-pragmatic content analyses. These procedures provide, in advance, specific research questions and schemata of categories derived from them. And if we go back to a broad definition of content analysis, even the procedures of critical discourse analysis may be seen as multidimensional and multi-stage content analyses. In any case, the techniques of content analysis may well be used within the framework of critical discourse analysis.

The ethnomethodological methods (MCD, conversation analysis) are clearly distinguished from content analysis since they dispense completely with data categorization. Differences between content analysis and functional pragmatics, and between objective hermeneutics and DTA all have a similar basis.

5.8 LITERATURE

The choice of primary literature is particularly difficult in such a well-established method as content analysis, which has been exhaustively discussed for several decades. Here we shall attempt to present a number of 'milestones' in the development of the method:

Bales, Robert F. (1950), *Interaction Process Analysis*, Cambridge: Addison-Wesley.

Bales develops here a clear example of semantic-pragmatic content analysis with broad objectives. The IPA laid the foundation of Bales's reputation as one of the leading exponents of group sociology and saw in SYMLOG (see Bales & Cohen 1979, and Chapter 10) a further development.

Berelson, Bernhard (1952), *Content Analysis in Communication Research*, New York: Hafner.

Berelson (1952) is the first comprehensive and synoptic work exclusively devoted to content analysis, and constitutes an important landmark in the development of the method.

Holsti, Ole R. (1969), *Content Analysis for the Social Sciences and Humanities*, Reading, MS: Addison-Wesley.

What Berelson (1952) achieved can also be said of Holsti; following the Annenberg Conference, the state of the art in content analysis at the beginning of the 1970s is summarized here.

Kracauer, Siegfried (1952), 'The Challenge of Qualitative Content Analysis', *Public Opinion Quarterly*, 16: 631–42.

The Kracauer-Berelson controversy is a landmark in the historical development of content analysis. The trigger was this short article by Siegfried Kracauer, in which he presents some important objections to a purely counting and measuring orientation in content analysis.

Krippendorff, Klaus (1969), 'Models of Messages: Three Prototypes', in George Gerbner, Ole Holsti, Klaus Krippendorff, William J. Paisley & Philip J. Stone (eds), *The Analysis of Communication Content. Development in Scientific Theories and Computer Techniques*, New York: Wiley, 69–106.

In his contribution to this collection, which summarizes the findings of the Annenberg Conference, Krippendorff asks fundamental questions about the communication model of content analysis and exposes the selectivity of the treatment of information.

Krippendorff, Klaus (1980), *Content Analysis. An Introduction to its Methodology*, Beverly Hills, CA: Sage.

Krippendorff (1980) provides one of the first summative accounts of methods, in which his discussion of the quality criteria of content analysis is particularly significant.

Lasswell, Harold D. (1941), *Describing the Contents of Communication. Experimental Division for the Study of Wartime Communication*, Doc. No. 9, Washington, DC: Library of Congress.

Lasswell, Harold D. (1946), 'Describing the Contents of Communication', in Bruce L. Smith, Harold D. Lasswell and Ralph D. Casey (eds), *Propaganda, Communication and Public Opinion*, Princeton, NJ: Princeton University Press, 74–94.

This article by Harold D. Lasswell (first published 1941, reprinted with minor amendments 1946) offers good insight into the aims of the pioneers of content analysis.

Lazarsfeld, Paul, Berelson, Bernhard & Gaudet, Hazel (1955), *The People's Choice. How the Voter Makes up his Mind in a Presidential Campaign*, (2nd edn), New York: Columbia University Press.

This key investigation of electoral behaviour, which also formulates the 'two-step-flow' model of communication, includes one of the first exemplary applications of content analysis.

McClelland, David C., Atkinson, John W., Clark, Russell A. & Lowell, Edgar L. (1953), *The Achievement Motive*, New York: Appleton Century Crofts.

McClelland and his collaborators develop a theory of achievement motivation and design a schema of categories for content analysis to be used in motivation research.

Osgood, Charles E. (1959), 'The Representational Model and Relevant Research Methods', in Ithiel de Sola Pool (ed), *Trends in Content Analysis*, Urbana, IL: University of Illinois Press, 33–88.

Osgood, Charles E., Saporta, Sol & Nunnally, Jum (1954), *Evaluation Assertive Analysis*, Chicago, IL: University of Chicago Press.

In the idea of 'evaluation assertive analysis' Osgood and his team, following the Allerton House Conference, present a schema of categories for content analysis which proved to be very fruitful for a variety of research questions.

Schramm, Wilbur (1954), *The Process and Effects of Mass Communication*, Urbana, IL: University of Illinois Press.

Schramm's work presents the widely accepted communication-theory basis for classical content analysis. Schramm reformulates here Shannon & Weaver's (1949) technological information model for the sphere of mass communication.

Shannon, Claude E. & Weaver, Warren (1949), *The Mathematical Theory of Communication*, Urbana, IL: University of Illinois Press.

5.9 SECONDARY LITERATURE

5.9.1 Manuals

Content analysis is included in almost all method manuals, although admittedly it is losing its unique position in more recent editions. For instance, in the latest edition of the *Handbook of Social Psychology* (Lindzey & Aronson 1985) there is no entry for content analysis. In place of this the authors have included a more general account by Clark (1985), 'Language Use and Language Users', which also outlines linguistic theories and methods (such as speech act analysis, conversation analysis). It can even be seen from the heyday of secondary publications on content analysis – the 1970s and early 1980s – that the lifecycle of the method has passed its peak and that a phase of differentiation has now begun.

Herkner, Werner (1974), 'Inhaltsanalyse', in Jürgen von Koolwijk & Maria Wieken-Mayser (eds), *Techniken der empirischen Sozialforschung*, vol. 3, München: Oldenbourg, 158–91.

Herkner's contribution to this manual gives a comprehensive overview of the emphases, the theoretical foundations and the procedures employed in content analysis research.

Holsti, Ole R. (1968), 'Content Analysis', in Gardner Lindzey & Elliot Aronson (eds), *The Handbook of Social Psychology*, (2nd edn), vol. 2, *Research Methods*, Reading: Addison-Wesley, 596–692.

Holsti provides, almost as a summary of his methodological book (1969), an overview of essential questions and procedures used in content analysis.

> Mayring, Philip (1991), 'Qualitative Inhaltsanalyse', in Uwe Flick, Ernst von Kardorff, Heiner Keupp, Lutz von Rosenstiel and Stefan Wolff (eds), *Handbuch Qualitative Sozialforschung*, München: Psychologie-Verlags-Union, 209–13.

Philip Mayring's contribution, which briefly outlines his 'qualitative content analysis', is included in this German manual of qualitative social research.

> Silbermann, Alphons (1974), 'Systematische Inhaltsanalyse', in René König (ed.), *Handbuch der empirischen Sozialforschung*, vol. 4, Komplexe Forschungsansätze, Stuttgart: Enke, 253–339.

Alphons Silbermann's contribution is particularly impressive for its thorough presentation of the historical development of the method. As fields of application, Silbermann describes the analysis of cultural and social thought systems, literary analysis, the analysis of stereotypes and symbolic representations, and the use of content analysis in warfare and politics. An overview of content analysis research in mass communication is followed by a section on the further development of the method and a short account of techniques.

5.9.2 Other descriptions of methods

> Lamnek, Siegfried (1989), *Qualitative Sozialforschung*, vol. 2, Methoden und Techniken, München: Psychologie-Verlags-Union, 202–13.

Lamnek gives a brief account of Marying's (1988) qualitative content analysis and contrasts this, as a genuinely qualitative method, with objective hermeneutics.

> Lisch, Ralf & Kriz, Jürgen (1978), *Grundlagen und Modelle der Inhaltsanalyse*, Reinbek: Rowohlt.

Ralf Lisch and Jürgen Kriz attempt a state of the art description and a critique in which they concentrate on the methodological foundations and the problems of sampling and categorizing, together with questions of validity and reliability. Further sections deal with content analysis and computing, with measurement of direction and intensity, and with the statistical analysis of trends, association structures and readability research.

> Mayring, Philip (1988), *Qualitative Inhaltsanalyse. Grundlagen und Techniken*, Weinheim: Deutscher Studienverlag.

In this work Mayring gives the clearest presentation of the general conception of his qualitative content analysis. At the centre are the 'techniques' (which he calls the 'objectives') of qualitative content analysis: summary, explication and structuring.

Merten, Klaus (1983), *Inhaltsanalyse. Einführung in Theorie, Methode und Praxis*, Opladen: Westdeutscher Verlag.

Klaus Merten succeeds in this book in providing probably the fullest and most detailed German account of content analysis. In addition to matters dealt with in other method descriptions (history and development, theoretical principles, problems of inference), this book is characterized by a typology of very different procedures and by an attempt to update the communication theory basis and to integrate some more recent social science approaches (Niklas Luhmann).

Ritsert, Jürgen (1972), *Inhaltsanalyse und Ideologiekritik. Ein Versuch über kritische Sozialforschung*, Frankfurt: Athenäum.

Jürgen Ritsert is concerned with the question of the place value of content analysis in an ideologically critical research programme based on the critical theory of the Frankfurt school.

Weber, Robert Philip (1990), *Basic Content Analysis,* (2nd edn), Newbury Park, CA: Sage (Quantitative Applications in the Social Sciences Series).

Weber treats questions from the creation of a simple coding scheme to an elaborate computer-aided analysis of content. He makes his points with numerous well-chosen pieces of text: US political party platforms, and Korean War editorials from American newspapers. At the end of each chapter, he provides a useful discussion of current literature. He finishes with a sensitive discussion of the unresolved problems in measurement, indication, representation and interpretation.

Wersig, Gernot (1968), *Inhaltsanalyse. Einführung in ihre Systematik und Literatur. Schriftenreihe zur Publizistikwissenschaft*, Vol. 5, Berlin: Volker Spiess.

Gernot Wersig's publication is noteworthy for a comprehensive and systematic bibliographic overview of investigations in content analysis.

5.9.3 Examples of studies

In 1968 Gernot Wersig was already able to list 1,400 publications on content analysis. If one discounts the communication theory or methodologically focussed contributions, there still remain more than a thousand examples of applications of content analysis. At the very least we can claim that it is the method of mass communication research. It is therefore all the more difficult to highlight individual studies as particularly exemplary. Moreover, this task is made even more difficult by the complexity of content analysis procedures. The only remaining possibility is to point again to a number of classical studies that have already been discussed (for example Lazarsfeld et al. 1955, Osgood et al. 1954).

Examples of didactically–oriented applications of 'classical' content analysis may be found in Merten (1983: 312–28), while examples for qualitative content analysis are given in Mayring (1988).

CHAPTER 6

GROUNDED THEORY

O ur own bibliometrical (see Chapter 15) and other findings (see Coffey et al. 1996, Lee & Fielding 1996) would suggest that grounded theory is the most prominent among the so-called 'qualitative' approaches to data analysis. This does not necessarily mean that the methodologies developed by Anselm Strauss and Barney Glaser are used to any great extent: 'When qualitative researchers are challenged to describe their approach, reference to 'grounded theory' has the highest recognition value' (Lee & Fielding 1996: 3.1).

6.1 THEORETICAL ORIGINS

One of the roots of grounded theory (hereafter GT) is American pragmatism, and in particular the work of John Dewey, 'including its emphases on action and the problematic situation, and the necessity for conceiving of method in the context of problem solving' (Strauss 1987: 5). Truth is therefore a 'pragmatic' concept: usefulness, value and success are the criteria. What works in practice is true. As a further source, Strauss indicates the Chicago School of Sociology, which gave central importance to field observation and in-depth interviews as methods of data collection and to social interactions and processes as objects of research. 'In addition the Chicago School, almost from its inception, emphasized the necessity for grasping the actor's viewpoints for understanding interaction, process and social change' (Strauss 1987: 6).

As a student in Chicago, Anselm Strauss – together with Barney Glaser, the founder of GT – became acquainted with Herbert Blumer who coined the term 'symbolic interactionism'. Strauss, however, refused to allow himself to be labelled a symbolic interactionist. Barney Glaser, on the other hand, studied with Paul Lazarsfeld and thereby brought to GT his own experiences and his dissatisfaction with standardized methods and multivariate analysis. For a better understanding of the background to GT, Strauss recommends the works of Dewey (1937) and Hughes (1993).

6.2 BASIC THEORETICAL ASSUMPTIONS

GT does share with symbolic interactionism a number of basic assumptions about communication and interaction: George H. Mead (1938a, 1938b) who, like Dewey, taught in Chicago, had already brought the subjective, language-related components of interaction processes to the attention of sociological theory. In this way, actors react to social objects on the basis of meanings which they attribute to them. These meanings arise in interactions, and are developed and permanently modified in the course of an interaction process. They are, however, 'objectivized' and become a framework or frameworks of conditions for human behaviour. Language and communication are, of course, not an explicit theme of GT, but there are many indications that interactions are primarily investigated with reference to linguistic communication.

Although GT procedures are equally applicable to non-textual data, a central importance is attributed to text as data material in the form of interview transcripts, observers' notes, books, newspaper articles, etc. (see Strauss 1987: 26f., Strauss & Corbin 1990: 46). The most prominent application of GT, therefore, is probably text analysis. Within the framework of GT, however, one will look in vain for a theory of text and for any more explicit understanding of the term text.

GT is not a method that can be clearly demarcated but a school of social science methodology whose research strategies may be summarized as follows.

- The *individual case* as an independent unit of investigation: autonomous units of action, which have a history, should first be reconstructed according to their own logic, with some theoretical goal – that is, concepts should be formulated on the basis of a case which can explain the circumstances of the particular case.

- Sociological interpretation as a '*Kunstlehre*': the process of theory generation is similar to artistic activity, where two conflicting approaches – one the impartial view, the other the scientific arrangement of reality – should be united.

- The *continuity* between everyday and scientific thought: everyday knowledge is not structurally different from scientific knowledge. It is an indispensable resource for the scientific process and must be made useful to it.

- *Openness* in social science terminology: GT does not deliver any incontrovertible theories. The terms, concepts, categories and hypotheses which it develops must repeatedly demonstrate their suitability for the scientific decoding of reality.

6.3 OBJECTIVES OF THE METHOD

Text analysis using GT always tries to conceptualize data-based assumptions. The focus is on exploration and the generation of hypotheses, while the testing of hypotheses receives less attention:

> Grounded theory is a detailed grounding of systematically and intensively analysed data, often sentence by sentence, or phrase by phrase of the field note, interview or other document; by constant comparison, data are extensively collected and coded, . . . thus producing a well-constructed theory. The focus of analysis is *not* merely on collecting or ordering a mass of data, but on organizing many ideas which have emerged from analysis of the data. (Strauss 1987: 22; see also Glaser 1978)

> A Grounded Theory is one that is inductively derived from the study of the phenomenon it represents. That is, it is discovered, developed, and provisionally verified through systematic data collection and analysis of data pertaining to that phenomenon. Therefore, data collection, analysis, and theory stand in reciprocal relationship with each other. One does not begin with a theory and then prove it. Rather, one begins with an area of study and what is relevant to that area is allowed to emerge. (Strauss & Corbin 1990: 23)

6.4 OUTLINE OF THE METHOD

This outline of GT relies upon the two books by Strauss (1987) and Strauss & Corbin (1990). According to these, GT is a research programme that integrates research planning, execution and analysis. The main focus of the following presentation is, of course, on its applications in text analysis. To achieve this, GT again focuses on the development of concepts or categories on the basis of text data. Nevertheless we ought to attempt to give a brief overview of the central procedures and rules of GT (see, for example, Strauss 1987: 23).

6.4.1 Data collection

The application of GT requires no specific methods of data collection. Observation and interviews are often mentioned (see Strauss 1987: 26, Strauss & Corbin 1990: 30f.), but data can also be collected in other ways (for example from documents). In any case, within the rubric of GT, data collection is not considered to be a specific phase that must be completed before analysis begins; after the first collection exercise it is a matter of carrying out the first analyses, finding indicators for particular concepts, expanding concepts into categories and, on the basis of these results, collecting further data (*theoretical sampling*).

In this mode of procedure, data collection is never completely excluded, since through the processes of coding and memo-writing (preparation of written analysis reports related to the development of the theory, see Strauss & Corbin 1990: 197f.) new questions always arise which can only be dealt with if new data are collected or earlier data are re-examined (Strauss 1987: 56).

6.4.2 Concepts and indicators

GT is based on a concept-indicator model with the help of which empirical indicators are coded according to concepts (Strauss 1987: 25). Concepts are designations or labels which are attached to individual events (indicators) (see Strauss & Corbin 1990: 61). In this it is not a matter of the a priori operationalization of theoretical concepts (as, for example, in classical content analysis) but of looking for indicators of provisional concepts in the data. Strauss (1987: 14ff.) gives the example of an investigation of in-patient treatments in a hospital, where the concept 'dependency on medical equipment' was identified as significant. The researcher investigates – and compares with others – many indicators (modes of behaviour, events) and then 'codes' and classifies them as indicators of a class of events.

With concepts it is primarily a matter of so-called *sensitizing concepts* or central ideas which are transformed into a provisional research question. The next stage is to elaborate the researchers' preliminary understanding to cover the field of relevant objects; for this the procedures of 'brainstorming', group discussion among the researchers and study of appropriate literature are recommended.

A framework of (theoretical) concepts is now offered which is seen as a stimulus to the coding process. This sort of framework of concepts, which Glaser (1978) calls *coding families*, may include the following:

- c-families – causes, consequences, correlations, constraints;

- process family – stages, phases, durations, passages, sequences, careers;

- degree family – measure, degree, intensity, level, boundary value, critical value;

- type family – types, classes, genres, classifications;

- strategy family – strategy, tactics, techniques, mechanisms, management;

- interaction family – relations, interactions, symmetry, rituals;

- identity family – identity, self-image, change of identity, alien images;

- culture family – norms, values, socially shared attitudes;

- consensus family – contract, agreement, definition of situation, conformity, homogeneity;

- mainline family – social control, agreement, socialization, organization, institution.

This is, therefore, a summary of collective and abstract concepts (causes, effects, phases, etc.) which may become relevant for the most varied fields of investigation and types of problem. On the basis of these coding families – and for any concrete case only a few will be appropriate and relevant – frameworks of theoretical concepts will then be developed from the sensitizing concepts, with continual reference to the indicators. During this process different indicators are investigated and compared with one another, and similarities and differences are considered. On the basis of this analysis of the indicators, concepts are finally specified – a procedure which is central to grounded theory. Here the theoretical concepts are dimensionalized, that is to say, any differences in the concepts – or distinctive features – are determined. 'Changing indicators, thereby generating new properties of a code will proceed only so far before the analyst discovers saturation of ideas through the *interchangeability of indicators*' (Strauss 1987: 26). The more numerous the indicators that are of equal significance for a concept, the higher the degree of saturation of the properties of that concept for the emerging theory.

6.4.3 Coding procedure

The coding procedure is undoubtedly central to GT, and in this it distinguishes itself clearly from classical content analysis. On the basis of texts and contextual knowledge, concepts are developed, categorized and dimensionalized. Simultaneously they are enriched with indicators (textual examples). The basis for coding is provided by the coding families mentioned above which count as the first heuristic clues. Strauss designates one section of these *coding families* (see section 6.4.2) – the conditions, interactions, strategies and tactics, together with consequences – as the main constituents of his 'coding paradigm' (Strauss 1987: 27), which all coding procedures ought to bear in mind.

By means of permanent comparison of the concepts, using the associated text units, they are successively *categorized* (that is related to each other, ordered, for example put into a hierarchy) and *dimensionalized*, that is broken down into dimensions, while variables are established at different scalar levels.

During the coding process the investigator is permanently switching between inductive and deductive thinking (Strauss 1987: 11ff.), and constant alternation between setting up and testing concepts and hypotheses is one of the essential features of GT. For this purpose GT proposes a number of coding procedures (Strauss & Corbin 1990: 57ff.), see below.

6.4.3.1 Open coding

GT understands open coding as the process of breaking down, examining, comparing, conceptualizing and categorizing data (Strauss & Corbin 1990: 62). This is the first step in the procedure of text interpretation. The goal is therefore to develop concepts based both on the data and also on the researcher's contextual knowledge (Strauss 1987: 28). During this process comparisons must be made and questions formulated (Strauss & Corbin 1990: 62), while open coding starts with the analysis of single passages of texts and phrases (that is at a delicate level of analysis). The following questions occupy the initial stages of the coding process: (a) What actually happens in the text? and (b) What category does the textual passage suggest?

After this there will be a search for *in vivo* codes (interpretations recognizable in the text itself) and for traditional categories, such as age, gender, social level. Strauss recommends that open coding should analyse very exactly and investigate the text with microscopic precision in order to minimize the risk of overlooking important categories (Strauss 1987: 30). At the same time, he avoids making any recommendations about possible units of analysis. He does, however, demonstrate an 'elementary line-by-line analysis' (Strauss 1987: 82ff.). During the coding process, theory memos should be written to record the development of concepts, categories and dimensions.

The asking of questions; the precise analysis of words, phrases and sentences, together with a continuous process of comparison (using polar oppositions, systematically but perhaps also in a far-fetched way); these will all help to increase the 'theoretical sensitivity' and creativity of the coding process (Strauss & Corbin 1990: 75).

6.4.3.2 Axial coding

GT uses this term to refer to procedures which, on the basis of the above mentioned 'coding paradigm', reassemble the results of open coding by creating new relationships between concepts (Strauss & Corbin 1990: 96ff.). It therefore assists in the refinement and differentiation of already available concepts, whereby these first acquire the status of categories. It then works along the 'axes' of these categories. After open coding it is normally not yet clear whether a particular concept has to do with a condition, a strategy or a consequence. Each single concept, together with its indicators, is therefore analysed and assigned according to the points of the 'coding paradigm' (Strauss 1987: 32, Strauss & Corbin 1990: 99ff.):

(a) What are the conditions for the events comprised in the concept?
(b) How can the interaction between the actors be described?
(c) What strategies and tactics can be determined?
(d) What are the consequences of the events?

During the coding process, which begins with open coding, axial coding becomes increasingly predominant: either individual text locations are extracted and interpreted 'axially', or several text locations are interpreted in comparison with one another. In such cases the procedure is similar to open coding: formulate a question (see above), dimensionalize, etc. (Böhm 1994: 130).

In axial coding the properties of a category are first elaborated, which means that the category is dimensionalized either explicitly or implicitly. Then, assumptions about conditions, interactions, strategies and consequences are specified and tested, which increases the relationships to other categories (Strauss 1987: 64). The links between the categories should be recorded in representations of networks, and the investigator should capture, in the form of coding notes and theory memos, as many as possible of the thoughts which have occurred during the process.

6.4.3.3 Selective coding

GT uses this term to refer to the process of selecting the core category, system-atically linking this core category to other categories, validating this linking process, and the filling of other categories which require further refinement and development. A core category is that central phenomenon around which all other categories are integrated (Strauss & Corbin 1990: 116). As the starting point for this final stage, coding lists, memos and network models should be reviewed and theoretically sorted.

In addition, Strauss & Corbin (1990: 116) recommend enquiring about the 'story' contained in the data. The essential events should be brought together by answering the following questions:

● What is the most striking feature of the field of investigation?

● What do I consider to be the main problem?

● What is the central theme of the story?

● Which phenomena are represented again and again in the data?

The central story extracted in this way rotates about the core category and shows its relationships to other categories. In the simplest case the core category may already be recognized from the network model and has already been identified, while in the most difficult case it must be completely newly identified, refined with regard to its properties, and its location established in the network of rela-tionships. The (provisional) results should be examined continually with reference to the textual data. In this way, step by step, a grounded theory will emerge.

6.4.4 Further procedures and rules of grounded theory

Theoretical sampling means the selection of samples or texts and segments of texts on the basis of the concepts in the developing theory. This is an aspect of comparative analysis that facilitates the desired search for and recognition of indicators in texts. The basis for this is provided by relevant concepts which appear repeatedly during comparison or which are quite clearly not present. Theoretical sampling can be applied within all three coding procedures:

- 'open sampling', characterized by openness and, to a lesser extent, by speci-ficity in open coding;

- sampling of relationships and variations with the aim of finding the most extreme differences at the dimensional level, in axial coding; and

- 'discriminating sampling', with the aim of confirming the main theme, of maximizing relationships between categories and of filling underdeveloped categories, in selective coding (Strauss & Corbin 1990: 176).

The *conditional matrix* is a tool proposed by Strauss & Corbin (1990: 158ff.) to record the conditions and consequences of individual concepts or categories at different levels (for example levels of social aggregation). For completion, Strauss & Corbin (1990: 195ff.) particularly recommend memos (coding notes, theoretical notes) and diagrams for the visual representation of relations between categories.

6.4.5 The debate on grounded theory

The development of the GT research programme was surrounded by disagree-ments. There are currently a number of fundamental differences between the positions of Barney Glaser (1978, 1992) and Anselm Strauss and Juliet Corbin (1990). The discussion, at times rather heated, is summarized in Kelle (1994: 333ff.):

- While Strauss & Corbin insist on tackling an object of study with 'open' questions, Glaser prefers that investigators approach their field without either research problems or questions.

- Glaser requires that an empirical field should be addressed with no prior contact with any of the scientific literature. All background knowledge is viewed as harmful. Strauss & Corbin on the other hand, permit – even rec-ommend – intensive study of the relevant literature before the empirical work begins.

- The multi-stage open coding procedure proposed by Strauss & Corbin is strongly criticized by Glaser. Strauss & Corbin suggest allocating a code to every event at the outset and then summarizing these codes on the basis of a comparison with categories. Glaser argues for an ongoing process of com-parison while coding is taking place. He is, however, aware that for this to be possible dimensions of comparison must be available. Glaser proposes his 'coding families' as the only dimensions of comparison.

- While Corbin & Strauss (1990) make a number of serious attempts to develop criteria for the verification of results, Glaser (1992: 106) considers this to be superfluous. He sees the value of GT in the development of hypotheses, and claims that these only have to comply with standards of plausibility.

- Axial coding, where coded events are ordered systematically as members of a chain of actions (context conditions, action strategies, intervening conditions, consequences, etc.), is firmly rejected by Glaser on the grounds that this superimposes the researchers' concepts on the data (see Glaser 1992: 82, Kelle 1994: 338).

All in all, this controversy provides a number of different answers to the question of whether it is in any way possible to embark on empirical work with an inductivist research strategy without any kind of theoretical concepts (Kelle 1994: 338ff.).

6.5 QUALITY CRITERIA

Grounded theory views itself as a methodology for generating theories on the basis of data. The hypothesis testing aspect is accordingly in the background. The 'usual criteria of "good science" . . . significance, theory-observation, compatibility, generalizability, consistency, reproducibility, precision and verification' should be redefined 'in order to fit the realities of qualitative research and the complexities of social phenomena' (Strauss & Corbin 1990: 250).

Corbin & Strauss (1990) attempt to develop specific evaluation criteria for GT oriented studies in which, however, the canonization of the methodology is central and the criteria presented incline to GT research strategy: these 'criteria' attempt, in question form, to assess (a) the adequacy of the research process, and (b) the empirical grounding of the findings (Corbin & Strauss 1990: 16ff.).

The first set of questions is designed to allow readers to judge whether the selected methodology and the developed theory are adequate for the object of study. A well-documented GT study should, in any case, make it possible to answers these questions:

- *Criterion #1* How was the original sample selected? On what grounds (selective sampling)?

- *Criterion #2* What major categories emerged?

- *Criterion #3* What were some of the events, incidents, action, and so on which indicated some of these major categories?

- *Criterion #4* On the basis of what categories did theoretical sampling proceed? That is, how did theoretical formulations guide some of the data collection? After the theoretical sample was carried out, how representative did these categories prove to be?

- *Criterion #5* What were some of the hypotheses pertaining to relations among categories? On what grounds were they formulated and tested?

- *Criterion #6* Were there instances when hypotheses did not hold up against what was actually seen? How were the discrepancies accounted for? Did they affect the hypotheses?

- *Criterion #7* How and why was the core category selected? Was the selection sudden or gradual, difficult or easy? On what grounds were the final analytical decisions made? How did extensive 'explanatory power' in relation to the phenomena under study, and 'relevance', as discussed earlier, figure in the decisions?

A second set of questions attempts to examine the empirical foundation of the ultimately derived theories (Corbin & Strauss 1990: 17ff.):

- Are concepts generated?

- Are the concepts systematically related?

- Are there many conceptual linkages and are the categories well developed? Do the categories have conceptual density?

- Is there much variation built into the theory?

- Are the broader conditions that affect the phenomenon under study built into its explanation?

- Has 'process' been taken into account?

- Do the theoretical findings seem significant and to what extent?

Apart from these questions Strauss & Corbin (1990: 247f.) also modify 'conventional' quality criteria:

(a) *Reproducibility* could mean that 'given the same theoretical perspective of the original researcher and following the same general rules for data gathering and analysis, plus a similar set of conditions, another investigator should be able to come up with the same theoretical explanation about the given phenomenon' (Strauss & Corbin 1990: 251).

(b) *Generalizability* in GT means that the conditions and consequences according to which particular interactions are related to some phenomena must be specified, and that the results can then be transferred to all those situations which correspond to these preconditions. 'Naturally, the more systematic and widespread the theoretical sampling, the more conditions and variations that will be discovered and built into the theory, the greater its generalizability (also therefore its precision and predictive capacity)' (Strauss & Corbin 1990: 251).

Whatever the case, GT oriented research should fulfil the criteria of validity, reliability and credibility of data, theory plausibility and value, as well as appropriateness of the research process.

6.6 PRECONDITIONS AND AREAS OF APPLICATION

For Strauss (1987: xii, 3) the whole field of the social sciences and the humanities is suitable for the application of GT. 'GT is suitable whenever the understanding of larger quantities of text, or a deepening of understanding, is required, or when new ideas, contexts, consequences and recommendations for action for a subject area have to be derived from texts' (Böhm 1994: 123).

A research objective oriented towards generating a theory is undoubtedly a precondition for the application of GT modes of procedure; it is only where the phenomena of a particular subject area cannot be sufficiently and satisfactorily explained with existing theories or models that the extravagant methodology of GT appears reasonable. The high investment of time and personnel is a result of, on the one hand, the detailed analytical requirements of open coding, and, on the other, the need for complete re-analysis of previously coded texts whenever new concepts and categories are discovered and labelled.

The data material usually consists of texts, transcribed interviews, and field notes and observation reports. Transcription norms are not given in the GT literature. The extent to which information content and/or form, verbal, para-verbal and non-verbal phenomena should be reflected in the analysis will depend ultimately on the concepts developed and the indicators attributed to them.

There is now a range of computer programs for qualitative data analysis (see Weitzman & Miles 1995 for an overview). Of these, the OSR (NUDIST QSRN Vivo programs and ATLAS/ti, see Muhr 1994) make particular reference to the basic premises of GT.[1] They support the extravagant coding procedure by assisting the analysts to maintain an overview of the system of categories they have developed, by displaying the allocation of text locations to categories and by simplifying the management of memos (definitions of, and remarks on, categories). A check on the consistency of coding in larger quantities of text can be made only with this kind of computer support. The second achievement of these programs consists of their being able – without recoding – to create higher order categories and summaries of categories. Thirdly the programs provide the possibility of conducting simple quantitative measurements. For example, it is possible to calculate what percentage of the total number of lines of text has been treated in the coding process and what proportion of text is allocated to what codes.

The use of such software packages in text analysis is no longer accepted without question. For example, Coffey et al. (1996, 7.4–7.5) fear that the coding aspect is over-emphasized: 'Grounded theorizing is more than coding, and software can be used to do more than code-and-retrieve textual analysis.'

6.7 SIMILARITIES AND DIFFERENCES IN COMPARISON WITH OTHER METHODS

Before comparing grounded theory with other methods it must again be pointed out that with GT it is less a matter of a specific method of analysis than of an approach to the development of (text-data based) concepts and theories (of small or middle range). It is therefore a question of a research strategy.

Ethnographic methods pursue similar goals, but do not have at their disposal such a carefully elaborated set of coding rules as GT. The differences, however, are by no means clear-cut.[2] Perhaps this also explains why various qualitative studies recommend proceeding according to the principles of GT, but often use only a small part of its repertoire. With reference to GT, it is stressed that texts should not be approached using ready-made concepts, rather these should be developed on the basis of the material itself. Ethnography and GT are a good match inasmuch as GT focuses on data analysis whereas ethnography focuses on data gathering.

The major difference with ethnomethodological approaches generally concerns the research goal. While GT certainly sets out to find, on the basis of the research material, theoretical concepts and explanations of which the actors are not (or need not be) aware, ethnomethodological approaches attempt to reconstruct the explanatory and meaning pattern of 'members'. With MCD and conversation analysis it is a question of the ordering principles that are relevant to participants, whereas with GT it is the concepts of the (text analysing) observers that are of interest.

Compared to methods of content analysis, GT emphasizes the development of concepts and categories rather than their application. Both SYMLOG and narrative semiotics, unlike GT, use schemata of categories which are fixed in advance and theoretically supported. GT oriented methods can, however, be used as an interim stage in the research process of content analysis, since their main focus is on the discovery rather than the testing of hypotheses.

In contrast to the more strongly hermeneutic methods (functional pragmatics, discourse analysis), the application of GT may be classified as fully object- or text-oriented. The ground rules of GT create on the one hand the necessary distance from the text, and on the other hand they bring it into the foreground and regulate the influence of the 'interpreting subject'. GT distinguishes itself from hermeneutic methods, but also from distinction theory text analysis, in that the former deliberately dispense with any categorization of text components whereas GT is concerned expressly with the development of concepts and categories.

Although a GT oriented text analysis may investigate linguistic categories (for instance, as indicators of concepts), it is not (compared to ethnography of communication, functional pragmatics and discourse analysis) an explicitly linguistic approach, since the relationship between cohesion and coherence is not of primary interest.

6.8 LITERATURE

The following distinctions may be made in the recommended literature on GT: (a) works of philosophy or theory of science that Barney Glaser and Anselm Strauss refer to (Dewey 1937, Mead 1938a, 1938b, Hughes 1993); (b) the first method-founding work in grounded theory (Glaser & Strauss 1967); (c) further developments and methodological controversies (Glaser 1978, 1992, Corbin & Strauss 1990); and (d) introductions and instructional presentations (Strauss 1987, Strauss & Corbin 1990).

Corbin, Juliet & Strauss, Anselm (1990), 'Grounded Theory Research: Procedures, Canons and Evaluative Criteria', *Qualitative Sociology*, 13: 3–21.

Dewey, John (1937), *Logic. The Theory of Inquiry*, New York: Wiley.

Glaser, Barney G. (1978), *Theoretical Sensitivity*, Mill Valley, CA: Sociology Press.

Glaser, Barney G. (1992), *Emergence vs. Forcing. Advances in the Methodology of Grounded Theory*, Mill Valley, CA: Sociology Press.

Glaser, Barney G. & Strauss, Anselm L. (1967), *The Discovery of Grounded Theory. Strategies for Qualitative Research*, Chicago, IL: Aldine.

Hughes, Everett C. (1993), *The Sociological Eyes* (2nd edn), New Brunswick, NJ: Transaction Books.

Mead, George H. (1938a, German edition 1968), *The Philosophy of the Act*, Chicago, IL: University of Chicago Press. (German title: *Geist, Identität und Gesellschaft*, Frankfurt: Suhrkamp.)

Strauss, Anselm (1987, German edition 1994), *Qualitative Analysis for Social Scientists*, Cambridge: Cambridge University Press. (German title: *Grundlagen qualitativer Sozialforschung*, München: W. Fink UTB.)

Strauss, Anselm & Corbin, Juliet (1990, German edition 1996), *Basics of Qualitative Research*, Newbury Park, CA: Sage. (German title: *Qualitative Sozialforschung*, Weinheim: Psychologie-Verlags-Union.)

6.9 SECONDARY LITERATURE

6.9.1 Handbooks

Strauss, Anselm & Corbin, Juliet (1994), 'Grounded Theory Methodology: An Overview', in Norman K. Denzin & Yvonna S. Lincoln (eds), *Handbook of Qualitative Research*, Thousand Oaks, CA: Sage, 273–85.

In this handbook contribution, the authors concentrate on the stance of grounded theory and discuss similarities and differences with regard to other strategies of qualitative social research. As a central difference they identify the emphasis on the aspect of theory development. The development of GT is then outlined, its theoretical base is specified and the relationship between theory and interpretation is discussed.

Wiedemann, Peter (1991), 'Gegenstandbezogene Theoriebildung', in Uwe Flick, Ernst von Kardorff, Heiner Keupp, Lutz von Rostenstiel & Stephan Wolff (eds), *Handbuch Qualitative Sozialforschung*, München: Psychologie-Verlags-Union, 440–5.

In this German handbook the contribution on GT is found in the section on 'testing and generalization' ('Überprüfung und Verallgemeinerung'). Wiedemann presents the central concepts and procedures of GT, although because of its brevity the presentation remains sketchy.

6.9.2 Other presentations of method

Böhm, Andreas (1994), 'Grounded Theory – Wie aus Texten Modelle und Theorie gemacht werden', in Andreas Böhm, Andreas Mengel & Thomas Muhr (eds), *Texte verstehen: Konzepte, Methoden, Werkzeuge. Schriften zur Informationwissenschaft* 14, Konstanz: Universitätsverlag, 121–40.

In this collection, in which GT is given prominence in other contributions, Böhm manages to give an introductory presentation of the bases of GT in which the emphasis is on the differences in coding procedures (open, axial, selective).

Kelle, Udo (1994), *Empirisch begründete Theoriebildung: zur Logik und Methodologie interpretativer Sozialforschung*, Weinheim: Deutscher Studienverlag, 283–349.

In this methodological treatise grounded theory occupies a substantial position in which – as the title promises – there is less focus on methodological niceties and more on the research orientation of GT. The author discovers and clarifies a number of differences between the approaches of Barney Glaser on the one hand and Anselm Strauss and Juliet Corbin on the other.

> Lamnek, Siegfried (1988), *Qualitative Sozialforschung. Band 1. Methodologie*, München: Psychologie-Verlags-Union, 106–23.

Lamnek contrasts GT with Barton & Lazarsfeld's (1979) concept of social research and discusses the approaches as different methodologies while focussing on the theoretical understanding of GT. Unlike Barton & Lazarsfeld, Glaser & Strauss would refuse to view qualitative research as merely a preliminary to quantitative research.

> Muhr, Thomas (1991), 'ATLAS/ti – A Prototype for the Support of Text Interpretation', *Qualitative Sociology*, 14 (4): 349–71.

> Muhr, Thomas (1994), 'ATLAS/ti: Ein Werkzeug für die Textinterpretation', in Andreas Böhm, Andreas Mengel & Thomas Muhr (eds), *Texte verstehen: Konzepte, Methoden, Werkzeuge. Schriften zur Informationswissenschaft* 14, Konstanz: Universitätsverlag, 317–24.

> Richards, Tom & Richards, Lyn (1991), 'The NUDIST Qualitative Data Analysis System', in *Qualitative Sociology*, 14 (4): 307–24.

These articles are concerned with outlines of the ATLAS/ti and NUDIST software packages, which both take explicit account of GT and support its methods.

6.9.3 Sample applications

To select as examples any individual studies that rely on GT may appear, in view of the multiplicity and diversity of the investigations, to be a difficult undertaking. No other method in the field of qualitative social research has been so intensively adopted. Those studies which triggered the development of the method come from the field of medical sociology. In the early 1960s Barney Glaser and Anselm Strauss investigated the interaction between clinical personnel and dying patients:

> Glaser, Barney G. & Strauss, Anselm L. (1965), *Awareness of Dying*, Chicago, IL: Aldine.

> Glaser, Barney G. & Strauss, Anselm L. (1968), *Time for Dying*, Chicago, IL: Aldine.

In his introductory book Anselm Strauss provides a series of didactically processed examples of applications which are similarly concerned with medical-sociological problems (dealing with pain, dependency on medical technology, etc.).

> Strauss, Anselm (1987, German edition 1994), *Qualitative Analysis for Social Scientists*, Cambridge: Cambridge University Press. (German title: *Grundlagen*

qualitativer Sozialforschung, München: W. Fink UTB, 72–89, 95–100, 124–50, 153–70, 200–22.)

Anselm Strauss and Juliet Corbin edited a collection containing ten recent studies based on GT, most of them dealing with medical sociology.

Strauss, Anselm & Corbin, Juliet M. (eds) (1997), *Grounded Theory in Practice*, Thousand Oaks, CA: Sage.

Finally, in Böhm's collection on text analysis (see above) there are a number of sketches of GT applications which summarize the results of larger research projects.

NOTES

1 More detailed information on these and further programs can be found on the Internet under http://www.scolari.com/
2 An indication of the fluid boundaries: when it is a matter of data analysis Hammersley & Atkinson (1995, esp. 216ff.) refer regularly, in their ethnographic primer, to Glaser & Strauss (1967).

CHAPTER 7

ETHNOGRAPHIC METHODS

Within ethnography a distinction can be made between, on the one hand, various ethnographically oriented, more or less elaborated methods of analysis which can be applied to texts (including grounded theory, in the opinion of many authors), and, on the other hand, Dell Hymes's (1962) 'The ethnography of speaking'.

7.1 THEORETICAL ORIGINS

The theoretical roots of ethnographic methods are to be found in the anthropological and ethnological works of Bronislaw Malinowski, Franz Boas and in the linguistic studies of Edward Sapir. The core of ethnographic methodology is its 'fundamental reflexivity'. All social research is based upon the human capacity for participant observation and the capability for reflecting upon it. 'We act in the social world and yet are able to reflect upon ourselves and our actions as objects in that world' (Hammersley & Atkinson 1995: 21). The epistemological basis of many ethnographic methods is presented in the social phenomenological approaches of Alfred Schütz and in the work of Peter Berger and Thomas Luckmann (1967).

In linguistics John Gumperz and Dell Hymes presented their 'ethnography of communication', or 'ethnography of speaking' in a special number of the *American Anthropologist* (1964), both as a method and as a theory that regards communicative patterns as part of cultural knowledge and behaviour. Hymes attempts, in his work, to exploit the formal models of linguistics for the interpretation of human behaviour in cultural contexts. In so far as he stresses the descriptive aspect of ethnography, he is following Malinowski and Sapir and consciously opposing Lévi-Strauss and Chomsky: Hymes criticizes Lévi-Strauss for over-emphasizing the comparative perspective. Chomsky is criticized for 'analysing language without reference to communication, where only grammaticality has to be explained', as well as for his 'nativistic tendency to postulate universals' (Coulmas in the Foreword to Hymes 1979: 14).

7.2 BASIC THEORETICAL ASSUMPTIONS

Ethnography analyses language and text in the context of culture: culture 'denotes an historically transmitted pattern of meanings embodied in symbols, a system of inherited conceptions expressed in symbolic forms by means of which men communicate, perpetuate and develop their knowledge about and attitudes towards life' (Geertz 1973: 89). 'So culture patterns provide such programs for the institution of the social and psychological processes which shape public behavior' (Geertz 1973: 92). They also provide, therefore, programmes for language and text.

The question of the relationship between culture and language is the starting point of the 'ethnography of speaking'. It is uncontested that language exists in a cultural context, but it remains open how the relationship is to be specified: does language function as the expression of culture and is it determined by the non-linguistic features of culture (in Radcliffe-Brown's sense)? Are linguistic and non-linguistic components of culture different in principle from one another? Or does language have a determining influence on culture as an organizational principle of the material world (Sapir-Whorf hypothesis)? The last mentioned viewpoint does not seem tenable without ambiguity (Coulmas 1979: 18, Coulmas 1997), although work is currently being done on a rehabilitation of the Sapir-Whorf hypothesis (Lucy 1992, Gumperz & Levinson 1996, Lee 1996).

The ethnography of speaking seeks to describe modes of speech according to the ways in which they construct and reflect social life within particular speech communities (Fitch & Philipsen 1995: 263). Dell Hymes contrasts grammaticality, which Chomsky seeks to explain, with acceptability (Coulmas 1979: 14), and focuses on the **communicative competence** of speakers: 'A necessary step is to place speaking within a hierarchy of inclusiveness: not all behavior is communicative, from the standpoint of the participants; not all communication is linguistic; and linguistic means include more than speech' (Hymes 1962).

Ethnography of speaking seeks to provide a framework within which both anthropological and linguistic studies of communication can be carried out. It shares with traditional ethnographic approaches an interest in complete explanations of meanings and behaviour, which are embedded in a broad structure of values, actions and norms (Schiffrin 1994: 140).

7.3 GOALS OF THE METHOD

It is probably a common feature of all ethnographic methods to interpret texts against the background of cultural structures or to use texts to reconstruct those cultural structures.

> Doing ethnography is like trying to read (in the sense of 'construct a reading of') a manuscript – foreign, faded, full of ellipses, incoherences, suspicious emendations, and tendentious commentaries, but written not in conventionalized graphs of sound but in transient examples of shaped behavior. (Geertz 1973: 10)

> So, there are three characteristics of ethnographic description: it is interpretive; what it is interpretive of is the flow of social discourse; and the interpreting involved consists in trying to rescue the 'said' of such discourse from its perishing occasions and fix it in pursuable terms. (Geertz 1973: 20)

> In its most characteristic form it involves the ethnographer participating, overtly and covertly, in people's daily lives for an extended period of time, watching what happens, listening to what is said, asking questions – in fact, collecting whatever data are available to throw light on the issues that are the focus of the research. (Hammersley & Atkinson 1995: 1)

A central issue in ethnographic analysis is, as Hymes states, 'We must know what patterns are available in what contexts, and how, where and when they come into play' (1962: 20). Hymes accepts totally Lévi-Strauss's structuralism, but broadens the objectives of structural analysis:

> By structural analysis is meant more than the placing of data in an articulated set of categories. Such placing is a necessary starting point, and also a desired outcome, when systems that have been individually analysed are studied comparatively. But for the individual system, structural analysis means a scientific and moral commitment to the inductive discovery of units, criteria, and patternings that are valid in terms of the system itself. . . . The categories presented here for an ethnography of speaking must be taken as ways of getting at individual systems, as analogous to a phonetics and perhaps part of a practical phonemics. The intent is heuristic, not *a priori*. (Hymes 1962: 22)

7.4 OUTLINE OF THE METHOD

To begin, a number of specific features of ethnographic methods should be established. First, the emphasis in ethnographic methods is on *data collection*, in which participant observation is the most important method of collection: the 'royal way'. Text analyses are found only in fringe areas (documents) or else fulfil an auxiliary function in the analysis of observation reports (see Silverman 1993: 30f., Schlobinski 1996: 218f.).

Second, data analysis is not a separable phase in the research process: a dialectic interplay of data collection and data analysis is postulated (Hammersley & Atkinson 1995: 205).

Third, text analysis is carried out in the form of questions which are asked about the text. Cicourel uses the analysis of psychiatric interviews (Pittenger et al. 1960: 210) as an example in which the following questions arise:

What does each participant say? Why does he say it? How does he say it? What impact does it have on the other participant? When and how is new material brought into the picture and by whom? What is being communicated out of awareness? How does the orientation of each participant change as the transactions continue? and why? And how do we know? and if he does, by virtue of what evidence? (Cicourel 1964: 172)

Fourth, similar questions are asked by Hammersley & Atkinson about documents to be analysed:

How are the documents written? How are they read? Who writes them? Who reads them? For what purposes? On what occasions? With what outcomes? What is recorded? What is omitted? What does the writer seem to take for granted about the reader(s)? What do readers need to know in order to make sense of them? (1995: 173)

Fifth, in the investigation of linguistic structures from an ethnographic perspective the involvement of context is of central importance, where context means not only the linguistic and more narrowly defined situational context but also 'facial expression, gesture, bodily activities, the whole group of people present during an exchange of utterances and the part of the environment in which these people are engaged' (Malinowski 1966: 22).

Finally, all ethnographic analyses are concerned with discovering cultural and linguistic patterns and key events. For the visualization of these patterns it is often suggested that 'maps, flowcharts and matrices all help to crystallize and display consolidated information' (Fetterman 1989: 95).

The attempt to give a compressed overview of ethnographic methods of text analysis breaks down on account of the heterogeneity of the analytical methods covered by this label. To achieve this it will be necessary first to examine the summarized introductions to the analytical process contained in a current textbook (Hammersley & Atkinson 1995), and then to consider the specifically sociolinguistic 'ethnography of speaking'.

7.4.1 General ethnographic text analysis

In Hammersley & Atkinson's (1995: 205f.) data analysis, parallels may be seen with grounded theory (see Chapter 6), although grounded theory is worked out in considerably more detail with regard to its rules and coding procedures. An important instrument of ethnographic analysis consists of 'analytical categories' (Hammersley & Atkinson 1995: 208f.), which must be developed for any application. The first step is a matter of developing concepts which help the investigator 'to make sense of what is going on in scenes documented by the data' (Hammersley & Atkinson 1995: 209). These concepts may be 'folk terms' or 'observer identified' (Hammersley & Atkinson 1995: 211): 'Reading through the corpus of data and generating concepts which make sense of it are the initial stages of ethnographic analysis' (Hammersley & Atkinson 1995: 212).

Using these concepts the text is then coded. 'Needless to say, the process of coding the data is a recurrent one; as new categories emerge, previously coded data must be recoded to see if they contain any examples of new codes' (Hammersley & Atkinson 1995: 212f.). The aim of the data analysis is first to develop a stable set of categories, and then to code the whole of the data using these categories.

Next, those categories which reflect the central and most important concepts for a particular piece of analysis must be analysed in detail, in order to explore their precise meaning and their relationship to other categories (see Hammersley & Atkinson 1995: 213).

The 'constant comparative method' (Glaser & Strauss 1967) is another borrowing from grounded theory; for each unit of analysis that has been coded and thereby allotted to a category, the researcher determines similarities to, and differences from, other units which have been coded in the same category. In this way, on the one hand existing categories are given a more precise meaning, and on the other hand sub-categories may be distinguished (Hammersley & Atkinson 1995: 213). To increase the validity of results, *triangulation measures* are suggested in a number of places (Fetterman 1989: 89ff.). Triangulation – a term borrowed from navigation – means in general the comparison of results on the basis of different data (for example qualitative and quantitative) and using differing methods. 'Theoretical triangulation' (Denzin 1970) requires that data should be approached from different perspectives and with different hypotheses. The question asked is: 'What in the individual theories makes it possible to understand the data?' Theories are used here to provide different focuses for the analysis.

This concept of theoretical triangulation has been much criticized (see Fielding & Fielding 1986, Silverman 1993: 157ff.), and Denzin has been accused of eclecticism and theoretical vagueness. It would be better, say the accusers, to proceed from a particular theoretical perspective and select methods and sources of data which give information about meanings and structures that are postulated within the chosen theoretical perspective. 'The major problem with triangulation as a test for validity is that, by counterposing different contexts, it ignores the context-bound and skilful character of social interaction and assumes that members are "cultural dopes" who need a sociologist to dispel their illusions' (Silverman 1993: 158, referring to Garfinkel 1967 and Bloor 1978).

7.4.2 The ethnography of speaking

The central concepts of the approach of Hymes (1962, 1972), which derives in its main components from Jakobson (1960), are *speech community*, *speech situation*, *speech event*, *speech act* and *setting*. The ethnography of speaking investigates speech acts within culturally specified speech events, and the core of the method consists of systematic analysis of context as a general framework within which a particular form fulfils particular functions. This is because form alone does not explain the illocutionary force of a speech act (Schiffrin 1994: 145). The units of analysis are, therefore, speech situations, speech events and speech acts (Saville-Troike 1989: 26).

For the categorization of speech events, Hymes (1962: 24) suggests the following questions:

- What are instances of speech events?

- What classes of speech events are recognized or can be inferred?

- What are the dimensions of contrast, the distinctive features, which differentiate them? (This will include reference to how factors are presented and functions served.)

- What is their pattern of occurrence, their distribution vis-à-vis each other and externally (in terms of some total behavior or selected aspect)?

Here an analysis of words that denote speech events can also be of use within the framework of oppositions. The 'speaking grid' (see Table 7.1) provides a crude analytical framework for speech events.

The resulting research questions are as follows: Who speaks, with whom, when, where and in what code, about what? The factors listed by Hymes (1962: 26, 1972: 58), which designate 'components' within a speech event and take on a certain prominence as a speaking grid, are to be understood as 'merely an initial heuristic framework':

Table 7.1   SPEAKING grid

S	Setting, scene	physical circumstances, subjective definition of an occasion
P	Participants	speakers, sender, addressor, hearer, receiver, audience, addressee
E	Ends	purposes and goals, outcomes
A	Act sequence	message form and content
K	Key	tone, manner
I	Instrumentalities	channel (verbal, non-verbal, physical), forms of speech drawn from community repertoire
N	Norms	norms of interaction and interpretation, specific properties attached to speaking, interpretation of norms within cultural belief system
G	Genre	textual categories

With the aid of this speaking grid, though a crude analytical schema, local (that is culturally specified) communication units should be identified: speech situations (for example conference), speech events (for example question and answer sequence), and speech acts. 'For any group, the indigenous categories will vary in number and kind, and their instances and classes must be empirically identified' (Hymes 1962: 25).

Speech events and speech acts should be analysed with regard to their functions, and for this Hymes (1962: 31) offers an extended catalogue of possible communicative functions:

- expressive, emotive;

- directive (cognitive, pragmatic, persuasive, opinion-influencing);

- poetic;

- contact function (concerns transmission contact);

- metalinguistic;

- representational or reference function (concerns topic content);

- contextual function.

Here the unit of analysis is the individual speech act. The analysis of the manner in which specific speech acts (for example questions) can be used within a speech event illustrates the cultural knowledge of linguistic structure and function, and the organization of social interactions and social roles (Schiffrin 1994: 181).

7.5 QUALITY CRITERIA

What quality criteria are appropriate for the assessment of ethnographic research has been the subject of controversy within the ethnographic tradition (see Hammersley & Atkinson 1995: 227ff., Silverman 1993: 145). Essentially there are two distinct strains to the argument: first, the total rejection of 'positivist scientific' quality criteria such as validity, reliability, objectivity or inter-subjectivity; and second, the acceptance in principle of these quality criteria, albeit in a modifed form to suit the object of investigation (cultural or social structures) and the qualitative research strategy.

Adherents of the first line of argument plead for a rejection of the criteria of validity and reliability in favour of intensive personal involvement. They also plead for the abandonment of traditional scientific control, for an improvising style of research which can face situations uninfluenced by the investigators, and for the ability to learn from repeated errors (cf. Agar 1986: 12). The critics of this position then enquire about the difference between ethnography and certain forms of journalism, and draw attention to defects in ethnographic studies which can be traced back to this research orientation (cf. Silverman 1993: 153): (a) the data have been selected in such a way as to fit an idealized (pre-)conception; and (b) the criterion for data selection is mainly its exotic or dramatic quality. Accordingly ethnography should attend to the quality of its pronouncements in order to guarantee a basis for discussion and not fall back on prejudice, irrationality or the romantic ways of thinking of the nineteenth century (cf. Silverman 1993: 154).

Hammersley (1992: 50f.) suggests, under the heading 'subtle form of realism' an adaptation of the concept of validity:

- validity means trust in results, rather than absolute certainty;

- reality is viewed as independent of the opinions of the investigator;

- reality is regularly illuminated from varying perspectives.

The validity of statements is therefore governed by three criteria: (a) plausibility, (b) credibility, and (c) empirical evidence. Since (a) and (b), however, might encourage conservatism and the acceptance of 'common-sense knowledge', validity is mostly decided on the basis of the third criterion (c). Popper's postulate on formulating hypotheses and seeking to falsify them seems also, in Silverman's opinion (1993: 153f.), to be of central importance in ethnographic research, although it is too seldom practised.

For the testing of assumptions, two different approaches are often proposed (cf. critically Hammersley & Atkinson 1995: 227ff., Silverman 1993: 156ff.). The first is *triangulation of data and methods*. Using this approach provisional research results are tested with the help of a variety of data (text types) and methods (for example quantitative content analysis). The illumination of results from different theoretical perspectives is also suggested (cf. Denzin 1970). Triangulation seems problematic, however, in that the context-bound nature of social interaction is not sufficiently considered (cf. Silverman 1993: 158). The second approach is *respondent validation*. This procedure allows the objects of an investigation, or 'members', whose interactions were the subject of the research, to be confronted with the results. Whether their acceptance should be a precondition of validity, however, remains highly contested. An open 'respondent validation' would only be possible in cases where the results are compatible with the self-image of the persons investigated.

Since these methods/approaches also have striking weaknesses, in Silverman's opinion (1993: 160) the only remaining possibility is a very careful selection of units of investigation, in order to ensure at least some generalizability of statements. The problem of representativity is a matter of concern to all qualitative social research. Since no solution is available that is comparable to random sampling procedures, the following alternatives are discussed (Silverman 1993: 160):

- comparison of relevant aspects of the case with those of a larger population;

- additional quantitative analysis of random samples;

- co-ordination of a number of ethnographic studies.

Silverman (1993: 160) is of the opinion that generalization with regard to theoretical concepts is more appropriate than attempting to make inferences from individual cases about larger populations. 'Theoretical sampling' should, therefore, be conducted and cases should be selected against the background of interesting concepts. (See also Chapter 3.)

The criterion of reliability has also been discussed. Hammersley (1992: 67) understands this as 'the degree of consistency with which instances are assigned to the same category by different observers or by the same observer on different occasions'. In accordance with this Silverman (1993: 145) distinguishes between diachronic and synchronic reliability. In face of the radical rejection of the reliability criterion on the basis of the 'infinite flux' of social phenomena, Silverman points out that there would be no foundation for systematic social research without the acceptance of certain at least temporarily stable qualities in social phenomena. In the area of text analysis, transcription conventions are suggested for the preparation of the material; for the analysis itself, he suggests multiple codings to guarantee reliability, and the use of intra- and inter-coder coefficients to measure it.

It remains to be noted that the sociolinguistic 'ethnography of communication' has not conducted any comparable discussion of quality criteria. Hymes (1976) mentions only 'empirical adequacy of field investigation' without further explanation of this criterion. This method does seem, however, to take its orientation from current quality criteria:

> Complete escape from subjectivity is never possible because of our very nature as cultural animals; however, the constraints and guidelines of the methodology are intended to minimize our perceptual and analytical bias. The tradition of participant-observation is still basic for all ethnography, but it may be augmented by a variety of other data collection and validation procedures. (Saville-Troike 1989: 4)

7.6 CONDITIONS AND AREAS OF APPLICATION

Ethnographic analyses always seem appropriate when it is not only textual patterns but also their relationships with cultural constraints that are of interest. In this all forms of ethnographic analysis presuppose a considerable measure of contextual knowledge; the analysis of context is an integral component of text analysis. There is a corresponding importance of (overt or covert) participant observation as the means of data collection, in order to understand the organization of social actions in specific settings (Silverman 1993: 60). In any case, this contextual information must, in addition, be collected during text analyses.

For ethnographic text analyses a range of computer programs have now been developed (Hammersley & Atkinson 1995: 193ff.), which simplify in particular the storing and locating of specifically coded text segments and which are intended to replace the manual 'cut and paste' operation. Such 'code-and-retrieve' procedures (Weitzman & Miles 1995: 148ff.) provide, for example, The Ethnograph, Kwalitan, MAX, but also the so-called 'code-based theory-builders'(Weitzman & Miles 1995: 204ff.) such as NUDIST and

ATLAS/ti, which also make possible the linking of codes and concepts with 'grounded theories'. (See also http://www.scolari.com/products.htm for further information on ATLAS, The Ethnograph, NUDIST, QSR N Vivo and Am Mex.)

The ethnography of speaking is often understood as an integrative but extravagant approach to text analysis (see Schiffrin 1994: 181). The 'speaking grid' puts far-reaching questions which are partly related to the subjective observation of the interaction partners, and which can probably only be answered provisionally and hypothetically. Although in the process of distinguishing speech events the greatest selectivity is attributed to the factors 'participants', 'ends' and 'act sequence', in the analysis of 'key' and 'instrumentalities' a very delicate system of recording and transcription is needed which can also capture para-verbal and non-verbal events.

7.7 SIMILARITIES AND DIFFERENCES IN COMPARISON WITH OTHER METHODS

The general ethnographic method displays similarities to methods based on grounded theory and ethnomethodology. As far as the discovery of concepts is concerned, however, grounded theory has been elaborated in greater detail. It concentrates on the coding procedure and can accordingly be looked upon as a complement to ethnographic text analysis. Ethnomethodological methods are different from ethnography in their objectives; in the former it is a matter of discovering normal patterns of explanation and rationalization for the 'members' of social units, whereas ethnography is directed towards explaining cultural patterns with concepts that are not used by the actors themselves.

There are clear differences from all those methods which approach texts with concepts fixed in advance (content analysis, etc.). Ethnographic methods do indeed also work with categories, but these tend to have a provisional character. Precise operationalization, selectivity, independence and unambiguousness are not criteria that ethnographic categories have to meet, and little value is placed on quantification.

Unlike hermeneutic methods, ethnographic approaches may be characterized as fully object-oriented: the material, rather than the interpretative power of the investigators, is of central importance. Unlike text analysis based on distinction theory, ethnographic methods also dispense with any possibilities that arise from an experimental approach to texts, particularly deconstruction and reconstruction. This systematic-heuristic component has no place in ethnography.

Striking similarities are found between the speaking framework of 'ethnography of communication', the framework concepts of grounded theory (see Chapter 6, 6.4.2) and the categories of content analysis suggested by Holsti (1968: 645) and Berelson (1952: 147ff.) as relevant to any text analysis (see Chapter 5, 5.4.1.3).

Ethnography of communication differs from linguistic methods such as discourse analysis and functional pragmatics primarily because of the relatively low value it places on linguistic categories (cohesion). Although in this respect ethnography of communication resembles conversation analysis, there is a clear difference in the broader understanding of context used in ethnographic analyses.

7.8 LITERATURE

7.8.1 On Ethnography

The references given here should be understood as only a selection from the enormous wealth of ethnographic literature. In addition to a much-quoted classical source which also pays explicit attention to linguistic analysis (Malinowski 1966), three works are introduced which have achieved a certain prominence because of their treatment of general problems of ethnographic method and methodology (Geertz 1987), or of ethnographically oriented social research (Denzin 1970, Hammersley 1992). Finally, our selection includes a number of introductory presentations of ethnographic method which also deal with ethnographic text analysis (Agar 1986, Fetterman 1989, Hammersley & Atkinson 1995).

Agar, Michael (1986), *Speaking of Ethnography,* Qualitative Research Methods Series, No. 2, London: Sage.

Denzin, Norman (1970), *The Research Act in Sociology*, London: Butterworth

Fetterman, David M. (1989), *Ethnography Step by Step*, Newbury Park, CA: Sage

Geertz, Clifford (1973), *The Interpretation of Cultures*, New York: Basic Books.

Hammersley, Martyn (1992), *What's Wrong with Ethnography. Methodological Explanations*, London: Routledge.

Hammersley, Martyn & Atkinson, Paul (1995), *Ethnography. Principles in Practice*, (2nd edn), London: Routledge.

Malinowski, Bronislaw (1966 [1935]), *Coral Gardens and their Magic*, Vol. II, The Language of Magic and Gardening, London: Bloomington [New York: American].

7.8.2 On the 'ethnography of communication'

With regard to the extensive literature on the ethnography of communication, attention should be given to the special number of the *American Anthropologist* by John Gumperz and Dell Hymes (1964), to their collection of papers (Gumperz & Hymes 1972), and to Saville-Troike's introductory work (1989):

Gumperz, John J. & Hymes, Dell (1964) (eds), 'The Ethnography of Communication', *American Anthropologist* 66 (6).

Gumperz, John J. & Hymes, Dell (1972) (eds), *Directions in Sociolinguistics. The Ethnography of Communication*, New York: Holt, Rinehart and Winston.

Hymes, Dell (1962), 'The Ethnography of Speaking', in Thomas Gladwin & William C. Sturtevant (eds), *Anthropology and Human Behavior*, 13–53.

Hymes, Dell (1972), 'Models of Interaction of Language and Social Life', in John J. Gumperz & Dell Hymes (eds), *Directions in Sociolinguistics. The Ethnography of Communication*, New York: Holt, Rinehart and Winston, 35–71.

Hymes, Dell (1976), 'The State of the Art in Linguistic Anthropology', in Anthony F.C. Wallace (ed.), *Perspectives on Anthropology*, Washington: American Anthropological Association.

Hymes, Dell (1979), *Soziolinguistik: Zur Ethnographie der Kommunikation* (ed. Florian Coulmas), Frankfurt: Suhrkamp.

Saville-Troike, Muriel (1989), *The Ethnography of Communication. An Introduction*, (2nd edn), Oxford: Blackwell.

7.9 SECONDARY LITERATURE

7.9.1 Contributions to handbooks

Atkinson, Paul & Hammersley, Martyn (1994), 'Ethnography and Participant Observation', in Norman K. Denzin & Yvonna S. Lincoln (eds), *Handbook of Qualitative Research*, Thousand Oaks, CA: Sage, 248–61.

In this contribution to Denzin & Lincoln's handbook, Atkinson & Hammersley are concerned with the agenda and theoretical stance of ethnography. For them the most significant method of ethnographic data collection – participant observation – is of central importance.

Fitch, Kristine & Philipsen, Gerry (1995), 'Ethnography of Speaking', in Jef Verschueren, Jan-Ola Östman & Jan Blommaert (eds), *Handbook of Pragmatics. Manual*, Amsterdam: Benjamins 263–9.

In their article, Fitch and Philipsen concentrate on the essential concepts of Dell Hymes and on a summary of current debate. Of special note is their attempt to give an overview of concrete research projects.

Saville-Troike, Muriel (1987), 'The Ethnography of Speaking', in Ulrich Ammon, N. Dittmar & K.J. Mattheier (eds), *Sociolinguistics. An International Handbook of Science of Language*, Vol. 1, Berlin and New York: de Gruyter, 660–71.

Saville-Troike also summarizes the goals, the theoretical assumptions, and the fundamental interests of Dell Hymes's 'The Ethnography of Speaking'. After an outline of a selection of studies that use this methodology, she deals more fully with the method's 'descriptive framework'.

7.9.2 Other presentations of method

Schlobinski, Peter (1996), *Empirische Sprachwissenschaft*, Opladen: Westdeutscher Verlag, 218–33.

In this introductory work, in addition to content analysis, discourse analysis and conversation analysis, Schlobinski presents ethnographic analysis as a 'qualitative' analysis of linguistic data. In this he restricts himself to Dell Hymes's approach which he illustrates with sample analyses.

Schiffrin, Deborah (1994), *Approaches to Discourse*, Oxford: Blackwell, 137–89.

Schiffrin also restricts herself to the 'ethnography of communication'. She does, however, give a very detailed presentation of the method, fully illustrated with interview texts. This makes it clear that, even within Hymes's framework, no detailed procedures are provided but that procedure always emerges from a concrete research question.

Atkinson, Paul & Coffey, Amanda (1997), 'Analysing Documentary Realities', in David Silverman (ed.), *Qualitative Research*, London: Sage, 45–62.

Baszanger, Isabelle & Dodier, Nicolas (1997), 'Ethnography: Relating the Part to the Whole', in David Silverman (ed.), *Qualitative Research,* London: Sage, 8–23.

Whereas Baszanger & Dodier concentrate upon general ethnographic methodology and observation techniques, Atkinson & Coffey deal with the analysis of documents.

Silverman, David (1993), *Interpreting Qualitative Data. Methods for Analysing Talk, Text and Interaction*, London: Sage, 60–71.

Silverman gives a general overview of ethnographic text analysis, paying particular attention to the types of text that can provide valuable supplementary material (for example databases, statistical data, public records). Here it is not a matter of statistical parameters but of the reason why these and not other types of data were collected.

7.9.3 Sample applications

Examples of applications that illustrate the procedures of the 'ethnography of communication' are found in the following descriptions of method:

Saville-Troike, Muriel (1989), *The Ethnography of Communication. An Introduction*, (2nd edn), Oxford: Blackwell, 161–80.

Saville-Troike gives a very detailed illustration of the use of 'speaking'-oriented analysis of a speech event, using data from a traditional village meeting in Mali.

Schriffrin, Deborah (1994), *Approaches to Discourse*, Oxford: Blackwell, 149–85.

Using 'speaking', Schiffrin seeks to analyse questions that were put to librarians in public libraries during book research and social science interviews. She discovers that questions about ends, participants and the act sequence lead to especially informative results and provide the clearest differentiation of the speech events which were investigated.

Apart from these very didactically motivated examples of analyses, applications of 'ethnography of communication' are particularly to be found in the area of cross-cultural and cultural studies. Examples are in the following:

Blom, Jan-Petter & Gumperz, John J. (1972) 'Social Meaning in Linguistic Structure: Code-switching in Norway', in John J. Gumperz & Dell Hymes (eds), *Directions in Sociolinguistics. The Ethnography of Communication*, New York: Rinehart and Winston, 407–37.

Blum-Kulka, Shoshana (1990), 'You Don't Touch Lettuce with your Fingers', *Journal of Pragmatics*, 14: 259–88.

Phillipsen, Gerry (1992), *Speaking Culturally*, New York: State University Press

Willis, Paul (1977), *Learning to Labour*, Columbia: Columbia University Press.

CHAPTER 8

TWO ETHNOMETHODOLOGICALLY ORIENTED METHODS OF TEXT ANALYSIS: MEMBERSHIP CATEGORIZATION DEVICE ANALYSIS AND CONVERSATION ANALYSIS

8.1 THEORETICAL ORIGINS

Garfinkel's 'ethnomethodology' – influenced by the 'phenomenology' of Alfred Schütz (and by his concept of the everyday world or the world of daily life) – unlike other branches of sociology does not investigate social order per se. Instead it seeks to identify those everyday procedures which members of a society use to create their own social order.

The philosophical roots of this direction in sociology are found not only in Husserl's phenomenology but also in Wittgenstein's philosophy, and in particular in his concept of the language game. Wittgenstein draws attention to the connection between speaking and way of life in his philosophical research: 'The word "language game" is used here to emphasize the fact that speaking a language is part of some activity or way of life' (Wittgenstein 1984: 250, see also Kenny 1974: 186ff.).

Ethnomethodology proceeds on the basis that participants in an interaction create social order in any current situation, that is to say 'locally'. The world of social facts is created through the continuing practice of its members. Ethnomethodology is concerned with the investigation of everyday rationality, colloquial language and everyday events. 'Hence ethnomethodology is the study of the methods used by members of a group for understanding communication, making decisions, being rational, accounting for action, and so on' (Mullins 1973: 182).

Harold Garfinkel – a student of the émigré Viennese social scientist Alfred Schütz – was, together with Aaron Cicourel, the initiator of ethnomethodological theory. Garfinkel (1974) reports that he developed the basic concepts of ethnomethodology in a project designed to investigate tape-recorded reports of jury deliberations using the system initiated by Bales (1950). This interaction process analysis (see Chapter 5, 5.4.1 and Chapter 10), however, was inadequate to deal with the richness of the material, as a result of which ethnomethodology was developed. After Garfinkel moved to UCLA there emerged – throughout the different universities in California – a circle of sociologists, ethnologists and linguists to which Harvey Sacks also belonged. Membership categorization device analysis (MCD) is one of the first methods of ethnomethodology, and from this conversation analysis subsequently developed (Mullins 1973). Its strong relationship with ethnomethodology is evident in its normal designation as 'ethnomethodological conversation analysis'.

> I want to propose that a domain of research exists that is not part of any other established science. The domain is one that those who are pursuing it have come to call Ethnomethodology/Conversation Analysis. That domain seeks to describe methods persons use in doing social life. (Sacks 1984: 21)

This establishes a clear distinction from non-ethnomethodological conversation analysis which, in many German sources, is taken to refer to approaches that analyse natural texts empirically.

In the 1960s and 1970s conversation analysis developed as an independent research direction in the group led by Harvey Sacks, and it was his 'Lectures', together with the classic studies of Emanuel A. Schegloff and Gail Jefferson, that laid the foundations of the method (Jefferson 1972, Sacks 1972a, Schegloff et al. 1977, Sacks et al. 1978, Sacks & Schegloff 1979). This early work in conversation analysis already addresses, as a main research focus, the regulatory principles of sequencing in social interaction, such as turn-taking organization – the principles underlying speaker change – or repair strategies, that is the mechanisms that are employed by participants to overcome communicative disturbance and to achieve inter-subjective understanding.

The growth of conversation analysis in the 1970s coincided with two developments in linguistics and had a considerable influence on them (see Streeck 1983, Bergmann 1994). These developments were, in the first place, the move away from Chomsky's idealized speaker-hearer model and the interest in authentic language; and, in the second place, the investigation of speech actions that was motivated by pragmatics, discourse analysis and speech act theory.

8.2 BASIC THEORETICAL ASSUMPTIONS

Since MCD and conversation analysis acquire their specific character because of ethnomethodology, the theoretical assumptions can only be understood with reference to ethnomethodological principles. Four essential assumptions of ethnomethodology will be presented here as influential: (a) the performative nature of social reality, (b) the indexicality, (c) reflexivity, and (d) demonstrability of actions.

The performative nature of social reality: Harold Garfinkel, in a dissertation supervised by Talcott Parsons, is interested in the 'conditions under which a person makes continuous sense of the world around him' (Garfinkel 1952: 1, quoted in Bergmann 1994: 5). He views social reality as a 'performance reality' which is not objectively determined but is constantly produced 'locally' by participants and intersubjectively ratified. In this, Garfinkel associates himself explicitly (even in his later work) with Alfred Schütz's phenomenology and, in particular, with the idea of 'everyday' life (Garfinkel 1972). He is interested in the 'seen but unnoticed backgrounds of everyday activities' (Garfinkel 1972: 3) to which participants refer when they negotiate reality locally and interactively. In the opinion of ethnomethodologists researchers must seek to discover those indicators which are significant to the participants themselves. Aaron Cicourel even makes the validity of research results dependent upon an implicit agreement between the indicators used by the 'man in the street' and those of the social scientist. The consequence of this is that ethnomethodological analysis avoids from the outset all generalizations and stereotyping in order to capture the categorizations that participants themselves make in interactions (Heritage 1984: 292). 'The study of common sense knowledge and common sense activities consists of treating as problematic phenomena the actual methods whereby members of a society doing sociology, lay or professional, make the social structures of everyday activities observable' (Garfinkel 1972: 30). Both MCD and conversation analysis conclude from the performative nature of reality that meaning and order in conversations are created in the interaction currently in progress. Language, like all other activities, is a situational product of rules and systems.

Indexicality means that all observed phenomena are bound to the situational conditions of their production. The meaning of linguistic expressions is also indexical, therefore, which means that it resides in the use of language by particular people in quite specific contexts. The sense of linguistic utterances, therefore, is always primarily accessible with reference to the concrete context of use. Even such contexts are not viewed by ethnomethodologists as objectively determined. They are themselves part of the interaction process.

Reflexivity is related to this: it refers to the fact that actions and context are reciprocally constituted. For conversation analysis this notion of context means that only what is meaningful for participants in the current communicative situation should be counted as part of the context. Language is context-bound in two ways, since an utterance not only occurs in the context of its production and interpretation, but simultaneously contributes to the context of the next utterance (Heritage 1984: 242). This reflexive context orientation characterizes the interlinking of utterances and is significant for the local creation of order.

Related to reflexivity is *demonstrability*: this refers to the rules used by participants to make actions demonstrable and recognizable (Schiffrin 1994: 234).

On the basis of these theoretical assumptions, ethnomethodology has developed specific methods of text analysis whose particular field of application is everyday conversation and everyday stories. MCD analysis attempts to reconstruct the tools used by participants for description and categorization. Conversation analysis is concerned 'briefly, with the communicative principles of the *(re-)production of social order* in situated linguistic and non-linguistic interaction' (Bergmann 1994: 3; emphasis in original).

8.3 OBJECTIVES OF THE METHOD

8.3.1 Objectives of MCD analysis

The goal of MCD analysis is to understand when and how members of society make descriptions in order subsequently to represent the mechanism used to produce appropriate and suitable descriptions (Silverman 1993: 80).

> What one ought to seek is to build an apparatus which will provide for how it is that any activities, which members do in such a way as to be recognisable as such to members, are done and done recognisable. (Sacks 1992b: 236)

8.3.2 Objectives of conversation analysis

Conversation analysis seeks to find those generative principles and procedures which participants use to produce the characteristic structure and order of a communicative situation (Bergmann 1994: 7).

> The kinds of phenomena we are going to be dealing with are always transcriptions of actual occurrences in their actual sequence. And I take it our business is to try to construct the machinery that would produce those utterances. That is, we will find and name some objects and find and name some rules for using those objects, where the rules for using those objects will produce those occurrences. (Sacks 1985: 13)

The goal is therefore to discover the 'machinery' that can reproduce what the participants do. In this way the discovery, through ethnomethodology, of every-day phenomena is also present in conversation analysis. In seeking participants' knowledge of their own everyday circumstances, conversation analysis attempts to discover how particular aspects of conversation are viewed by the speakers themselves. Behaviour is therefore analysed, and from this analysis units, patterns and rules are derived and formulated (Schiffrin 1994: 236). An example of observable phenomena whose underlying mechanisms are of fundamental interest to conversation analysis is speaker change: participants speak individually and rarely at the same time, one speaker may nominate the next speaker, or the next speaker may be self-nominated, etc. The underlying rules of this everyday behaviour have been presented by Harvey Sacks, Emanuel Schegloff and Gail Jefferson as a simple system, and this will be described in more detail below (Sacks et al. 1978; see also section 8.4.2).

It is also part of the theoretical basis that conversation analysis is concerned with the analysis of texts from natural rather than experimental situations. The method is context-bound and the idea of text relates closely to the ethnomethodological tradition. Text is understood as an interactive product and the result of the mutual interpretations of partners in a conversation. Interaction is structured: one example of such structuring is found in adjacency pairs. These are a sequence of two utterances produced by different speakers and ordered as first and second part, so that the first part implies a second part, for instance in question-answer sequences.

Related to this is the idea of context, which similarly has an ethnomethodological orientation. The assumption of this prospective-retrospective attribution of meaning binds each utterance to the context of the previous one and views it simultaneously as the context for the next: 'the significance of any speaker's communicative action is doubly contextual in being both *context-shaped* and *context-renewing*' (Heritage 1984: 242). Factors other than these context-creating factors in the text itself are not of primary importance: 'the fact that they are "in fact" respectively a doctor and a patient does not make those characterizations *ipso facto* relevant' (Schegloff 1987: 219). The only thing that counts as context is what is evident in the text for the participants. The idea of context used by conversation analysis is therefore founded upon the text.

8.4 OUTLINE OF THE METHOD

8.4.1 Outline of MCD analysis

The starting point for MCD analysis consists of small textual units which are mostly single statements or sentences. The following two sentences have achieved a measure of fame through the work of Sacks (1972b):

The baby cried. The mommy picked it up.

MCD analysis attempts to ascertain what lies behind the understanding of such small units by members of a particular group. If we examine our everyday understanding it becomes clear that we understand that it is the mother of that particular baby who picks it up because it is crying. The task of picking up the baby is allotted to her. The text is understood in this way, even though the following questions are not explicitly answered:

● Is this indeed the mother of the child in question?

● Did the baby cry before it was picked up?

● Was the baby picked up because it cried?

Apparently, however, the sequence of two sentences is understood in the same way by all potential listeners, even though they do not know exactly which baby and which mother are referred to, whether the baby cried before being picked up and what the mother's motives were.

MCD analysis then seeks to construct the 'machinery' that will show how it is that listeners understand this fragment in predominantly the same way. This mechanism – the membership categorization device – consists, according to Sacks (1972b), of the following components (see Sacks 1972a):

(a) *categories*, which are used for the description of objects or persons, for example 'mother';
(b) *collections*, that is of categories which are perceived as belonging together – for example the categories 'mother', 'father' and 'baby' belong to the collection 'family';
(c) *category bound activities*, which are those actions which are normally attributed to the members of a category – so 'crying' is attributed to 'baby', and 'picking up the baby' to its mother.

In applying these components members are normally guided by two rules (Sacks 1972a, 1972b):

(a) *consistency rules*. Whenever a speaker uses two or more categories and it is possible to understand these categories as belonging to one *collection*, they will be understood in this way; in this way 'mother' and 'baby' belong in the same family. Once a category from a particular *collection* has been used, there is a preference for relating other previously uncategorized members to categories from the same *collection*.
(b) *efficiency rule*. Every person is allocated to only one category, and when all persons have been allocated the interpretation is complete.

The task of MCD analysis is then to reconstruct this mechanism in texts, whereby observational and evaluative schemata of groups (or members) may be discovered.

8.4.2 OUTLINE OF CONVERSATION ANALYSIS

8.4.2.1 Rules and the course of the analysis

In the introduction to the classic collection of papers on conversation analysis, Jim Schenkein speaks of a common 'analytic mentality' in the studies contained in the book (Schenkein 1978a: 1). The ethnomethodological orientation implies that it is a matter of reconstructing reality from the point of view of the participants to an interaction. Related to this is the requirement to discover those methods that are used by the participants themselves in the production of the object. The particular procedure used in the analysis must therefore be adapted to the specific object of investigation. For this reason conversation analysis does not formulate any general and binding methodology. However, its analysis is systematic and rule-governed. As examples of generally binding ground rules for any conversation analysis we may take the requirements formulated by Harvey Sacks:

> A first rule of procedure in doing analysis, a rule that you absolutely must use or you can't do the work, is this: In setting up what it is that seems to have happened, preparatory to solving the problem, do not let your notion of what could conceivably happen decide for you what must have happened. (Sacks 1985: 15)

> There is no necessary fit between the complexity or simplicity of the apparatus you need to construct some object and the face-value complexity or simplicity of the object. (Sacks 1985: 15–16)

This means that in any analysis the reconstruction of reality from the participants' viewpoint should not be hidden by the investigators' ideas, and that simple everyday matters may not necessarily be described with equal simplicity. As an example of this, Harvey Sacks cites an English grammar, where precisely those sentences which a six-year-old child can routinely produce could not be adequately accounted for (Sacks 1985: 16).

In addition to these ground rules, the steps in the analysis can be described only in very general terms since they derive from the behaviour of the participants and are only gradually formulated as the structure of the particular object is discovered. According to Werner Kallmeyer (1988: 1101) sequential procedure, precise observation of ordered nature of activities, and the elaboration of reciprocal interpretations are the hallmarks of the method.

The type of description used in conversation analysis approaches the sound and visual documents step by step – that is sequentially. Bergmann (1994: 11) recommends that, as a first step, a relatively small segment of data should be analysed by an interpretation group, without jumping backwards or forwards in the transcript. Interpretation hypotheses are developed, rejected or validated jointly. The work of interpretation consists only of identifying objects (that is linguistic and non-linguistic utterances) and understanding them as components of an ordered event created by the participants. Conversation analysis understands the ordered nature of activities to be a result of the methodical solving of some structural problems in the social organization of interaction, in other words as the answer to a preceding question. Proceeding from hypotheses about the underlying structural problem, it reconstructs those everyday methods used by participants to solve the particular problem and thereby to produce the observable order of the activities. To test the validity of the interpretation, a series of cases are finally examined. The starting point is always the participants' notion of relevance; it is therefore not a question of what speakers might intend by a particular utterance, but of how this utterance was handled in the conversation. At the end there is a classification of the techniques used in the conversation by the participants to the interaction. Categorizations are, therefore, typically only undertaken as a final step.

> We would want to name those objects and see how they work, as we know how verbs and adjectives and sentences work. Therefore we can come to see how an activity is assembled, as we see a sentence assembled with a verb, a predicate, and so on. Ideally, of course, we would have a formally describable method, as the assembly of a sentence is formally describable. The description not only would

handle sequences in general, but particular sentences. What we would be doing, then, is developing another grammar. And grammar, of course, is the model of routinely observable, closely ordered social activities. (Sacks 1984: 24f.)

In this way conversation analysis locates itself in the border area between sociology and linguistics; even though language is being investigated, grammatical categories and structures are not of interest to the analysis, since no categories are formulated that are not relevant for the speakers in current conversation (see Schiffrin 1994: 239).

At the centre of interest are the regulatory mechanisms for organizing the course of social interaction. Classic objects of investigation are the organization of speaker change and the sequential organization of conversations which links two successive utterances as an interaction sequence. The organization of speaker change as a central component in the interaction system provides an example of the procedure followed by conversation analysis (see Sacks et al. 1978: 7–55). In their classic article Sacks, Schegloff and Jefferson claim to have found here a context-free and context-sensitive system for the organization of contributions to conversations (see Sacks et al. 1978: 10): context-free, because a formal system is available that can be applied to all possible conversational situations, and context-sensitive in that it copes simultaneously with contextual factors (see Figure 8.1). The system comprises two components, namely the turn-construction component and the turn-allocation component, as well as rules for combining them. The word 'turn' is used in conversation

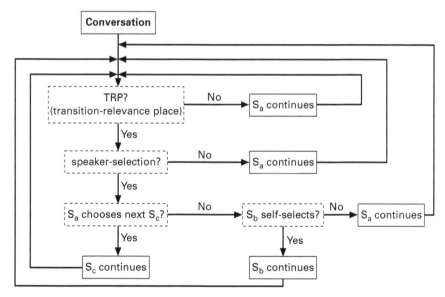

S_a: current speaker
S_b: next speaker (self selection)
S_c: next speaker (selection by other)

FIGURE 8.1   System of speaker change (Source: Schlobinski 1996: 209)

analysis to refer to an utterance (or sequence of utterances) from a single speaker from taking over the right to speak until it is yielded to the next speaker. The turn-construction components may, for example, be sentences. They are recognized by the listeners as such and make it possible for them to assess the further development of the contribution. The first possible conclusion of construction types are the so-called 'transition-relevance places' (TRP). With turn-allocation components, a distinction is made between those by means of which current speakers choose the next speakers, and those by means of which a subsequent contribution comes about through self-selection. In addition two rules are formulated. Rule one is divided into three: (a) If the contribution contains a device for speaker selection, then the speaker who is thereby selected has the right to take over the next contribution. (b) If the turn contains no device for 'selection by other', self-selection is possible, and the one who first begins to speak obtains the next turn. (c) If the turn contains no device for 'selection by other' the current speaker may continue, except when some other person takes over the talk. Rule two states: if, at the first transition-relevant place, the current speaker has selected no one and no one else has taken over the turn, and if the current speaker continues, then the rules described in rule one (above) will apply recursively at the next transition-relevant place. The system of speaker change is presented in Figure 8.1.

Schlobinski illustrates this underlying system with the example of a sequence from a purchasing conversation:

(1) Seller: a pound of apples, right (.)

(2) Buyer: and four pears please.

A pause indicates here the transition-relevance place at the end of the seller's turn. The next speaker interprets this herself as a TRP and self-selects.

(1) Seller: a pound of apples, right (.) anything else?

(2) Buyer: and four pears please.

Here the current speaker yields the right to speak to the next speaker, and intonation plays a decisive role in this. The next speaker accepts the 'selection by other' by beginning his or her own turn.

Conversation analysis places at a higher level than the organization of speaker change the principle of sequential organization, that is the joining of two adjacent utterances into an interaction sequence, and it also analyses the forms of different interaction sequences that go beyond that. To deal with this the concepts of conditional relevance and preference organization were developed. Conditional relevance denotes a dependency relationship between two turns. A question, for example, expects an answer and a greeting anticipates a counter-greeting. Through conditional relevance so-called adjacency pairs are formed (see Schegloff & Sacks 1973).

Convervation analysis uses the term preference organization to describe the fact that not all possible reactions to a linguistic activity are of equal value, and makes a distinction between preferred and dispreferred activities. The preferred structure after a question is an answer, but equally the dispreferred option of a counter-question might be selected. An early study of preference organization was that of Schegloff et al. (1977), which analyses the preference for self-correction (that is self-correction by the speaker) over correction by other speakers. By means of the categories of conditional relevance and preference organization, conversation analysis can certainly deal with complex and wide-ranging contexts (see also Kallmeyer 1988: 1099).

8.4.2.2 Critical discussion

The criticism of conversation analysis was stimulated particularly by its understanding of context (cf. Cicourel 1992, Kotthoff 1996, Gruber 1996, Mey 1993). In a response to Schegloff's lecture 'Whose Text? Whose Context?' (see Schegloff 1998), Teun van Dijk[1] explains why he considers as illusory the unconditional study of the 'text itself' postulated by conversation analysis. Researchers always project their own categories on to texts in order simply to be able to understand them. Participants in an interaction can implicitly take as given categories such as gender. In addition van Dijk believes that the boundary between what belongs to the text itself and all other influences cannot be clearly defined since there is much in a text which is implied and presupposed. Finally, the transmission of the rich sociocultural knowledge of cognitive processes must also be considered. In van Dijk's opinion it is now a matter of developing explicit theories which capture the relationship between the properties of the text itself and the manifold social, cultural and cognitive contexts, since such relationships cannot simply be taken as given or transparent.

Kotthoff's (1996) criticism is in the same general direction: when conversation analysts claim to find all relevant macro-phenomena such as social level, age, etc. in a single conversation (Schegloff 1987), they presuppose in the investigators a knowledge of those procedures which make cultural and power differences and so on relevant in a conversation. Kotthoff sees this argument as circular since only a systematic comparison of conversations can reveal distinctions which may be due, for example, to power differences (Kotthoff 1996: 187). Gruber (1996) and Cicourel (1992) show that the shared background knowledge of participants together with its cultural and organizational conditions are revealing in an understanding of conversations. This criticism, and also the fact that classical ethnomethodologists such as Harold Garfinkel and Harvey Sacks (in his 'Lectures') referred to the background knowledge of participants, has led, within conversation analysis itself, to a broader notion of context (see especially Atkinson & Heritage 1984, Bilmes 1993).

From the ethnomethodological restriction on the 'here and now', Flader and von Trotha (1988) derive a serious academic limitation: if one is looking at the procedures used by participants in problem-solving, then the results are restricted to the participants in the conversation and have no explanatory power beyond the individual case (cf. Wodak et al. 1990: 43, Rehbein 1988: 1183).

There has also been critical discussion of the relationship between linguistic and interactive structures, and the meaning attributed in the analysis to linguistic units (Kallmeyer 1988: 1100). The role of linguistic structures is seriously undervalued by the treatment of language as a guest in interaction structure. An attempt is being made to take acount of this criticism in more linguistically oriented studies (see for instance Gülich & Kotschi 1987).

8.5 QUALITY CRITERIA

If one accepts the judgement of Mullins (1973: 190), the most important programmatic stimulus for ethnomethodology came from Aaron Cicourel's (1964) *Method and Measurement in Sociology* where he claims:

> The recipes of everyday life consist of a set of analogies, which are constantly being masked, altered, and created during the course of interaction. The study of cultural meanings, with their invariant and innovative properties, remains empirically open. Our methods often follow the assumptions of the measurement systems we would like to use, and we are led into their application without asking whether alternative modes of measurement are possible or even demanded because of the structure of events under study. (Cicourel 1964: 224)

Of course Cicourel avoids discussing 'classical' quality criteria or formulating new ones, but his recommendations for fieldwork (1964: 68ff.) may nevertheless be used to derive a number of 'criteria' for ethnomethodologically oriented text analysis:

- Research goals should be formulated as explicitly as possible, theoretical claims should be studied and hypotheses should be tested.

- Every additional piece of knowledge of the research situation should be obtained. All types of information that are necessary for the research goals should be made explicit. This rule, which Cicourel formulates for ethnomethodological research in general, has not been adopted by conversation analysis.

- Careful notes concerning all stages of the research should make transparent any discrepancies between '(1) explicit and implicit plans, (2) theory and methodology and (3) changes of position over the course of time'.

- 'Whereas a researcher may have started with a very meager research design and vague notions about the problem under investigation, by means of a detailed specification of his methodological procedures as well as of their limitations, he may come to test some very specific hypotheses, if the conditions of the setting permit it' (Cicourel 1964: 69).

If one accepts these rules one can also find in ethnomethodology relics of the criteria of validity, reliability and, in particular, replicability of results. Sacks (1972a: 33) defines 'participants' adequacy' as a central criterion for ethnomethodological analyses. Schegloff (1992: 107ff.) discusses this criterion of 'relevance', comparing a 'positivistic' and an 'alternative' variant. In the sense of the former, success in the categorization of participants can be attributed to a particular 'technology' – be it statistical significance or historical evidence; the 'alternative' solution is based on the fact that the characterization of participants depends on aspects which are clearly not relevant for the persons themselves. This notion of validity – even though Sacks and Schegloff do not explicitly identify it as such – seems to suggest a kind of 'participant validation' (cf. Chapter 7, 7.5).

8.6 AREAS OF APPLICATION AND PRECONDITIONS

8.6.1 For MCD analysis

Ethnomethodology always means devoting oneself to the search for everyday reality. It is therefore concerned with the explanation of social phenomena with 'ethno'-concepts. Originally MCD was developed for the analysis of everyday situations, conversations and interactions. There is, however, no reason why the analytical framework should not be applied to other texts. In the variant proposed by Sacks, however, MCD analysis is only applicable to small quantities of text. Although this is not foreseen in the actual methodology, the results of a MCD analysis can serve as the starting point for (theoretically supported) interpretations, devoted to the question of what social structures could lie behind the categorization mechanisms that have been discovered in the analysis.

8.6.2 For conversation analysis

Bergmann (1994) sees conversation analysis as a victim of the misunderstanding that it is only concerned with the analysis of 'conversations' in the sense of informal everyday talk. In fact, everyday types of talk, without pre-structuring, and where the distribution of turns, the sequence of themes and the length of contributions is not fixed, are of central interest as a basic form of linguistic interaction (Heritage 1984); they also form the basis for the analysis of all other texts (see Silverman 1993: 134). The foundation for a wide ranging area of application was already laid in Jim Schenkein's (1978a) collection:

> There are conversations held over telephones and intercoms; into hidden recorders and open microphones; in living rooms and factories; out of doors and aboard ship; over a meal and under arrest; among strangers, co-workers, intimates, and others; delivering news, conducting business, offering praise, registering complaints, selling insurance, giving instructions, calling the police, telling stories, making excuses, working through therapy, exchanging small talk and so on. Within obvious limits, it is a highly varied corpus of materials. (Schenkein 1978b: 2)

As a result of this, analyses of institutional communication were quick to develop (see for example Atkinson & Drew 1979, Drew & Heritage 1992).

The heterogeneity of the potential areas of application implies strict preconditions which the data material must meet (Kallmeyer 1988: 1102ff.): preparatory ethnographic studies must make the field of investigation accessible and help in the discovery and – if possible – selection of relevant phenomena. This is of particular importance if the field of research is not part of the researchers' life experience and if specific situations, such as court dealings and the like, are being dealt with rather than general mechanisms. The extent to which ethnographic studies themselves spill over into the analysis depends on the underlying notion of context. The data material is not experimental but derives from natural interaction. As far as possible the work is carried out with transcribed texts and film material rather than with reductive and interpreting data. The communicative phenomena being investigated should be fully recorded, including the beginning and the conclusion, since these are often important for the reconstruction of some sequentially ordered coherence. In principle this is also true for so-called sample analyses where it is not specific communicative events such as therapy talk that are being investigated but collections of such data as question and answer sequences or repair devices. Here too, every example from a particular sample should be reconstructed as an individual case.

Finally the recorded data are prepared for analysis using a specific system of transcription which was developed mainly by Gail Jefferson (see Schenkein 1978a: xi). It is important to give the fullest possible attention to phonetic and non-verbal phenomena, since from the point of view of conversation analysis nothing is prejudged as irrelevant. For example square brackets indicate overlaps, and dashes indicate the lengthening of sounds. Punctuation marks are used to indicate intonational phenomena: a full stop shows falling intonation, a comma shows continuing (level) intonation, and a question mark denotes rising intonation; an abrupt cessation is indicated by a hyphen and an intensive tone by an exclamation mark. Arrows represent a particularly prominent change in rising or falling tone. Underlining is used to mark emphasis, and other comments are inserted in round brackets. In Jim Schenkein's collection (1978a: xi) this system of transcription is explained at the beginning with a number of examples:

```
TOM:     I used to smoke a lot when I was young
         [[
BOB:     I used to smoke Camels
```

The double square brackets indicate that the two utterances happen simultaneously.

```
TOM:     I used to smoke a lot more than this=
                  [
BOB:                   You used to smoke
TOM:     =but I never inhaled the smoke
```

The single square bracket indicates where two or more utterances begin to overlap and '=' shows where in the transcript an utterance continues.

ANN: It happens to be *mine*
BEN: It's not either yours it's *mine*
ANN: AND I DON'T KNOW WHY YOU'RE SO HARD ON THIS

Emphasis is indicated by italic script and is reinforced by bold typeface or capitals. 'I used to ((cough)) smoke a lot': – comments are inserted in round brackets in the text.

8.7 SIMILARITIES AND DIFFERENCES IN COMPARISON TO OTHER METHODS

8.7.1 MCD analysis

The main point that distinguishes MCD analysis from other methods of text analysis is its specific research question, its search for the categorization mechanism used by individuals in their function as members of social units. Perception schemata, for instance, are also a principle focus in the research goal of text analyses using distinction theory.

The difference between MCD, with its strong text and interpretation orientation, and the categorizing procedures of content analysis is clear at first glance. MCD analysis could, of course, be seen as a quantitative sort of content analysis. The concepts of collections, categories and activities are set up (either deductively or inductively) and illustrated, making it possible to give quantitative evaluations. For this purpose text-retrieve programs with powerful 'keyword-in-context' functions (for example WordCruncher) may be used.

8.7.2 Conversation analysis

The most important data source (although other forms such as audio and film documents can and should be used in a supplementary way) consists of texts in written form, in particular transcriptions of oral communication. There are also some individual suggestions that the method can be applied to other text-types (Knauth et al. 1990/91). In this way conversation analysis differs in principle from other methods where the field of application is not restricted to oral communication. Apart from this, conversation analysis, unlike most other methods, analyses only those texts that are produced by more than one person. As with critical discourse analysis and functional pragmatics, a very precise transcription – taking account of overlaps, para-verbal and non-verbal phenomena – is an absolute prerequisite for the analysis.

A further difference is to be found in the understanding of context, which is very different from that of other methods and which belongs to the eth-nomethodological tradition. The reflexive context-orientation means that every utterance is shaped by the context of the preceding utterance and simultaneously provides the context for the following utterance: an utterance is therefore not only contextually shaped but is also context-modifying. The classic form of conversation analysis sees context as part of the text itself. It therefore proceeds on the basis of a much narrower understanding of context than other methods which include features of speakers and situation, historical facts, and macro-social relationships in their analyses of context. (In ethnographic terms this would be described as 'whatever data are available', cf. Hammersley & Atkinson 1995: 1.) We may observe, however, that criticisms of this definition of context in conversation analysis have led to further developments and to a broader notion of context in some conversation analysis studies (see Gruber 1996, Kotthoff 1996, Cicourel 1992).

The local context-orientation in conversation analysis implies, moreover, that macro-social phenomena such as level, age and so on are recorded when they are relevant in a particular conversation. This concentration on the immediate locality means that, unlike other methods, conversation analysis does not conceptualize any theoretical link between language and society. Fairclough's critical discourse analysis uses this link, following Foucault, in his so-called orders of discourse (for example Fairclough 1995a); and the discourse-historical method is able to incorporate the social framework in the socio-psycholinguistic theory of text-planning (for example Wodak et al. 1990). Functional pragmatics accounts for these links with reference to language-external purposes, which underlie all speech actions, and to their transmission by institutions (Ehlich & Rehbein 1986).

A similar relationship to the theoretical background is seen in the fact that conversation analysis does not rely on pre-defined concepts; in this sense it operates in much the same way as ethnography and grounded theory. Both of these attempt to approach their data material as impartially as possible, and deny themselves the use of pre-defined concepts and theories. The impartiality of conversation analysis takes the ethnographic principles to the point where it uses no linguistic categories that are not relevant for the speakers themselves in a current conversation.

We propose that there should be a distinction between all 'linguistic' methods that incorporate (text-)linguistic starting points and theories. Fairclough starts with Halliday's multifunctional theory of language; his analytical model also includes the analysis of content and 'form', or texture. Wodak bases her discourse-historical method on a socio-psycholinguistic theory of text-planning; her analytical model also includes, in the forms of the linguistic realizations, a textual level. Functional pragmatics also falls back on grammatical categories in its 'means of expression' for 'procedures'.

In respect of the practical relevance of different methods there is a clearly defined boundary between conversation analysis on one side and functional pragmatics and critical discourse analysis on the other. Whereas the latter two expect their results to lead to more or less explicit changes in the behaviour of participants, conversation analysis seeks only to discover the generative procedures used by participants and does not seek to influence or change those procedures.

8.8 LITERATURE

8.8.1 On ethnomethodology

For ethnomethodological sociology we should first of all draw attention to the contribution of Nicholas Mullins (1981, 1973), who describes the origin and growth of the discipline from an historical and sociological perspective. Garfinkel's *Studies in Ethnomethodology* (1967) and Cicourel's *Method and Measurement in Sociology* (1964) should also be mentioned as foundation works. A number of different contributions to ethnomethodology are also to be found in Turner's (1974) collection:

Cicourel, Aaron V. (1964), *Method and Measurement in Sociology*, Glencoe, IL: The Free Press.

Garfinkel, Harold (1967), *Studies in Ethnomethodology*, Englewood Cliffs,NJ: Prentice Hall.

Mullins, Nicholas C. (1973), *Theory and Theory Groups in Contemporary American Sociology*, New York: Harper & Row.

Mullins, Nicholas C. (1981), 'Ethnomethodologie: Das Spezialgebiet, das aus der Kälte kam', in Wolf Lepenies (ed.) *Geschichte der Soziologie: Studien zur kognitiven, sozialen und historischen Identität einer Disziplin*, Frankfurt: Suhrkamp.

Turner, Roy (ed.) (1974), *Ethnomethodology*, Harmondsworth: Penguin.

8.8.2 On MCD analysis

There is no single work exclusively devoted to MCD analysis and the procedures used in this method. Instead Sacks refers in a number of different places to the 'Membership Categorization Device', normally also in relation to conversation analysis, and in each of these he introduces individual aspects of the method:

Sacks, Harvey (1972a), 'An Initial Investigation of the Usability of Conversational Data for Doing Sociology', in David Sudnow (ed.) *Studies in Social Interaction*, New York: The Free Press, 31–73.

In this contribution Sacks describes the 'Collections of Membership Categories' as one of the basic concepts to account for the material that has arisen from counselling conversations with persons in danger of suicide. He develops systematically the rules which the 'Categorization Device' employs.

Sacks, Harvey (1972b), 'On the Analysability of Stories by Children', in John J. Gumperz and Dell Hymes (eds), *Directions in Sociolinguistics*, New York: Holt, Rinehart and Winston, 325–45.

Here Sacks illustrates the function of MCDs with the frequently quoted example 'The baby cried. The mommy picked it up.' He gives pointers for the identification of collections, categories and category-bound activities; with the section on the sequential organization of conversations he moves on to conversation analysis.

Sacks, Harvey (1992a, 1992b), *Lectures on Conversation*, 2 Vols, Gail Jefferson (ed.), Cambridge, MA: Blackwell.

In these two volumes of posthumously published lectures, which Sacks gave between 1964 and 1979, MCD is also mentioned in several places (see Sacks 1992a: 40ff., 169ff., 175ff., 568ff., 578ff., 584ff., 589ff.), and it becomes clear that Sacks devoted himself in his early lectures to MCD, whereas in later ones he attended more to matters of sequential organization and therefore conversation analysis.

8.8.3 On conversation analysis

The starting point of ethnomethodological conversation analysis is to be found in the lectures of Harvey Sacks (1992a, 1992b) edited by Gail Jefferson. In addition a distinction may be made between general considerations of objectives and methodology (Sacks 1984, 1985) and the classic collections with sample applications of the conversation analysis method (Drew & Heritage 1992, Atkinson & Heritage 1984, Psathas 1979, Schenkein 1978a, Sudnow 1972). These also include the most prominent studies (such as Sacks et al. (1978): 'A simplest systematics for the organization of turn taking for conversation' in J. Schenkein (ed.), (1978a), *Studies in the Organization of Conversational Interaction*, New York: Academic Press, 7–55). Many linguists were first made aware of conversation analysis by Levinson (1983).

Atkinson, J. Maxwell & Heritage, John C. (eds) (1984), *Structures of Social Action: Studies in Conversation Analysis*, Cambridge: Cambridge University Press.

Levinson, Stephen C. (1983), *Pragmatics*, Cambridge: Cambridge University Press.

Sacks, Harvey (1984), 'Notes on Methodology', in J.M. Atkinson & J.C. Heritage (eds), *Structures of Social Action: Studies in Conversation Analysis*, Cambridge: Cambridge University Press, 21–7.

Sacks, Harvey (1985), 'The Interference-Making Machine: Notes on Observability', in Teun A. van Dijk (ed.), *Handbook of Discourse Analysis*, vol. 3, Discourse and Dialogue, London: Academic Press, 13–23.

Sacks, Harvey (1992a, 1992b), *Lectures on Conversation*, 2 vols, Gail Jefferson (ed.), Cambridge, MA: Blackwell.

Schegloff, Emanuel A. (1992), 'On Talk and its Institutional Occasions', in Paul Drew & John Heritage, *Talk at Work. Interaction in Institutional Settings*, Cambridge: Cambridge University Press, 101–34.

Schenkein, Jim (ed.) (1978a), *Studies in the Organization of Conversational Interaction*, New York: Academic Press.

Sudnow, David (ed.) (1972), *Studies in Social Interaction*, New York: Free Press.

8.9 SECONDARY LITERATURE

8.9.1 Handbooks

A range of chapters in handbooks are concerned with the ethnomethodological background, and three representative examples may be cited:

Firth, Alan (1995), 'Ethnomethodology', in Jef Verschueren, Jan-Ola Östman & Jan Blommaert (eds), *Handbook of Pragmatics: Manual*, Amsterdam: Benjamins, 269–78.

Holstein, James & Gubrium, Jaber F. (1994), 'Phenomenology, Ethnomethodology and Interpretative Practice', in Norman K. Denzin & Yvonna S. Lincoln (eds) *Handbook of Qualitative Research*, Thousand Oaks, CA: Sage, 262–72.

Streeck, Jürgen (1987), 'Ethnomethodologie', in Ulrich Ammon, Norbert Dittmar & Klaus Mattheier (eds), *Soziolinguistik: ein internationales Handbook zur Wissenschaft von Sprache und Gesellschaft*, vol. 1, Berlin: de Gruyter, 672–9.

In the last mentioned chapter Holstein and Gubrium sketch the development of qualitative social research with a phenomenological and ethnomethodological orientation. The chapter seeks to give an overview of 'a variety of aspects of social order' that are investigated by ethnomethodology. The foundations and assumptions of conversation analysis are described, but more recent developments and research emphases (such as 'collective representations', and 'rhetorics of everyday life') are also discussed.

The following articles concentrate on conversation analysis:

Hutchby, Ian and Drew, Paul (1995), 'Conversation Analysis', in Jef Verschueren, Jan-Ola Östman & Jan Blommaert (eds), *Handbook of Pragmatics: Manual*, Amsterdam: Benjamins, 182–9.

This article gives a short overview of the theoretical origin and the areas of application of conversation analysis and describes, with examples, the turn-taking system, the interactive production of meaning, and conditional relevance.

Kallmeyer, Werner (1988), 'Konversationsanalytische Beschreibung', in Ulrich Ammon, Norbert Dittmar & Klaus Mattheier (eds), *Soziolinguistik: ein internationales Handbuch zur Wissenschaft von Sprache und Gesellschaft*, vol. 2, Berlin: de Gruyter, 1095–108.

Werner Kallmeyer describes in detail how the individual theoretical and methodological principles of ethnomethodology find an expression in conversation analysis, and demonstrates the analytical process and its preconditions.

Bergmann, Jörg R. (1994), 'Ethnomethodologische Konversationsanalyse', in Gerd Fritz & Franz Hundsnurscher (eds), *Handbuch der Dialoganalyse*, Tübingen: Niemeyer, 3–16.

In addition to the history and the theoretical background Jörg Bergmann presents the central themes of conversation analysis.

8.9.2 Other presentations of method

Silverman, David (1993), *Interpreting Qualitative Data. Methods for Analysing Talk, Text and Interaction*, London: Sage, 80–9, 125–33.

Silverman sketches both MCD and conversation analysis, relating the former to text analysis and the latter to the analysis of transcripts. In this he takes account of the primary area of application of conversation analysis. He illustrates MCD analysis with newspaper headlines, contact advertisements and fragments of conversations. The latter are used to present conversation analysis, and in this he goes more deeply into the sequential ordering of conversations, conversational openers, and the structure of turn taking. In addition to this standard thematic area in conversation analysis, Silverman gives particular attention to studies of institutional conversations. Overall, Silverman succeeds in giving a clear, intelligible yet concise introduction.

Schlobinski, Peter (1996), *Empirische Sprachwissenschaft*, Opladen: Westdeutscher Verlag, 207–17.

In the chapter on conversation analysis, the system of speaker change, conversational sequencing and basic structures are presented, with examples, as three themes that are of central interest in conversation analysis.

Malmkjaer, Kirsten (1991b), 'Discourse and Conversational Analysis', in Kirsten Malmkjaer (ed.), *The Linguistics Encyclopedia*, London: Routledge, 100–10.

In this article conversation analysis is presented alongside the system of discourse analysis developed in Birmingham University. The presentation is limited to one main focus of interest in conversation analysis, namely the system of adjacency pairs.

Finally, the contribution of Knauth et al. (1990/91) is worthy of mention: this not only sketches the methodological orientation of conversation analysis, but also discusses its usability in text analysis and illustrates this with psychiatric expert opinions.

Knauth, Bettina, Kroner, Wolfgang & Wolff, Stephan (1990/91), 'Konversationsanalyse von Texten', *Angewandte Sozialforschung*, 16 (1–2: 31–43).

8.9.3 Sample studies

All of Harvey Sacks's works on MCD also contain examples that illustrate the method:

Sacks, Harvey (1972b), 'On the Analysability of Stories by Children', in John J. Gumperz and Dell Hymes (eds), *Directions in Sociolinguistics*, New York: Holt, Rinehart and Winston, pp. 325–45.

Sacks, Harvey (1992a, 1992b), *Lectures on Conversation*, 2 vols, Gail Jefferson (ed.), Cambridge, MA: Blackwell.

As already indicated, Silverman illustrates MCD analysis with newspaper headlines, contact advertisements and short conversational sequences:

Silverman, David (1993), *Interpreting Qualitative Data. Methods for Analysing Talk, Text and Interaction*, London: Sage, 80–9.

All of these examples pursue predominantly didactic goals. More comprehensive examples of applications using MCD analysis are not to be found in the literature.

For conversation analysis we may refer to the collections discussed in 8.9.2 (above), since these contain a plethora of case examples. Other examples of applications are to be found in volume 3 of van Dijk's handbook on discourse analysis (van Dijk 1985c):

Heritage, John (1985), 'Analysing News Interviews: Aspects of the Production of Talk for an Overhearing Audience', in Teun A. van Dijk (ed.), *Handbook of Discourse Analysis*, vol. 3, Discourse and Dialogue, London: Academic Press, 95–131.

Atkinson, J. Maxwell (1985), 'Refusing Invited Applause: Preliminary Observations from a Case Study of Charismatic Oratory', in Teun A. van Dijk (ed.), *Handbook of Discourse Analysis*, vol. 3, Discourse and Dialogue, London: Academic Press, 161–81.

Schiffrin (1994) contains an example of an application of conversation analysis with a didactic background:

Schiffrin, Deborah (1994), *Approaches to Discourse*, Oxford: Blackwell, 149–85.

After a brief general outline of the method, the author demonstrates the methodology of conversation analysis with a concrete example ('there + be + ITEM').

A more comprehensive example using conversation analysis as its principal method is found in Wilke (1992). This author analyses psychoanalytical initial conversations, using conversation analysis, to show a variety of types of opening. She subsequently also uses the themes introduced by the clients as the basis of a content analysis:

Wilke, Stefanie (1992), *Die erste Begegnung: eine konversations- und inhaltsanalytische Untersuchung der Interaktion im psychoanalytischen Erstgespräch*, Heidelberg: Asanger.

NOTE

1 Personal communication.

CHAPTER 9

NARRATIVE SEMIOTICS (SÉMANTIQUE STRUCTURALE)

Narrations can be understood as stories with a beginning, a middle, and an end that contains a conclusion or some experience of the storyteller. Telling a story is normally connected with some unusual event and some complication in the course of the events depicted. The narrative genre depends on temporal principles of ordering (Labov & Waletzy 1967, Gülich & Quasthoff 1985).

Narrative analyses exist in different methodological variants, which are distinct from each other in respect of their degree of formalization and their deductive and inductive procedure. Deductive variants proceed from a set of rules and principles and attempt to use these to clarify the meaning of a text. Inductive variants are mostly of ethnographic provenance, and attempt to identify context-dependent units in a text and to reconstruct the structure as well as the effect of a story. A great majority of narrative methods are 'rather loosely formulated, almost intuitive, using terms defined by the analyst' (Manning & Cullum-Swan 1994: 464f.). This verdict is not true of the narrative semiotics of the French semioticist and structuralist Algirdas Julien Greimas which will be presented here in more detail.

9.1 THEORETICAL ORIGINS

The theoretical basis of narrative semiotics is to be found in the semiotic studies of Charles S. Peirce, Charles Morris and in the structural linguistics of Ferdinand de Saussure. Semiotics views language as only one of many possible systems of signs with differing standards, applicability and complexity. Saussure's linguistics emphasizes on the one hand the relational aspect of language: the relations between signs are the source of meaning. On the other hand, Saussure introduces a distinction between *langue* and *parole*, that is between the underlying rules and conventions (*langue*) and the actualized and concrete act of speaking (*parole*).

The narrative component of Greimas's method derives from Russian formalism (Roman Jakobson, Viktor Sklovskij), and in particular from Vladimir Propp's (1958) analysis of Russian fairy tales, in which there is an emphasis on the role of form in the transmission of meaning. Fairy tales set up narrative structures which are central to all stories. In an analysis of more than a hundred fairy tales Propp identifies 31 'functions' (such as injury, hindrance), that can be taken on by different performers. These functions are in particular relations with one another and thereby constitute seven spheres of action (for example villain, supporter, true hero, false hero), the presence or absence of which yields a total of only four plots for fairy stories (Silverman 1993: 74). Greimas reduces the total of possible functions and spheres of action. In the construction of his *actants*, who occupy the roles or forces that drive the narration, Greimas (1983: 215ff.) also involves psychoanalytic and psychodramatic concepts.

9.2 BASIC THEORETICAL ASSUMPTIONS

Greimas's method proceeds from a semiotic understanding of communication. Communication, therefore, consists of semiotic processes, that is the linking of sign and signified through meanings:

- According to Peirce, semiosis means 'an action, an influence, which is, or involves, a cooperation of *three* subjects, such as a sign, its object, and its interpretant, this tri-relative influence not being in any way resolvable into actions between pairs' (Charles S. Peirce, *Collected Papers* 1934, 5: 484, quoted in Eco 1991: 29). The component 'meaning' (or 'interpretant'), therefore, mediates between the *signified* (object) and *signifier* (sign), and here reference is also made to convention or *sociality* (Eco 1991: 29f.): signs have no 'natural' connection with the signified. The relationships are conventional.

- Signs are not autonomous entities but achieve their meaning only through their position in a semiotic system and through their distinctiveness from other signs. In Saussurean linguistics, signs are in relation to each other in two different dimensions: on the one hand there are combinatory possibilities by means of which signs can be ordered according to some meaningful totality, for example as chains. These are termed *syntagmatic relations*. On the other hand there are mutually exclusive signs which are in some sense, however, different representations of one category and can, for example, be ordered as a pair of opposites (yes/no). These are termed *paradigmatic relations*.

For semiotics, texts are systems of signs which always consist of two components: the surface structure at the level of syntax and words, and the underlying meaning. For narrative semiotics this model always appears as follows (see Greimas & Rastier 1968, Fiol 1990: 380):

- The *surface structure* is deemed to be the immediately recognizable and readily accessible forms of a text. These are the structures that are regularly investigated in traditional text and content analysis.

- The *deep structure* means the fundamental system of values embedded in a text, and this consists of norms, values and attitudes which are universal in that they reflect in the text the value and norm structures of specific social systems.

As a link between these two levels narrative semiotics constructs a third level, the structures of manifestation, which are concerned with the narrative structures: 'the generation of meaning does not first take the form of the production of utterances and their combination in discourse; it is relayed, in the course of its trajectory, by narrative structures and it is these that produce meaningful discourse articulated in utterances' (Greimas 1987: 64f.). Narrative structures use these to produce and organize the meanings of the surface structure. They may be derived from a series of choices, basic conditions and roles that may occur in text.

9.3 OBJECTIVES OF THE METHOD

Narrative semiotics is concerned with reconstructing the narrative structure and the meaning-bearing deep structure of texts:

> we have to set in place those formal models by which we will be able to manipulate those contents and arrange them in such a way that they will be able to control the production and segmentation of the discourse and organize, under certain conditions, the manifestation of narrativity. (Greimas 1987: 65)

Consequently narrative semiotics seeks, as a first step, to identify the narrative structures of a text that form the bridge between the surface and the deep structure. Only an understanding of these intermediate structures makes possible the understanding of the deep structure (Fiol 1990: 380).

9.4 OUTLINE OF THE METHOD[1]

Narrative semiotics employs categories as instruments for the analysis of both narrative structure and deep structure, and its procedure is governed by the provision of predetermined steps and directives.

9.4.1 Narrative structure

The narrative structure of a text is characterized by six roles which Greimas (1983: 202ff., 1987: 106ff.) calls *actants*, and which direct the story:

(a) *Destinator*   This refers to the particular force which puts the rules and values into action and represents the ideology of the text.
(b) *Receiver*   This carries the values of (a). It therefore refers to the object on which (a) places value.
(c) *Subject*   The subject occupies the principal role in the narration.
(d) *Object*   The object of the narration is what the subject aspires to. It represents the goal to which the interest of the subject is directed.
(e) *Adjuvant*   This supporting force helps the subject in its endeavours concerning the object.
(f) *Traitor*   This impeding force represents everything that tries to deter the subject from its goal.

These *actants* do not necessarily have to be actors. Between these various forces only very particular relations are possible. The *subject* directs itself to the *object* and in this is supported by the *adjuvant* and impeded by the *traitor*. All of this takes place within the value structure of the *destinator*, which is imparted by the *receiver*. The ideology of the *destinator* is often represented by the narrator.

Two other influences that determine the plot are space and time. Greimas characterizes these influences as *isotopes* (1983: 78ff., 1974):

• The *isotope of space* categorizes the environment in which the story takes place. The inner space within which the *subject* acts is called *utopian*, while the vague and imprecisely defined surroundings are called *heterotopian*.

• The *isotope of time* characterizes displacements on the time axis, which means the orientation of the narrative towards past, present and future.

It is the task of an analysis of narrative structure to describe these six *actants* and the two isotopes in the course of the narration.

9.4.2 Deep structure

The analysis of the deep structure of a text seeks to identify the underlying values and norms. Different narrative structures may be based on a common deep structure. The components of the deep structure must (a) be sufficiently complex, logically consistent and sufficiently stable to give an adequate representation of the text, (b) fulfil an effective intermediary and objectifying function between the text and the analyst, and (c) be precise enough. A suitable model for this is the semiotic square (see Figure 9.1).

Love (+) S1	Hate (-) S2
No hate (+) S-2	No love (-) S-1

FIGURE 9.1   The semiotic square

The concepts arranged in the semiotic square in Figure 9.1 are marked in a text as either positive (+) or negative (−). The square incorporates two kinds of logical relationships: the relationship between S1 and S2 (and also between S-1 and S-2) is one of *opposites*, whereas the relationship between S1 and S-1, and also between S2 and S-2, is one of *contradiction*. From a static point of view the square represents the normative condition at a particular moment in the narration; from a dynamic viewpoint it can be used to illustrate different developments in values and norms.

In order to identify the static structure of every section of the narration, the textual content must be successively reduced, from the surface structure through the narrative structure. A set of rules are provided for this purpose (Fiol 1990: 383).

9.4.3 Analytical procedure

First phase   The first phase of the analysis should give a general feeling for the three levels of the text. In this process the text should first be broken down into thematic blocks, during which changes of theme or direction must be recognized. Then the essential forces in the story should be identified and classified as *actants*. Finally it is an opportunity to characterize the spatial and temporal isotopes.

Second phase   There now follows the more precise analysis of the individual thematic blocks. By means of formal rules that must be applied to each block, it should be possible to get at the deeper structures:

- First, the *actants* as well as time and space are analysed separately for each segment.

- Then, for each segment, the mood and the relationship between the *actants* is determined – are they more active or more passive, are they related to one another or not?

- As a third step, the movements of the *actants* are analysed. How can these movements be characterized? The list of possible movements includes acquisition, confrontation, suppression, cognition, extension and modification. These are used to specify the relationships between the *actants*.

- Next the goal and purpose of the particular segment should be determined. Here a distinction is made between cognitive involvement (that is acquisition of knowledge and skills) and pragmatic involvement (that is validation or application of knowledge and skills).

- In this final stage the original thematic segments are set against the results of the first four steps. Here the blocks that were defined thematically in the first phase should now be described as a narrative programme on the basis of the results. Are there, within these segments, any breaches in the relations between the *actants*? Do the moods of the *actants* change? If this should indeed be the case, the blocks must be redefined and the first four stages have to be repeated.

Third phase   Now the investigator should progress from the narrative structure into the deep structure of the text. In this way the surface structure is completely set aside so that the distance between the analyst and the text can be assured and work can proceed on the basis of the formalized narrative programmes – that is, the results of the second phase. The third phase is then much less rule-governed than the preceding phases.

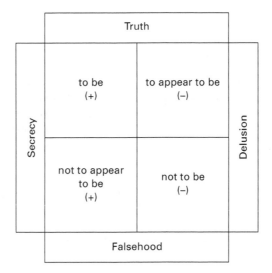

FIGURE 9.2   Carré de veridiction

On the basis of the narrative programmes, however, in which space, time, *actants*, moods, their interrelations and movements, and also the purpose of the programme are determined, it should be possible to highlight the underlying values and to locate them in semiotic squares. In this process a distinction should always be made between values belonging to the subject and the actual values represented by the *destinator* and *receiver*, for which an additional semiotic square – the so-called *carré de veridiction* – is provided (Greimas & Rastier 1968, see Figure 9.2).

In this way the development of the observed and 'actual' values can be represented. The conflict between observed and 'actual' values is related to the measure of association or dissociation between the subject and the other *actants*.

The output of a narrative semiotic analysis should at least provide some insight into the deep structure of a text, as represented in semiotic squares for all narrative programmes. The ways in which the observation of values by the subject is developed and the conflict with 'actual' values is resolved provide the ultimate insight into the purpose which underlies the narration.

9.5 QUALITY CRITERIA

As might be expected, traditional quality criteria receive no explicit mention in Greimas (1983). However, semantics also

> has the right to imagine establishing correlations, until then more or less neglected or unnoticed, between elements of systems and algorithms recognized in different micro-universes, which authorize the formulation of hypotheses and the constitution of models of description from partial structural concomitances. (Greimas 1983: 162)

Thus narrative semiotics also seeks to formulate and test hypotheses, in order to be able to represent structures in models.

Greimas (1983: 163ff.) formulates the demands made on a corpus. This is understood as a set of messages that is constituted by a linguistic model (see Greimas 1983: 163). It is the analysis, therefore, which construes the corpus. Corpora must meet the following requirements:

- They must be representative, by which Greimas does not refer to any statistical criterion but rather to a hypotactic subordinating relationship between the components and the totality of a discourse.

- They must be exhaustive, in the sense that they must implicitly comprise all elements of the model.

- They must be homogeneous. This depends on situational parameters where variations must be understood at the level either of the speaker or of the total scope of the communication.

In order to fulfil these deliberately abstract criteria, Greimas (1983: 163f.) suggests the following 'more economical means that would allow us to obtain the same guarantees of a faithful description of the corpus as those which exhaustiveness appears to offer':

- In a first phase the description should use only a (representative) segment of the corpus and construe a model on this basis.

- A second phase is concerned with 'verification of that temporary model', and for this Greimas offers two procedures: (a) 'Verification by saturation of the model (Vladimir Propp, Claude Lévi-Strauss)'. Here the remaining hitherto untouched part of the corpus is compared systematically with the model, or processed using the model, and the model is enriched with further elements until all the structural variations are exhausted and it cannot be changed further. (b) 'Verification through soundings (Jean Dubois)'. Here samples are taken from the untouched part of the corpus, and these are used to test the model. This can lead to rejection, confirmation or completion of the model.

Without explicitly mentioning them, therefore, Greimas also has notions of validity and reliability, and here he is guided, in the test measures that he presents, mainly by statistical procedures.

9.6 AREAS OF APPLICATION AND PRECONDITIONS

It will seem appropriate to apply narrative semiotics wherever stories are investigated to determine their underlying structures and values. A precondition for the use of narrative semiotics is, therefore, that texts can demonstrate narrative components. Examples always relate to 'typical' stories (particularly fairy tales), and the method is certainly not applicable to non-narrative texts. If one intends to apply the method beyond purely literary forms, then narrative and biographical interviews would seem to be a suitable area of application.

The scope of analysis is restricted if one compares narrative semiotics, for example with hermeneutic methods, since investigations concentrate on textual segments rather than the smallest semantic units. While the method is extremely manageable, provided that the focus is on the discovery of the narrative structure of a story, the step into the deep structure does require a measure of interpretative skill.

9.7 SIMILARITIES AND DIFFERENCES IN COMPARISON TO OTHER METHODS

Because of its concentration on narrative structure a comparison with other methods of text analysis seems difficult. The specific research question distinguishes narrative semiotics from all other methods presented in this book. Similarities can be found only if one uses more abstract criteria for comparison.

The method is deductive and proceeds on the basis of a semiotic-narrative theory of text and language. It uses types or categories derived from this as a research instrument. In view of this deductive procedure there are similarities with SYMLOG but also with (other) semantic procedures used in content analysis.

The method is reductive when it attempts to free itself from the surface structure of a text and to continue the investigation using the results of the categorial reduction of the first two phases of an analysis. In this respect we see further similarities with SYMLOG.

Like functional pragmatics and objective hermeneutics, it attempts to identify deep structures in texts. Whereas functional pragmatics views this as the goal-directedness of linguistic behaviour and objective hermeneutics views it as latent meaning, narrative semiotics understands deep structure as the fundamental values and norms which underlie a story.

9.8 LITERATURE

As primary literature we may note the landmark investigation of Russian folk tales by Vladimir Propp (1958), Algirdas Greimas's foundation of *Structural Semantics* (1983) and the work of Greimas and Rastier (1968).

Greimas, Algirdas J. (1974), 'Die Isotopie der Rede', in Werner Kallmeyer, Wolfgang Klein, Reinhard Meyer-Hermann, Klaus Netzer & Hans-Jürgen Siebert (eds), *Lektürekolleg zur Textlinguistik*, Frankfurt: Athenäum, 126–52.

Greimas, Algirdas J. (1983) [1966], *Structural Semantics. An Attempt at a Method*, Lincoln: University of Nebraska Press [original: *Sémantique structurale: Recherche de méthode*, Paris: Larousse].

Greimas, Algirdas J. (1987), *On Meaning. Selected Writings in Semiotic Theory*, London: Frances Pinter.

Greimas, Algirdas J. & Rastier François (1968), *The Interaction of Semiotic Constraints*, Yale French Studies: Game Play and Literature, New Haven, CT: Eastern Press.

Propp, Vladimir I. (1958) [1928], *Morphology of the Folktale*, The Hague: Mouton.

9.9 SECONDARY LITERATURE

9.9.1 Handbooks

In handbooks from sociology and linguistics Greimas's method does not figure prominently, but is sometimes discussed in relation to narrative analyses:

Gülich, Elisabeth & Quasthoff, Uta M. (1985), 'Narrative Analysis', in Teun A. van Dijk (ed.), *Handbook of Discourse Analysis,* vol. 2, Dimensions of Discourse, London: Academic Press, 169–97.

Manning, Peter K. & Cullum-Swan, Betsy (1994), 'Narrative, Content and Semiotic Analysis', in Norman K. Denzin & Yvonna S. Lincoln (eds), *Handbook of Qualitative Research*, Thousand Oak, CA: Sage, 463–77.

9.9.2 Other presentations of method

Fiol, C. Marlene (1990), 'Narrative Semiotics: Theory, Procedure and Illustration', in Anne Sigismund Huff (ed.), *Mapping Strategic Thought*, Chichester: Wiley, 377–402

In this article Marlene Fiol succeeds in giving a clear presentation of narrative semiotics, putting the emphasis less on its theoretical background and more on a brief description of the method with detailed illustrations.

Silverman, David (1993), *Interpreting Qualitative Data. Methods for Analysing Talk, Text and Interaction*, London: Sage, 71–80.

On the theme of 'narrative structures' Silverman discusses the approaches of both Propp and Greimas. The methods of analysis involved, however, are only sketched in a fragmentary way ('functions', 'sphere of action', 'structures'). Finally Silverman demonstrates a narrative analysis, loosely based on Propp and Greimas, of a past and future scenario of the British Labour Party as presented by trade union leaders.

9.9.3 Sample studies

The two presentations mentioned by Fiol (1990) and Silverman (1993) both contain examples of applications: Fiol presents a precise and gradual narrative analysis of the text of a fairy story. This example is didactic in intent and ensures the intelligibility of the method. Silverman (1993: 76ff.) uses an unpublished investigation of his own and shows how narrative analyses in the broader sense can be applied to texts which are not purely literary.

NOTE

1 Cf., on the systems of genres, schemas or frames Sandig & Rothkegel 1984, Swales 1991, Wodak 1986. A distinction is often made between narrative, argumentative, descriptive and instructive types of texts.

CHAPTER 10

SYMLOG AS A METHOD OF TEXT ANALYSIS

SYMLOG stands for 'A System for the Multiple Level Observation of Groups' (Bales & Cohen 1979: 3). In its original form it involved a framework for the observation of groups.[1] Other authors also recommend this schema for the content analysis of everyday descriptions of social interactions (see Schneider 1989). If Merten's (1983) suggested typology of content analysis procedures is followed, it is – like interaction process analysis – a semantic-pragmatic procedure focussing on the 'situation'.

10.1 THEORETICAL ORIGINS

Bales & Cohen (1979: 11) mention many theoretical backgrounds to their 'systematic multi-level field theory': different theories of social cognition (for example Fritz Heider's *Balance Theory*, Leon Festinger's *Dissonance Theory* and Harold H. Kelley's *Attribution Theory*), symbolic interactionism, theories of social exchange (Thibaut & Kelley, Blau and Homans), Talcott Parsons's (1951a, 1951b) action theory, and approaches to family therapy (Murray, Bowen, Salvador, Minuchin). Of particular importance are the theory of psychoanalysis and Kurt Lewin's field theory.

Robert F. Bales is one of the most prominent exponents of sociological small group research and has helped to shape the discipline since 1950 (see, for example, Bales 1950). In the course of their collaboration in the early 1950s, Bales and Talcott Parsons discovered that the categories developed by Bales in his instruments for the analysis of small group interactions were closely related to the 'pattern variables' set up by Parsons. That is to say, they comprised the same dimensions even though the two sets of categories were developed independently of each other. Parsons's schema requires the listing of general features of social systems, while Bales's categories do the same for the micro-world of the small group. The starting question was: what problems must a group overcome to ensure their equilibrium or even survival? The problems are attributable to two levels: the social-emotional domain and the area of problem-solving. At the social-emotional level every group must (a) integrate its members emotionally, must (b) overcome tensions which arise and must (c) take decisions. Each of these three categories can occur in the form of positive or negative reactions: for example either solidarity or hostility may be shown. At the second level – the problem-solving level – there are also three categories; to achieve a particular task the group must overcome the problems of (a) orientation, (b) evaluation, and (c) monitoring. In these categories there are always questions (for example, opinion-seeking) and attempts to reply (as in the expression of opinion). From this came the well-known observation schema with its 12 categories.

10.2 BASIC THEORETICAL ASSUMPTIONS

Bales & Cohen (1979: 13) characterize the 'systematic multi-level field theory' as a 'grounded theory' in the sense of Glaser & Strauss (1967), because it was formulated on the basis of extensive group-process observations. It is multi-level because it takes account of both the dynamics of groups and the dynamics of individual personalities, and it facilitates a systematic insight into the relations between personality dynamics and social field dynamics. Unlike Kurt Lewin's (1951) field theory, it distinguishes multiple fields: namely (a) fields of individual perception, (b) the multi-level behaviour of all individuals for themselves and, at particular points in time, (c) the interaction process between individuals irrespective of time, (d) the development of reciprocal relations between all pairs of individuals in the group, (e) the entire inner structure of the surrounding group, that is, the field of social interaction during a given time-frame, and (f) the dynamic changes in the field of social interaction over a period of time (Bales & Cohen 1979: 53).

The SYMLOG approach investigates first and foremost three levels (Schneider 1989: 10):

- verbal and non-verbal behaviour,

- the content of ideas imparted during the communication,

- values (pro and contra).

All three levels, however, may be localized in a common, three-dimensional observational and evaluative space, the SYMLOG space-model. The three dimensions, which are identified by factor analysis, are characterized as follows:

- Exertion of influence vs Refraining from influence (Upward – Downward).

- Emotional inclination vs Emotional distancing (Positive – Negative).

- Co-operation and goal-directedness vs Impulsiveness and emotionality (Forward – Backward).

If three possible variants are postulated for each of these dimensions, 26 spatial locations are achieved, which are always characterized by combinations of these six letters (Bales & Cohen 1979: 23). These 26 positions derive from all the possible combinations of the three dimensions, each in two variants (with the middle position unmarked), and they may be visualized in the form of the SYMLOG-cube (see Figure 10.1).

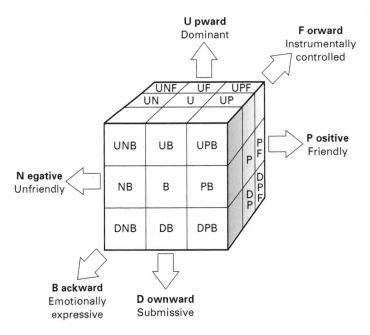

FIGURE 10.1   SYMLOG-spatial model (Source: Bales & Cohen 1979: 23)

To analyse the field of social interaction, the individual field diagrams of the participating members of the group are summarized in a group average diagram. Here *polarization* and *unification*, as important concepts from group theory, come into play (Bales & Cohen 1979: 32). Polarization means that a group tends to form sub-groups under certain conditions of imbalance. The members of such sub-groups may then remove the imbalance that relates to polarization by allocating roles to individuals who are forced into the role of either scapegoat or mediator. Unification, on the other hand, implies a 'coming together' of perceptions and ideas within a group.

10.3 GOALS OF THE METHOD

It [SYMLOG] is a set of methods for the study of groups – groups of many kinds, but basically small natural groups, such as families, teams, or classroom groups, where the personalities of the specific persons involved and their relationship with each other are the focus of interest. (Bales & Cohen 1979: 3)

10.4 OUTLINE OF THE METHOD

SYMLOG provides a coding procedure that incorporates behaviour, content and values in the form of 'messages' in a coding-form, recording the following variables:

1   time of the interaction;
2   name of actor;
3   name of addressee;
4   a simple language commentary on behaviour, or a summary of linguistically expressed idea;
5   the value expressed by the actor towards the idea (pro–contra);
6   coding of behavioural orientation within the SYMLOG space or coding of the orientation of the idea within the SYMLOG space (rating); and,
7   the allocation of the idea to one of six content classes (self, other, group, situation, society, fantasy).

Step 6 is called 'rating', and the other steps are characterized as signing. Ratings are given for subsequent description and are achieved in a standardized way; the function of signing is to provide detailed observation and description of individual participants (Bales & Cohen 1979: 4). As an analytical instrument Bales & Cohen provide a standardized 'Signing Form' (1979: 411) and an 'Adjective Rating Form' (1979: 21). The results of the rating procedure are normally shown in so-called field diagrams, with the P–N dimensions as the horizontal axis and the F–B dimensions on the vertical axis. The degree of influence-exerting (U–D) is shown by circles of different diameters (cf. Bales & Cohen 1979: 20, Orlik & Schario 1989: 24).

To demonstrate the application of SYMLOG to text analysis Orlik (1987, but see also Orlik & Schario 1989: 47ff.) provides a 'semantic atlas', which should be used to assist in the coding of written or spoken everyday language. Here the first step consists of allocating the unit of analysis to one of four basic behavioural types (retreat, conflict, sympathy, achievement). The 26 SYMLOG spatial categories are then distributed among these four basic types:

● retreat: D, DB, DNF, DN, DNB

● conflict: NF, N, NB, UNF, UN, UNB

● sympathy: UB, B, UBP, PB, DPB, UP, P, DP

● achievement: UPF, PF, DPF, U, UF, F, DF

The semantic atlas specifies adjectives for each of the spatial orientations which permits a precise allocation of the unit of analysis to one spatial orientation.

Orlik & Schario (1989: 21ff.) suggest the following procedure for a SYMLOG text analysis:

1 The behavioural information to be coded should, if possible, be a complete sentence with the actor as subject.
2 Using the SYMLOG atlas, the action presented in the sentence is translated into a suitable linguistic characterization.
3 The sentence is then allocated to one of the 26 orientation codes.
4 The evaluation takes place according to a checklist which gives the frequencies of each of the six orientations in the SYMLOG-space for each of the actors in the scene in question.
5 Using the formula provided by Bales & Cohen (1979: 462) the frequencies are transformed into co-ordinates:

$$L_i = 5 \cdot \left(\frac{m(p_i - n_i)}{P+N} + \frac{p_i - n_i}{p_i + n_i} \right)$$

L_i Position of actor i in Dimension P – N
m number of actors
p_i number P – codings of actor i
n_i number N – codings of actor i
P totals P – codings
N totals N – codings

6 Using the calculated co-ordinate values, the SYMLOG field diagram can then be drawn, locating all the actors that figure in the text.

10.5 QUALITY CRITERIA

The SYMLOG approach relies on the traditional criteria of validity and reliability, but uses, in view of its content analysis type of application, the specifications that are characteristic of this method (see Chapter 5, 5.5).

Bales & Cohen (1979: 241ff.) pay considerable and explicit attention to testing the reliability and validity of their mode of procedure, particularly the main procedures of the SYMLOG approach: adjective-rating and interaction-signing. As far as their observational procedure is concerned, they come to the following conclusion:

> The theoretical construct of the three-dimensional SYMLOG space is strongly supported by the findings from both methods, and the two methods tend to converge, implying that each method produces valid measures, although each produces some independent information. The inter-observer reliabilities are high enough for each of the two methods to reassure us that groups of a practical size for rotating observer teams can give results of satisfactory reliability. (Bales & Cohen 1979: 299)

Whether this optimistic assessment of reliability and validity is also true for text study, that is for the content analysis implementation of the SYMLOG schema, remains an open question. Orlik's (1987) SYMLOG-atlas undoubtedly makes a significant contribution to the improvement of inter-coder reliability.

10.6 AREAS OF APPLICATION AND PRECONDITIONS

Since the main focus of SYMLOG is on interaction analysis, the following are suitable areas of application:

- the analysis of transcribed interactions, particularly in small groups (for example group discussions);

- the analysis of observation protocols (from observations of interactions);

- the analysis of narratives, such as novels and fairy tales (Orlik & Schario 1989), but also narrative interviews;

- the analysis of stereotypes (Lobel 1989), systems of personal constructs (Sturm 1989) and free descriptions of persons (Becker-Beck 1989).

The use of the SYMLOG method requires a particularly thorough training of coders (Schneider 1989: 12). Sturm (1989: 106) reports, for example, that for the first-time user there is a considerable obstacle in the need 'first to devote substantial energy to learning the SYMLOG language in order to be able to work reliably with this model'.

10.7 SIMILARITIES AND DIFFERENCES IN COMPARISON WITH OTHER METHODS

When SYMLOG is used for text analysis it is a matter of a specific type of content analysis that – in Merten's (1983) typology – investigates the semantic-pragmatic level and focuses, in the process, on both receiver and situation. The tools used (schema of categories, repertoire of examples) also suggest a content analysis orientation.

Bales & Cohen (1979: 15f.) make a clear distinction between their approach and ethnographic and ethnomethodological methods:

> The present approach departs from the more extreme phenomenology of some symbolic interactionists, however, who tend to emphasize the subjectivity, uniqueness, and variability of meaning in the perception and behavior of each individual to such an extent that it seems hopeless to try to use any systematic method, any standardized approach, or to look for any general tendencies.

Unlike ethnographic and ethnomethodological methods, SYMLOG operates with standardized, theory-driven instruments – that is to say, deductively.

If we accept the formulation of Bales & Cohen (1979: 13), the theory underlying SYMLOG is a type of grounded theory – in other words, a theory founded on data and developed from data. SYMLOG is not concerned, however, with extending the theory but with applying it (deductively) to empirical fields.

Although SYMLOG and narrative semiotics come from totally different theoretical traditions – SYMLOG from field and small group sociology and narrative semiotics from structuralism – there are clear parallels between the two methods. Not only do both have a theory-driven deductive orientation, but both also seek to specify structures between actors or roles, and are therefore particularly well-suited to narrative types of text. For the classification of actors SYMLOG makes a more detailed framework available, whereas the analysis of deep structure is altogether missing in SYMLOG.

10.8 LITERATURE

Bales, Robert F. (1950), *Interaction Process Analysis*, Cambridge: Addison-Wesley.

Bales, Robert F. & Cohen, Stephan P. (1979), *Symlog: A System for the Multiple Level Observation of Groups*, New York: The Free Press.

Bales, Robert F. (1980), *Symlog Case Study Kit*, New York: The Free Press.

Bales's work on interaction process analysis should be seen as an early attempt at methodical and systematic observation of interactions in small groups. In the second work Bales and Cohen provide a broad introduction to the SYMLOG approach to multi-level group observation. In the first part they outline their 'systematic multi-level field theory'. They then provide guidelines to the SYMLOG system of interaction signing, compare interaction signing and adjective rating and demonstrate the use of SYMLOG in observation training and reporting to group participants. The book concludes with extensive examples of procedural technique. Their presentations are illustrated with examples from case studies.

Orlik, Peter (1987), 'Ein semantischer Atlas zur Codierung alltagssprachlicher Beschreibungen nach dem SYMLOG-Raummodell', *International Journal of Small Group Research*, 3: 88–111.

In his 'semantic atlas' Peter Orlik makes available a tool for the application of the SYMLOG-model to (German) text or content analysis, and this gives valuable guidance in its concrete example of coding.

Schneider, Johannes F. (ed.) (1989), *Inhaltsanalyse alltagssprachlicher Beschreibungen sozialer Interaktionen: Beiträge zur SYMLOG-Kodierung von Texten*, Saarbrücken-Scheidt: Dadder.

In this book edited by Johannes Schneider a number of different contributions to SYMLOG text coding are brought together.

10.9 SECONDARY LITERATURE

The contributions listed here are contained in the collection edited by Johannes Schneider. They provide examples of applications of SYMLOG text analysis in very different fields of investigation:

Becker-Beck, Ulrich (1989), 'Freie Personenbeschreibungen als interaktionsdiagnostische Methode', in Johannes F. Schneider (ed.), *Inhaltsanalyse alltagssprachlicher Beschreibungen sozialer Interaktionen: Beiträge zur SYMLOG-Kodierung von Texten*, Saarbrücken-Scheidt: Dadder, 109–39.

Lobel, Sharon A. (1989), 'Inhaltsanalysen von Tiefeninterviews', in Johannes F. Schneider, (ed.), *Inhaltsanalyse alltagssprachlicher Beschreibungen sozialer Interaktionen: Beiträge zur SYMLOG-Kodierung von Texten*, Saarbrücken-Scheidt: Dadder, 67–87.

Orlik, Peter & Schario, Reinhild (1989), 'Die Analyse sozialer Interaktionsfelder in der Romanliteratur', in Johannes F. Schneider (ed.), *Inhaltsanalyse alltagssprachlicher Beschreibungen sozialer Interaktionen: Beiträge zur SYMLOG-Kodierung von Texten*, Saarbrücken-Scheidt: Dadder, 19–51.

Sturm, Gabriele (1989), 'Strukturanalyse persönlicher Konstruktsysteme von Erstgebärenden', in Johannes F. Schneider (ed.), *Inhaltsanalyse alltagssprachlicher Beschreibungen sozialer Interaktionen: Beiträge zur SYMLOG-Kodierung von Texten*, Saarbrücken-Scheidt: Dadder, 89–108.

Hare, A. Paul & Naveh, David (1986), 'Conformity and Creativity: Camp David 1978', *Small-Group-Behavior*, 17 (3): 243–68.

This study by Hare & Naveh seems to be the only one published in English that applies SYMLOG to text analysis, although the method's presentation is not very intelligible. President Carter's description of his negotiations with President Sadat of Egypt and Prime Minister Begin of Israel at Camp David in 1978 was coded to illustrate the extent to which levels of creativity and types of pressure toward conformity were involved. One set of categories was based on the social-psychological literature on conformity, social power and social exchange. A second set of categories was the three-dimensional SYMLOG system.

NOTE

1 It is uncontested that SYMLOG is a method for the observation of groups (cf. Titscher 1995a).

CHAPTER 11

TWO APPROACHES TO CRITICAL DISCOURSE ANALYSIS

11.1 THEORETICAL ORIGINS

The term discourse analysis is used in various ways in the relevant literature (cf. Ehlich 1993: 145, 1994, Schlobinski 1996, Widdowson 1995). Similarly the term critical discourse analysis (hereafter CDA) is far from implying a homogeneous method within discourse analysis. Its general theoretical background, basic assumptions and overall goals may therefore be outlined, but its methodology can only be presented with reference to particular approaches and with regard to their specific theoretical backgrounds. Accordingly two approaches have been selected: critical discourse analysis in the form developed by Norman Fairclough, and the discourse-historical method of Ruth Wodak.

The theoretical framework – even when this is not explicitly stated – is derived from Louis Althusser's theories of ideology, Mikhail Bakhtin's genre theory, and the philosophical traditions of Antonio Gramsci and the Frankfurt School. Michel Foucault has also been a major influence on some exponents, including Norman Fairclough. In addition, Fairclough's CDA is related to Michael Halliday's systemic functional linguistics (Fairclough 1992a, Halliday 1978), whereas Ruth Wodak or Teun van Dijk have been more influenced by cognitive models of text planning (see Wodak et al. 1990, van Dijk 1984).

CDA is 'critical' in two senses: one sense is based on the ideas of the Frankfurt School (in particular the work of Jürgen Habermas) and the other on a shared tradition with so-called critical linguistics. According to Habermas a critical science has to be self-reflective – that is to say, it must reflect the interests on which it is based – and it must take account of the historical contexts of interactions. Habermas's concept of an ideal speech situation is the utopian vision of interactions or power relations. Through rational discourse, ideologically impaired discourse may be overcome and an approximation to the ideal speech situation may be achieved (Habermas 1970, 1971).

The term 'critical linguistics' first appeared in connection with Hallidayan studies of the use of language in organizations (see Fowler et al. 1979, Kress & Hodge 1979). The emergence of a critical perspective within linguistics should be understood as a reaction to contemporary pragmatics (for example speech act theory) and the quantitative-correlative sociolinguistics of William Labov (cf. Wodak 1995: 205). Jacob Mey (1985) speaks vehemently in favour of a critical direction in linguistic pragmatics. The view of Kress & Hodge (1979), that discourse cannot exist without social meanings, and that there must be a strong relation between linguistic and social structure, was subsequently accepted by researchers from different traditions, such as sociolinguistics, formal linguistics, social psychology or literary criticism. This was often developed with an emphasis on the interdisciplinary nature of the approach.

CDA is a young science and the majority of the references – particularly for the methods of Fairclough and Wodak which we have selected – date from the 1990s: Fairclough 1989, 1992a, 1993, 1994, 1995a and Wodak et al. 1990, 1994, 1998, Wodak & Matouschek 1993, Matouschek & Wodak 1995/96, Wodak 1996, Wodak & Reisigl 1999, Weiss & Wodak 1999a, 1999b, Straehle et al. 1999, Iedema & Wodak 1999, van Leeuwen & Wodak 1999.

11.2 BASIC THEORETICAL ASSUMPTIONS

The theoretical basis, with the sole exception of the ideas of Michel Foucault, may be described as neo-Marxist: it is claimed that cultural rather than merely economic dimensions are significant in the creation and maintenance of power relations. Moreover, there is no strict separation between infrastructure and superstructure.

According to Antonio Gramsci the political structure of a society is dependent upon a specific combination of political/institutional and civil society. To achieve the agreement of the majority to the pressure exerted by the political society, a collective will must be formed. This is achieved by means of ideologies (see also Matouschek & Wodak 1995/96: 42f., Fairclough & Wodak 1997). Ideologies achieve in discourse a 'real materiality in the linguistic sign' (Demirovic 1992: 38). Awareness is a type of meaning which participants in dialogue-processes give to particular signs. It is 'part of a complex process of discourse formation' (Demirovic 1992: 38). Meanings are produced and reproduced in a dialectic process of negotiation. The 'Concept of Mechanisms' (Gramsci 1983, Althusser 1971) finds in institutions, or social mechanisms, mediating devices between the complete mechanisms of a society and the phenomena of interactions. Ideologies are closely related to the practices embedded in these institutions. They are therefore also closely related to discourse, which may be understood as a type of social practice. Ideologies locate human beings in specific ways as social subjects.

CDA has been further influenced by the Russian theorists Mikhail M. Bakhtin and Valentin N. Volosinov. Their linguistic theory of ideology views every instance of language use as ideological. Linguistic signs are the domain of the class struggle, which is also a struggle concerning the significance of signs

(Volosinov 1975). Bakhtin stresses the dialogue properties of texts – their 'inter-textuality' as it is termed by Julia Kristeva (Moi 1986) – in that every text is viewed as part of a series of texts to which it reacts and refers, and which it modifies. Bakhtin's theory of genre was also adopted by CDA. This involves seeing every text as dependent on socially predetermined repertoires of genres (for example scientific articles), and means that differing genres can be mixed in creative ways as, for instance, in advertising.

The general principles of CDA may be summarized as follows (Wodak 1996: 17–20):

- CDA is concerned with social problems. It is not concerned with language or language use per se, but with the linguistic character of social and cultural processes and structures. Accordingly CDA is essentially interdisciplinary.

- Power-relations have to do with discourse (Foucault 1990, Bourdieu 1987), and CDA studies both power in discourse and power over discourse.

- Society and culture are dialectically related to discourse: society and culture are shaped by discourse, and at the same time constitute discourse. Every single instance of language use reproduces or transforms society and culture, including power relations.

- Language use may be ideological. To determine this it is necessary to analyse texts to investigate their interpretation, reception and social effects.

- Discourses are historical and can only be understood in relation to their context. At the metatheoretical level this corresponds to the approach of Wittgenstein (1984, §7), according to which the meaning of an utterance rests in its usage in a specific situation. Discourses are not only embedded in a particular culture, ideology or history, but are also connected intertextually to other discourses.

- The connection between text and society is not direct, but is manifest through some intermediary such as the socio-cognitive one advanced in the socio-psychological model of text comprehension (Wodak 1986).

- Discourse analysis is interpretative and explanatory. Critical analysis implies a systematic methodology and a relationship between the text and its social conditions, ideologies and power-relations. Interpretations are always dynamic and open to new contexts and new information.

- Discourse is a form of social behaviour. CDA is understood as a social scientific discipline which makes its interests explicit and prefers to apply its discoveries to practical questions.

11.3 OBJECTIVES OF THE METHOD

CDA conceptualizes languages as a form of social practice, and attempts to make human beings aware of the reciprocal influences of language and social structure of which they are normally unaware (see Fairclough 1989, van Dijk 1993, Wodak 1989).

The objectives may be derived from the theoretical foundations:

> Though in different terms, and from different points of view, most of us deal with power, dominance, hegemony, inequality, and the discursive processes of their enactment, concealment, legitimation and reproduction. And many of us are interested in the subtle means by which text and talk manage the mind and manufacture consent, on the one hand, and articulate and sustain resistance and challenge, on the other. (van Dijk 1993: 132)

CDA sees itself as politically involved research with an emancipatory requirement: it seeks to have an effect on social practice and social relationships, for example in teacher development, in the elaboration of guidelines for non-sexist language use or in proposals to increase the intelligibility of news and legal texts. The research emphases which have arisen in pursuit of these goals include language usage in organizations, and the investigation of prejudice in general, and racism, anti-semitism and sexism in particular.

Analyses are based on heterogeneous data in which a distinction is normally made between text and discourse (see Chapter 2). 'I use the term "text" for both written texts and transcripts of spoken interaction' (Fairclough 1993: 166). 'Text' is used to refer to the product of the process of text-creation, whereas the notion of 'discourse' is more informative and relevant than the term 'text', since CDA analyses not texts but discourses. Discourse has a wider application than text: 'But I shall use the term *discourse* to refer to the whole process of social interaction of which text is just a part' (Fairclough 1989: 24).

> Critical discourse analysis sees discourse – language use in speech and writing – as a form of 'social practice'. Describing discourse as social practice implies a dialectical relationship between a particular discursive event and the situation(s), institution(s) and social structure(s) which frame it. A dialectical relationship is a two-way relationship: the discursive event is shaped by situations, institutions and social structures, but it also shapes them. (Fairclough & Wodak 1997: 55)

From this complex meshing of language and social facts is derived the frequently unclear and hidden ideological effects of language use as well as the influence of power-relations. In discourse practice structures and ideologies are expressed which are not normally analysed or questioned. CDA is now seeking, by close and detailed analysis, to shed light on precisely these aspects.

Context, in contrast to the way the term is used in ethnomethodological text analyses, includes both intertextuality and sociocultural knowledge. Discourses are always related to those produced before, simultaneously and subsequently, and are only intelligible in terms of the underlying conventions and rules (together with their historical contexts in the discourse-historical method).

11.4 OUTLINE OF CRITICAL DISCOURSE ANALYSIS (FAIRCLOUGH)

11.4.1 Specific theoretical background

Fairclough bases his theoretical considerations and scheme of analysis on quite specific definitions of a number of concepts. The following key terms will be helpful in understanding his approach (Fairclough 1993: 138):

- *Discourse* (abstract noun) – 'language use conceived as social practice'.

- *Discursive event* – 'instance of language use, analysed as text, discursive practice, social practice'.

- *Text* – 'the written or spoken language produced in a discursive event'. Later Fairclough emphasizes the multi-semiotic character of texts and adds visual images and sound – using the example of television language – as other semiotic forms which may be simultaneously present in texts (see Fairclough 1995b: 4).

- *Interdiscursivity* – 'the constitution of a text from diverse discourses and genres'.

- *Discourse* (countable noun) – 'way of signifying experience from a particular perspective'.

- *Genre* – 'use of language associated with a particular social activity'.

- *Order of discourse* – 'totality of discursive practices of an institution and relationships between them'.

Fairclough understands CDA to be concerned with the investigation of the tension between the two assumptions about language use: that language is both socially constitutive and socially determined. He bases his ideas on the multifunctional linguistic theory embodied in Halliday's functional-systemic linguistics (Halliday 1978, 1985): every text has an 'ideational' function through its representation of experience and representation of the world. In addition texts produce social interactions between participants in discourse and therefore also display an 'interpersonal' function. Finally, texts also have a 'textual' function in so far as they unite separate components into a whole and combine this with situational contexts, for example by the use of situational deixis (Fairclough 1995a: 6).

Through the notion of the multifunctionality of language in texts, Fairclough operationalizes the theoretical assumption that texts and discourses are socially constitutive: 'Language use is always simultaneously constitutive of (i) social identities, (ii) social relations and (iii) systems of knowledge and beliefs' (Fairclough 1993: 134). The ideational function of language constitutes systems of knowledge; the interpersonal function creates social subjects or identities or the relationships between them. That implies that every text contributes – albeit in a small way – to the constitution of these three aspects of society and culture. Fairclough further maintains that identities, relationships and knowledge are always present simultaneously, although one aspect may take precedence over the others (Fairclough 1995a: 55).

For Fairclough language use is doubly constitutive, in both a conventional and a creative sense. Conventional constitution of identities, relationships and knowledge means, for him, the reproduction of these phenomena in language. Creativity, in this context, means the opposite: it denotes social change. Whether language use has a reproductive or a transforming function depends on the prevailing social circumstances – for example on the degree of flexibility in the power relations.

Language is not only socially constitutive, but is also viewed as socially determined. According to Fairclough this is a very complex relationship: on the one hand very different types of discourse may coexist within the same institution, while on the other hand the relationship between actual language use and the underlying conventions and norms is not a simple linear one (Fairclough 1993: 135). Fairclough approaches this complex relationship using the concept of 'orders of discourse' defined with reference to Foucault (1981): the 'order of discourse' of a social domain refers to the totality of discourse types and the relationships between them in this domain. For the social domain 'school' this would include the discourse types of the classroom, the school playground and the staffroom. The investigation of whether the different discourse types found within one order of discourse, or different orders of discourse, are strictly separate from one another, or whether they frequently overlap, may provide the key to conflicts and power struggles or social and cultural changes (Fairclough 1995a: 56). Within orders of discourse Fairclough distinguishes two categories of discourse type: discourses and genres. 'Discourses' are formed on the basis of specific areas of experience and knowledge; 'genres' are related to particular types of activity, such as job interview, media interview or advertising.

Discourse analysis means, therefore, the analysis of relationships between concrete language use and the wider social and cultural structures. In Fairclough's terminology this becomes the relationships between a specific communicative event, such as a television documentary, and the total structure of an order of discourse, as well as modifications to the order of discourse and its constituents, genres and discourses (Fairclough 1995a: 56).

11.4.2.1 Analytical framework

For the operationalization of the theoretical considerations Fairclough develops an analytical framework (Fairclough 1993, 1995a), and relates to this the concepts of *interdiscursivity* (that is, the combination of genres and discourses in a text) and *hegemony* (the predominance in and dominance of political, ideological and cultural domains of a society) (Fairclough 1995b: 76). He attributes three dimensions to every discursive event. It is simultaneously text, discursive practice – which also includes the production and interpretation of texts – and social practice. The analysis is conducted according to these three dimensions.

At the *textual level* content and form are analysed. Instead of form, Fairclough speaks of textual organization and texture, which relates to the work of Halliday and Hasan (1976). These two aspects of a text – content and form/texture – are, for Fairclough, inseparable: contents are realized by particular forms; different contents also imply different forms and vice versa. The form is therefore part of the content (Fairclough 1992b: 193). By linguistic analysis of a text Fairclough means phonology, grammar, vocabulary and semantics, but in addition such supra-sentential aspects of textual organization as cohesion and turn-taking.

The level of *discursive practice* is the link between text and social practice. It is to do with the socio-cognitive aspects of text production and interpretation. These are, on the one hand, formed by social practice and assist in its formation and, on the other hand, closely related to the textual level: text production leaves so-called *cues* in a text and interpretation takes place on the basis of textual elements. The analysis of discursive practice therefore includes not only a precise explanation of how the participants in an interaction interpret and produce texts, but also the relationships of discursive events to orders of discourse, that is the matter of *interdiscursivity* (Fairclough 1993: 136). Through these intertextual or interdiscursive components of text analysis, Fairclough's work is related to Mikhail Bakhtin's (1986) concept of interdiscursivity and Julia Kristeva's intertextuality (Moi 1986), in that he incorporates historical and social facts. Intertextual analysis enquires how these social and historical foundations are combined or modified by texts, and how discourses and genres blend together. Fairclough (1995a: 61) gives the example of widely known documentary texts in which the genres of information, persuasion and entertainment are combined. From the dynamics of discourse and genre types comes the idea that texts do not have to be linguistically homogeneous. They may, in fact, be very heterogeneous and display contradictory stylistic and semantic properties which are the concern of linguistic analysis (Maingueneau 1987, Kress & Threadgold 1988). Fairclough's intertextual or interdiscursive analysis, in contrast to descriptive linguistic analysis, is more strongly interpretative, since those investigators who are concerned with the creation of a relationship between texts and the social repertoire of discursive practices are more dependent on social and cultural insight (Fairclough 1992b, 1995a: 61f).

Interdiscursivity within text analysis has, for Fairclough, a bridging function between text and context: it is concerned with how the repertoires of genres and discourses are exploited within orders of discourse for text production and interpretation. How discourses and genres are combined, or how texts are ultimately produced and interpreted, depends upon the social context: a stable set of social relationships and identities implies a relatively orthodox and normative use of discourses and genres together with a respect for social conventions. For example, texts are semantically more homogeneous where social relationships are unstable. As an instance of unstable relationships Fairclough cites those between men and women in modern European and American society. The questioning of conventional inter-gender interactions leads to creativity and innovation in the use of orders of discourse and results in relatively heterogeneous texts (Fairclough 1992b: 215).

The analysis of the third dimension of a discursive event – that of *social practice* – relates to the different levels of social organization: the situation, the institutional context, the wider group or social context. Questions of power are of central interest; power and ideologies may have an effect on each of the contextual levels. Fairclough refers to Antonio Gramsci's (1971) concept of hegemony. He proceeds from an essential connection between discourse and hegemony, and views the control over discursive practices as a struggle for predominance over orders of discourse. Hegemony is understood as transitory and unstable, and orders of discourse are an area of potential cultural hegemony. To illustrate this Fairclough cites the example of the political predominance of Margaret Thatcher in the UK, which was used to a considerable extent to control discursive practices and their combination.

In this Fairclough relies centrally on the construction of the identity of Thatcher as a political leader, on that of the 'public' or the 'people', and the relationship between the leader herself and the people. Thatcherism, as a new political persuasion, first had to create for itself a political base of supporters, and this was constructed and reconstructed by politicians. A discursive construction of this sort is measured by the extent to which it is accepted and implemented by people. In a radio interview in 1985, Thatcher, while talking of the 'British People', mixed the liberal discourse of individual self-reliance with that of Conservatism by addressing the themes of family, community, and law and order: 'Britain is a country whose people think for themselves, act for themselves, can act on their own initiative, they don't have to be told and don't like to be pushed around, they are self-reliant' (Fairclough 1989: 173).

The connection of the types of discourse remains implicit and must be constructed by the addressees themselves. Thatcher's own identity is marked by the tension between masculine authority and a femininity emphasized by various devices such as her hairstyle. For the public or the listeners there is another type of tension – that between relationships of authority and solidarity. In Fairclough's view this is to be seen in the mixing of traditional political discourse and that of everyday experience. Fairclough analyses the relationship with the public as manifest in the use of pronouns. 'We' sometimes includes both the political party and the general public, sometimes it refers only to the Conservative Party, and often it is used in a deliberately ambivalent way. The inclusive *we* signals on the one hand solidarity, but on the other – and at the same time – authority, in that Thatcher takes upon herself the right to speak for the general public. By 'you' Thatcher means the public at large, and this makes no claim to authoritarian solidarity. 'You' tends to be the colloquial counterpart of the literary 'one', and is therefore the form which Thatcher uses to convey a shared world of life and experience. Through her use of *you* and *we*, therefore, Thatcher signals the mixing of political and everyday discourse.

Fairclough emphasizes the significance of the textual level in discourse analysis and criticizes the inadequate attention given to text analysis in the social sciences, despite the prominence of the supposed 'linguistic turn' (1992b: 212). He advances four arguments in favour of text analysis: theoretical, methodological, historical and political.

His theoretical foundation is that social structures such as class relations, which are of central interest to sociology, are in a dialectical relationship with social activities and that texts are a significant form of social activity. As a methodological justification for the great importance of text analysis, Fairclough points to the increasing use of texts as sources of data. His historical foundation is that texts are good indicators of social change. This consideration refers back to intertextuality and the linguistic heterogeneity of texts: texts give evidence of lasting processes such as the redefinition of social relationships, and the reconstruction of identities and of knowledge. For Fairclough an understanding of text analysis – that is, the analysis of content and texture – provides a counterbalance to strongly schematic types of social analysis which take too little account of the mechanisms of change. In this connection he is critical of the historical discourse studies of Foucault (Fairclough 1992a). His fourth foundation is political and relates to the critical orientation in discourse analysis: social control and

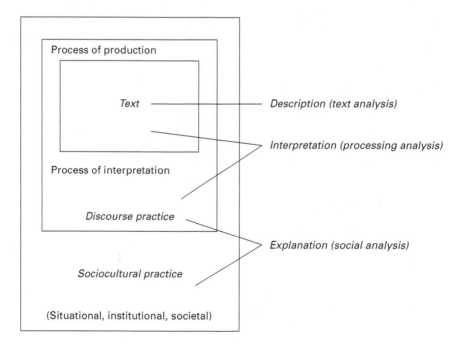

FIGURE 11.1   Dimensions of discourse and discourse analysis

power are exercised with increasing frequency by means of texts, so text analysis becomes an important part of critical discourse analysis.

11.4.2.2 Procedures

Fairclough's method is based on the three components *description, interpretation* and *explanation*. Linguistic properties are described, the relationship between the productive and interpretative processes of discursive practice and the text is interpreted, and the relationship between discursive and social practice is explained (Fairclough 1995b: 97). The dimensions on which the method is based are shown in Figure 11.1.

The procedure may be illustrated by means of a doctor–patient conversation (Fairclough 1995b: 98–101):

Patient:	but she really has been very unfair to me . got ⌈ no
Doctor:	⌊ hm
Patient:	respect for me at ⌈ all and I think . that's one of the
Doctor:	⌊ hm
Patient:	reasons why I drank s⌈o much you⌈ know ——
Doctor:	⌊ hm ⌊ hm hm
Patient:	a⌈ nd em ⌈
Doctor:	⌊ hm ⌊are you you back are you back on it have you
	started drinking⌈ again
Patient:	⌊ no
Doctor:	oh you haven't (unclea⌈r)
Patient:	⌊no . but em one thing that the lady on the
	Tuesday said to me was that . if my mother did turn me out of the
	⌈ house which she
Doctor:	⌊ yes
Patient:	thinks she may do ⌈ . coz . she doesn't like the way
Doctor:	⌊ hm
Patient:	I've been she has turned me ⌈out be ⌈fore . and em .
Doctor:	⌊hm ⌊hm
Patient:	she said that . I could she thought that it might be possible to me
	for me to go to a council ⌈flat
Doctor:	⌊right yes ⌈yeah
Patient:	⌊ but she said it's a very em
	she wasn't
Patient:	⌈ pushing it because . my mother's got to sign a
Doctor:	⌊ hm
Patient:	whole⌈ lot of ⌈things and e: . she said it's difficult
Doctor:	⌊hm ⌊ hm
Patient:	⌈and em . there's no rush over it . I I don't know
Doctor:	⌊hm
Patient:	whether . I mean one thing they say in AA is that you shouldn't
	change anything .
Doctor:	⌈for a year
	⌊hm
Doctor:	hm yes I think I think that's wise . I think that's wise (5 second pause)
	well look I'd like to keep you know seeing you keep . you know hearing how things are going from time to time if that's possible

At the textual level Fairclough notes contradictions which he illustrates by pointing out the difference between 'fact' – the content and pragmatic aspect – and 'manner' – the mode of linguistic realization. On the one hand the doctor asks questions, for example those about a possible relapse of his alcoholic patient, and requests him to come again for check-ups. But on the other hand he softens the authority thereby expressed by a variety of linguistic devices such as vagueness, reformulation, increased speech tempo (which Fairclough mentions but does not indicate in the transcript), and makes the important medical question about a relapse seem like a side issue.

At the level of discursive practice (in Halliday's terms *interpersonal function*) Fairclough uncovers two different discourses, namely the traditional medical and the counselling discourse. Traditionally a doctor dominates an interaction but here, by means of specific linguistic realizations, the doctor yields much of the control of the conversation to the patient and simultaneously indicates empathy. He thereby adds to the conventions of a traditional medical conversation those of a counselling discourse.

With regard to sociocultural practice (Halliday's *ideational function*) it may be explained at the institutional level that the doctor is a member of a group which is receptive to other practices than those of official medicine and which behaves in an anti-authoritarian way towards patients.

The specific mixing of two discourses analysed in this example is interpreted by Fairclough as the expression of a general characteristic of contemporary orders of discourse. He calls it the 'conversationalization of discourse'. This refers to the permeation of institutional discourse by elements from the private domain. This change gives institutional discourse a markedly informal character. The interaction no longer takes place between roles or statuses, as in traditional institutional discourse, but because of sharply divided conversation control and the reduction of asymmetries, it becomes more informal and democratic. According to Fairclough, 'conversationalization' is the discursive component of social and cultural change.

11.5 OUTLINE OF DISCOURSE-HISTORICAL METHOD

11.5.1 Specific theoretical background

The discourse-historical method sees itself as part of the research background to sociolinguistics and text linguistics (Wodak et al. 1990: 33). It uses the theory of linguistic activity to deal with the content and relational level of interviews, rounds of discussion and the like. One quite specific theoretical base is the theory of text planning, by means of which the intentions of speakers and the extralinguistic factors in text production are identified.

The starting point for the theory of text planning is a perceived shortcoming in the theory of linguistic activity, which takes no account of extralinguistic factors. But the speech situation, the status of participants, time and place, together with sociological variables (group membership, age, professional socialization) and psychological determinants (experience, routine, etc.) play an essential role in text production. These categories are incorporated into the socio-psycholinguistic 'Theory of Text Planning' developed by Ruth Wodak (Wodak 1981, 1984, 1986).

Wodak et al. (1990: 46–9) assume that consideration must be given to the social-psychological, cognitive and linguistic dimensions of text production (see Figure 11.2). The social-psychological dimension comprises various strategies for coming to terms with reality which are learned as part of the process of socialization. These include culture, gender and class membership, and speech situation, together with personality or psycho-pathogenesis as individual determinants. From this social-psychological preconditioning are derived 'frames' and 'schemata' for the structuring and perception of reality. Frames are understood as global patterns which summarize our general knowledge of some situation, such as a lecture; they are therefore the stored image of a particular situation. Schemata are exact patterns for the concrete realization of a situation or a text. For text production 'plans' are also of great significance: these are patterns which lead to an intended goal; also of significance are 'scripts', which are stabilized plans that – after frequent use – determine the role and expected actions of communicators (Beaugrande & Dressler 1981: 95–6).

The application of this theory may be illustrated with reference to the area of diplomacy: if a diplomat needs to produce a report to his or her own government about bilateral relations with the host country, he or she constructs a plan of the substance which he or she wishes to write about. The realization of this intention is first dependent on the diplomat's cognitive schema, which tells him or her what form a report to the central authority should take. In addition he or she is guided by the frame, or general knowledge about reports of this nature, which indicates what one is allowed to say and in what form. What the script of the report will ultimately look like depends upon the personality of the writer, the time, the place, and so on. This means that the same text-thematic macrostructure, such as recognition of the efforts of the minister in the area of bilateral relations, is

SCHEMA

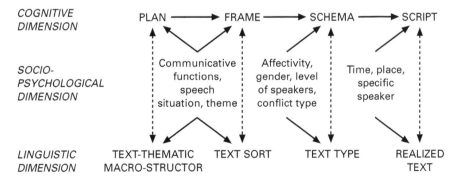

FIGURE 11.2   Text planning (Source: Wodak et al. 1990: 47)

realized through the influence of plans and frames in different text variants; these, in turn, are translated by immediate determinants into different text types.

Closely related to the concepts of frame, schema and script is the notion of strategy. In principle strategies are used to achieve goals. Wodak et al. (1998, Projektteam 1989: 93) do not define strategy as something ultimately and rationally intelligible. They present it rather as being dependent on subjective assessments and possibilities. Strategies are certainly goal-directed, but this does not mean that participants in an interaction are always conscious of them. They often work in an unconscious, irrational and emotional way. If speakers give voice to racist ideas they cannot, according to the theory of text-production, be accused of the conscious expression of these ideas. (This does not, of course, diminish the idea of responsibility for one's own utterances.)

The integrative model of comprehension (Lutz & Wodak 1987, Wodak 1996) is similar, although it should not be understood as a simple 'reversal' of the theory of text planning. Text comprehension is also dependent upon the socio-psychological influences which are important in text production. Hearers and readers first classify the text according to frames and approach the original text 'strategically'. They therefore interpret the text in order to construct its textual basis and ultimately to understand it. Wodak assumes that there is no general textual basis which is valid for all hearers and readers. The differences depend on the fact that hearers and readers construct not only the text but also the social context, and that text and context interact with one another. In this model text comprehension is understood as a cyclical and interpretative process.

Through the theory of text planning and comprehension it is possible to represent systematic differences in the shaping of the same dependency on theme, context and text variant. It is also possible to capture the differences between oral and written modes, and systematic differences in text reception. In this way Wodak illustrates empirically the theoretical claim that discourse must be viewed as social practice.

Recent research has led to further developments and refinements like the *concept of critique, the concept of discourse and field of action, the concept of recontextualization* and *the concept of context* (for further discussion see especially Wodak & Reisigl 1999; Weiss and Wodak 1999a and b). The *concept of social critique* embraces three interconnected aspects, namely that of *'text'* or *'immanent discourse critique'*, that of *'socio-diagnostic critique'* which is concerned with exposing the 'manipulative' character of discursive practices and, finally, the *prospective critique* associated with the ethico-practical dimension and nurtured ethically by a sense of justice based on a normative and universalist conviction concerning human rights.

The *concept of discourse*, in Wodak and Reisigl's most recent work (Wodak & Reisigl 1999), can be understood as a complex bundle of simultaneous and sequential interrelated linguistic acts which manifest themselves within and across the social fields of action as thematically interrelated semiotic tokens (that is texts) that belong to specific semiotic types (genres). *Fields of action* (cf. Girnth 1996) may be understood as segments of the respective societal 'reality' which contribute to constituting and shaping the 'frame' of discourse (see also Reisigl 1999, Reisigl and Wodak 1999).

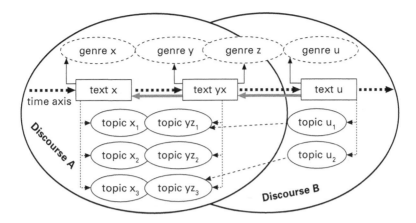

FIGURE 11.3   Interdiscursive and intertextual relationships between discourses, discourse topics, genres and texts

In Figure 11.3, interdiscursivity (for example the intersection of discourse A and discourse B) is indicated by the two large overlapping ellipses. Intertextual relationships in general – which are of an explicitly referential kind, a formally or structurally iconic (diagrammatical) kind, or in the form of topical correlations, evocations, allusions or (direct and indirect) quotations, etc. – are represented by bold double arrows. The assignment of texts to genres is signalled by simple arrows. The topics a text refers to are indicated by small ellipses which simple dotted arrows point to, the topical intersection of different texts is signalled by the overlapping small ellipses. Finally, the specific intertextual relationship of thematic reference of one text to another is indicated by simple broken arrows.

The *concept of re-contextualization* is linked both to *intertextuality* and to *interdiscursivity* (see 11.4.2.1 above). It is used to chart shifts of meaning either within a single genre – as in different versions of a specific written text – or across semiotic dimensions; in an organizational context, for example, a text may progress from discussion to monologue and thence to actions that may even belong to a different semiotic mode.

The discourse-historical approach now also embodies Cicourel's (1964) principle of triangulation to permit exploration of the interconnectedness of discursive and other social practices as well as structures. This is based on a concept of context which takes into account (a) the immediate, language or text-internal cotext and the local interactive processes of negotiation and conflict management; (b) the intertextual and interdiscursive relationship between utterances, texts, genres and discourses; (c) the language-external social/sociological variables and institutional frames of a specific 'context of situation' (that is formality, place, time, occasion, groups, roles of participants, and so on); and (d) the broader socio-political and historical context the discursive practices are embedded in and related to, that is to say, the fields of action and the history of the discursive event as well as the history to which the discoursal topics are related.

This notion of context is very important in the critical ethnographic approach which characterizes the aims of the Vienna School. In the exploration of organizations or political discourses, the recontextualization of arguments and *topoi* (namely, the obligatory parts of an argument) is pursued from one genre to the next, or from one public domain to the next (Wodak et al. 1998, 1999, Wodak 1996). This 'life of arguments' illustrates the power struggle about specific opinions, beliefs or ideologies. For example, in studies of the European Union and discourses on unemployment (Weiss and Wodak 1999a, 1999b, Straehle et al. 1999, Iedema and Wodak 1999), interviews, written texts, parliamentary debates and meetings were contrasted with each other. The difference of the Vienna School approach, therefore, compared to many other CDA approaches, lies specifically in three aspects: the emphasis on interdisciplinarity, the principle of triangulation, and the ethnographic approach to sources of data.

11.5.2 Method

11.5.2.1 Analytical apparatus

The discourse-historical method, following the models described above, works with a three-dimensional analytical apparatus (see Figure 11.4).

A fundamental distinction is made between contents, argumentation strategies, and forms of linguistic implementation as analytical levels. Under linguistic implementation a distinction is drawn between text, sentence and word levels. It is important to understand strategies as a set of processes which operate consciously or unconsciously at different levels of communication (Projektteam 1989: 3). Strategies, as more or less automated or conscious plans of action, mediate between the goals of different communicators and their realization (Heinemann & Viehweger 1991: 215). These three analytical dimensions are then completed independently of any particular object of investigation which has categories. Only at the level of content are the categories specific and non-transferable to other objects of investigation. In contrast, strategies and linguistic realizations, once identified, may in principle also be applied to other discourses.

In the context of discourses about migrants in the Austrian mass media from 1989–90, Matouschek et al. (1995: 60) produced the analytical apparatus shown in Figure 11.4 to account for the so-called discourses of difference.

11.5.2.2 Procedure

The procedure of the discourse-historical method is viewed as being hermeneutic and interpretative, with some influence from cognitive science (Wodak et al. 1990: 53, Wodak 1996). It should therefore be understood not as a sequence of separate operational steps but as a cycle in which the three analytical dimensions are systematically and recursively related to the totality of contextual knowledge. The exact description of individual texts and the analysis of larger corpora of

We-you-discourse	
Discourse of difference 1. Categorization and evaluation 2. We-discourse: – Constitution of 'we' – Positive self-portrayal	*Linguistic realization* 1. Content definition of groups 2.1. Grammatical cohesive elements 2.2. Disclaimers, self-assessment, norm-respect
Argumentation strategies/techniques (justification)	
Attribution of responsibility or guilt	*Denial of responsibility or guilt*
Black-white painting	Devaluation or defamation by distortion
Rejection of guilt	
Scapegoat strategy	
Victim-agent reversal	a) Exaggeration: for example theories of conspiracy
The above strategies and denials are also realized by certain 'techniques' of argumentation about distortions ➡	b) Playing down: balancing/rationalization
Goal: devaluation and defamation of the 'opponent's' viewpoint	c) Rejection, denial
Forms of linguistic realization		
● unreal scenarios	● rhetorical questions	Vagueness:
● comparisons	● introductory formulae	● generalizing reference
● analogies	● allusions, evocations	● speakers' perspectives
● evocations	(also at text and word level)	● stylistics/situationality
● equation/generalization	● assertions	● euphemisms
● discourse representation	● metaphors	● text coherence
● quotations	● predication	● metaphorical lexems

FIGURE 11.4   Analytical schema for the discourse-historical method
(*Source:* Matouschek, Wodak & Januschek 1995: 60)

data allow statements to be made, at both micro and macro levels, on the reconstruction of discourse contexts. The general principles of the discourse-historical method may be summarized as follows (Wodak et al. 1990: 57):

● Setting and context should be recorded as accurately as possible, since discourses can only be described, understood and interpreted in their specific context.

● The content of an utterance must be confronted with historical events and facts as well as presented reports (intertextuality).

- Texts must be interpreted by other subject specialists (sociology, history, psychology). All stages imply an interdisciplinary approach as an important characteristic of the discourse-historical method.

- Texts must be described as precisely as possible at all linguistic levels.

Representatives of the discourse-historical method appreciate the difference between their approach and that of other text and sociolinguistic studies, thanks to a profitable networking of various scientific approaches.

A first step in text analysis is to make certain generalizations which are then classified according to the analytical apparatus. This is then followed by a renewed analysis of the text, and so on. The discourse-historical procedure may conveniently be illustrated with reference to popular reporting of Austrian refugee policy:

Bundeskanzler: Wirtschaftshilfe für östliche Nachbarn / Haider: Gipfel über Unterbringung der Asylwerber
SEIT 11 JAHREN: 7,5 MILLIARDEN FÜR FLÜCHTLINGE
Lead: (6zeilig, doppelspaltig)
Welche finanziellen Opfer Österreich bringt, um seiner humanitären Verpflichtung der Flüchtlingshilfe nachzukommen, geht aus neuen Zahlen des Finanzministeriums hervor: von 1980 bis einschließlich 1990 wurden für die Flüchtlingsbetreuung (Unterkunft, Verpflegung) insgesamt 7,5 Milliarden Schilling flüssig gemacht.
Text: (3spaltig, 82zeilig)
Drei große Flüchtlingswellen hatte unser Land in 34 Jahren zu verkraften: (Abs. 1)
1956 kamen nach der blutig unterdrückten Revolution in Ungarn 180–432 Menschen über unsere Grenzen. (Abs. 2)
1968 flohen nach der Niederwalzung des Prager Frühlings 162.000 Tschechoslowaken auf unser Staatsgebiet. (Abs. 3)
1981 suchten nach der Verhängung des Kriegsrechtes in Polen 33.142 Flüchtlinge um politisches Asyl an. (Abs. 4)
Nächste Woche muß Österreich, wie gestern Innenminister Löschnak der 'Krone' gegenüber bekräftigte, auf die Notbremse steigen. (Abs. 5)
Der Ministerrat wird eine Visumpflicht für Rumänen, die vorwiegend als Wirtschaftsflüchtlinge einzustufen sind, beschließen. (Abs. 6)
Unsere Grenzen bleiben aber jenen Ausländern, die aus politischen, rassischen oder religiösen Gründen in ihrer Heimat verfolgt werden, weiterhin offen. (Abs. 7)
Immer wieder wird behauptet, die Flüchtlinge aus dem Osten seien daran Schuld, daß die Kriminalität in Österreich steige. Dazu stellte gestern das Innenministerium der 'Krone' gegenüber fest: (Abs. 8)
Die Kriminalitätsrate der legal beschäftigen Gastarbeiter ist niedriger als die der Österreicher. (Abs. 9)
Dafür werden aber von Ostflüchtlingen, die oft schwarz arbeiten, im Schnitt mehr Straftaten verübt als von unseren Landsleuten. (Abs. 10)
Kriminalität in Österreich steigt (Textschlagzeile in Fettdruck)
Tatsächlich ist die Kriminalität in Österreich von 1987 auf 1988 um 2, 5 bis 3 Prozent und von 1988 auf 1989 um 3, 5 bis 4 Prozent gestiegen. Diese alarmierende Entwicklung ist laut Innenministerium auf mehrere Faktoren zurückzuführen: (Abs. 11)

Auf das international zu beobachtende Ansteigen der Straftaten, auf die starke Zunahme des Bandenwesens, an dem Österreicher beteiligt sind, und auf die Ostflüchtlinge. (Abs. 12)

Zwei Spitzenpolitiker meldeten sich gestern zur Flüchtlingsproblematik zu Wort: Kanzler Vranitzky versicherte, Österreich bleibe ein Asyl- und Flüchtlingsland, man müsse aber zwischen politischem und wirtschaftlichem Flüchtling unterscheiden. Vranitzky bezeichnete es als beste Flüchtlingspolitik, der Wirtschaft unserer östlichen Nachbarn zu helfen. (Abs. 13)

FPÖ-Chef Haider forderte Innenminister Löschnak auf, eine Landeshauptleute-Konferenz über die Unterbringung der Flüchtlinge einzuberufen. Sozialminister Geppert müsse dafür sorgen, daß Asylanten beschäftigt würden. (Abs. 14)
Ende

Chancellor: Economic Aid for Eastern Neighbours / Haider: Summit on Accommodation of Asylum-seekers
IN 11 YEARS: 7.5 BILLION ON REFUGEES
Lead: (6 lines, 2 columns)
The financial sacrifices that Austria is making to fulfil its humanitarian obligations to aid for refugees can be seen in new figures from the Ministry of Finance: from 1980 to the end of 1990 7.5. Billion Schillings were released for care of refugees (Accommodation and welfare)
Text: (3 columns, 82 lines)
Our country has had to cope with 3 great waves of refugees over the past 34 years: (§ 1)
In 1956, after the Hungarian revolution, suppressed with considerable bloodshed, 182,432 people crossed our borders. (§ 2)
In 1968 after the crushing of the Prague Spring 162,000 Czechoslovaks fled to our territory. (§ 3)
In 1981 after the imposition of martial law in Poland 33,142 refugees sought political asylum.
Next week, as Interior Minister Löschnak confirmed to the *Krone* yesterday, Austria will have to step on the emergency brake. (§ 5)
The Cabinet will decide on a compulsory visa for Romanians, most of whom count as economic migrants. (§ 6)
But our borders will still be open to those who are being pursued in their homeland for political, racist or religious reasons. (§ 7)
It continues to be claimed that refugees from the East are responsible for rising crime in Austria. On that subject the Interior Ministry informed the *Krone* yesterday: (§ 8)
The crime rate amongst legally employed guest-workers is lower than among Austrians. (§ 9)
On the other hand Eastern refugees who work illegally are more likely on average to commit crimes than our own citizens. (§ 10)
Crime Rate in Austria Climbing (Headline in bold type)
The crime rate in Austria did indeed climb, from 1987 to 1988 by 2.5–3 %, and from 1988 to 1989 by 3.5–4%. This alarming development is, according to the Interior Ministry, the result of three factors: (§ 11)
The increase in criminal acts visible internationally; the sharp increase in gangsterism in which Austrians are involved; and refugees from the East. (§ 12)
Two top politicians commented yesterday on the refugee problem:
Chancellor Vranitzky guaranteed that Austria would remain a refugee and asylum

state, but a distinction would have to be made between political and economic migrants. Vranitzky said that the best refugee policy was to assist the economies of our eastern neighbours. (§ 13)

FPÖ leader Haider challenged Interior Minister Löschnak to call a conference of state governors on the accommodation of refugees. Social Services Minister Geppert would have to ensure that refugees are made to work.
(End)

(Textual example from Matouschek & Wodak 1995/96:57)

Setting and context   The text arises out of discussions concerning the housing of 800 Romanian refugees in the district of Kaisersteinbruch – the high point of an eighteen-month long discussion of Austria's responsibility to refugees and immigrants from the former Eastern Bloc. There had been some discourse of sympathy and imposition of will from pro-revolutionary reports of the sufferings of the Romanian people. This had already become a discourse concerning the expulsion of troublesome asylum-seekers. Because of this there arose a discourse of justification, in the sense that those whose sufferings had aroused sympathy were now to be excluded for matters of violence, crime and social parasitism.

Theme and content, intertextuality   The themes of this piece of reporting reflect those of prejudiced migration debates at the international level: stress on numbers of refugees, metaphors of threat ('streams', 'floods', 'masses'), illegality, criminality, dishonesty, and attribution of the status of 'economic migrants'. The emphasis on the theme 'criminality of refugees' is newly introduced in this article. The complete text corpus, beyond this short sample text, displays a xenophobic attitude in a wide range of text variants from a wide range of media. The differences are only in the degree of explicitness of the xenophobia. Even the more liberal media organs are unable to distance themselves unambiguously from this expulsion discourse. Groups were set up and ranged against each other: the we-group of helpful Austrians, overburdened by the numbers of refugees and their criminality, is presented in a positive light. Against them the *refugees, Eastern refugees, economic migrants*, and so on are clearly marked by negative content.

Confrontation with data and reported facts   The detailed contextual knowledge of other specialists provides information about distortion in the texts.

The most precise description possible of the text at all linguistic levels by means of a distinction between strategies and linguistic realizations   The prejudiced negative attitudes to the groups of foreigners are justified by the most varied strategies. Vague formulations (*Eastern neighbours, asylum-seekers, refugees*) and rationalization, by giving pseudo-objective facts to the detriment of the refugees, are already used in the headline and in the lead to justify refusal to the initially unnamed source. Austria is further represented as the victim (*victim-agent reversal*) of a wave of refugees. The acceptance of refugees from Romania is placed immediately after the waves of refugees of 1956, 1968 and 1981. The burden of the influx of refugees is conveyed by the deliberately vague discourse representation, with floating borders between the opinions of the author and other sources, by metaphors of threat ('emergency break'), and by the conceptualization of the group as 'economic migrants'. The construction of the link between the group of foreigners and criminality could be more precisely investigated in the same way.

Summary   The rejection and expulsion of Romanians is justified in the text in a quasi-objective manner. By including contextual knowledge about the discourse, the text can be situated in the total discourse. In any case the discourse about Romanians can only be understood with reference to previous discourses about difference in the more distant or recent past. Taking textual contextual knowledge and intertextuality into account, Matouschek and Wodak conclude 'that the discourse about Romanians (in the total discourse of media and politics) may be viewed as a kind of example. An example is made of the Romanians to stem the further flow of "foreigners" in general and Eastern Europeans in particular' (Matouschek & Wodak 1995: 62).

11.6 CRITICAL DISCUSSION

Criticism of CDA comes from conversation analysis – the 'reverse side' of the debate between conversation analysis (Schegloff 1998) and CDA (van Dijk, personal communication, email). Schegloff argues that CDA, even though it has different goals and interests than the local construction of interaction, should deal seriously with its material: 'If, however, they mean the issues of power, domination and the like to connect up with discursive material, it should be a serious rendering of that material.' This means it should at least be compatible with what is demonstrably relevant for the behaviour of participants in an interaction. Only when such categories as the gender of participants are made relevant – for instance by an explicit mention ('Ladies last') – are they important for an analysis. If CDA is understood in this way it would not, in Schegloff's opinion, be an *alternative* to conversation analysis but would require a conversation analysis to be carried out first. 'Otherwise the critical analysis will not "bind" to the data, and risks ending up merely ideological.' Van Dijk explains, in the critical appraisal of conversation analysis (cf. Chapter 8), that in his opinion the kind of analysis required by Schegloff of the 'text itself' is an illusion.

Alongside this general debate about the whole enterprise of CDA, a more specific discussion has developed between Norman Fairclough and Henry Widdowson. Widdowson criticizes the fact that the term discourse is as vague as it is fashionable: 'discourse is something everybody is talking about but without knowing with any certainty just what it is: in vogue and vague' (Widdowson 1995: 158). He also criticizes the lack of a clear demarcation between text and discourse. Furthermore – and here his criticism approaches that of Schegloff – CDA is an ideological interpretation and therefore not an analysis. The term critical discourse analysis is a contradiction in terms. Widdowson believes that CDA is, in a dual sense, a biased interpretation: in the first place it is prejudiced on the basis of some ideological commitment, and then it selects for analysis such texts as will support the preferred interpretation (Widdowson 1995: 169). Analysis ought to mean the examination of several interpretations and, in the case of CDA, this is not possible because of prior judgements. Fairclough (1996), in reply to this criticism, draws attention to the open-endedness of results required in the principles of CDA. He also points out that CDA, unlike most other approaches, is always explicit about its own position and commitment.

11.7 QUALITY CRITERIA

Critical discourse analysis must be intelligible in its interpretations and explanations. The way in which investigators have arrived at their results must be recognizable. In addition, the validity of CDA results is not absolute and immutable but always open to new contexts and information which might cause the results to change. The interplay of open-endedness and intelligibility, and of the interpretative and explanatory nature of its analysis, are important criteria for CDA. One further characteristic requirement which results must meet is that of practical relevance. CDA is concerned with social problems: the usability of its findings is a precondition.

11.8 AREAS OF APPLICATION AND PRECONDITIONS

The areas of application of CDA are closely related with its development out of the specific political context of ideological and political movements since the 1960s. CDA is interested in a very general way in dominance and power relations between social entities and classes, between women and men, between national, ethnic, religious, sexual, political, cultural and sub-cultural groups. Its potential areas of application are therefore all relationships and themes which are relevant to the analysis of social power: women's studies (Wodak & Benke 1997), anti-semitism (Wodak et al. 1990), fascism (Maas 1984), xenophobia (Matouschek and Wodak 1995/96), language in politics (Wodak & Menz 1990, Fairclough 1989, 1992a) or language in organizations (Wodak 1996). Its point of departure is always the assumption that inequality and injustice are repeatedly reproduced in language and legitimized by it.

Because of contextual meaning and the postulated intertextuality, CDA requires – as a precondition to any application – comprehensive information about prevailing social and historical conditions and historical chains.

For the approaches described here specific areas of application have developed. Fairclough's model is suited to analysis of the contexts of social and discursive change. This is analysed with reference to the combination of discourses and genres in texts, which leads to a restructuring of the relationships between different discursive practices within and beyond institutions, and also with reference to changes in the boundaries within and between 'orders of discourse'. As an example of discursive change, Fairclough analyses changes in the way universities in England are marketed (Fairclough 1993). In a range of texts, including reports of meetings, academic CVs and job advertisements, he finds a change in the discursive practices of modern universities, an end to stable institutional identities and a stronger investment in the construction of entrepreneurial identities (Fairclough 1993: 157). A further example of discursive change is the 'conversationalization' of public discourse, which implies a restructuring of the boundary between public and private life through a change in discursive practices. Fairclough illustrates this in doctor–patient conversations (Fairclough 1995b). His research has also focussed on media interviews and language teaching.

Ruth Wodak begins by applying the discourse-historical method to communication in organizations and to language barriers in courts, schools and hospitals. Later research focuses on sexism, anti-semitism and racism in settings with differing degrees of public accessibility. In particular she examines the construction of the concept of an enemy in public discourse. The discourse-historical approach seeks to facilitate the analysis of implicitly prejudiced utterances, and to assist in the decoding of allusions typically concealed in such utterances by referring to background knowledge. Examples of this are found in studies of post-war anti-semitism in Austria (Wodak et al. 1990), discourses on migrants (Matouschek et al. 1995), and attitudes to Central and Eastern European neighbours (Projekt team 1996). One important aim of this approach is the practical relevance of its findings. More recent studies have been concerned with the discursive construction of national identities (Wodak et al. 1998) and the complex organization of the European Union (Straehle et al. 1999, Iedema & Wodak 1999).

11.9 SIMILARITIES AND DIFFERENCES IN COMPARISON WITH OTHER METHODS

The differences between CDA, to which these two approaches belong, and other methods may be most clearly established with reference to the general principles of CDA. In the first place the nature of the problems with which CDA is concerned is different in principle from all those methods which do not determine their interest in advance, such as content analysis or grounded theory, but also from other methods which are explicit about their object of study. Here we may make a comparison with ethnomethodologically oriented text analysis, and in particular with conversation analysis. While CDA is interested in social problems, conversation analysis is concerned with structural problems in the organization of conversations.

Related to the object of investigation is the fact that CDA follows a different and critical approach to problems since it endeavours to make explicit power relationships which are frequently hidden, and from that to derive results which are of practical relevance. In this sense it approaches other critical approaches such as functional pragmatics. The latter, like CDA, is concerned with practical relevance of results but formulates this less explicitly as a goal of the method. Moreover, in functional pragmatics the analysis and discovery of power relations are less important than insight into the conditions of day-to-day activity which can lead to a situation where what seems obvious no longer has to be taken for granted. This includes those power relations which are normally taken for granted, but they do not occupy the same central position as in CDA. This kind of critical orientation is missing in ethnomethodological text analysis, which is primarily concerned with the reconstruction and description of the routine behaviour of participants. The critical claims of discourse analysis are derived from its theoretical background.

One more important difference arises from the assumption of CDA that all discourses are historical and can, therefore, only be understood with reference to their context. Other methods proceed on a similar basis: ethnography is interested in language in its cultural context. Functional pragmatics deals, not with context, but with general social settings, and investigates these by means of its assumption of some underlying purpose in all linguistic behaviour. Common to all of these approaches is that they take context, or settings, to refer to such extralinguistic factors as culture, society or ideology, which is also important in CDA. The strong form of conversation analysis does not admit these influences and locates context within a text. In our outline of conversation analysis, however, it has already been shown that there is now a development in the direction of a broader understanding of context. In any case, the notion of context is broadest in CDA, since this explicitly includes social-psychological, political and ideological components and thereby postulates an interdisciplinary procedure. This interdisciplinary procedure often remains eclectic, however, since the data are frequently not representative.

Beyond this, CDA – using the concepts of intertextuality and interdiscursivity – analyses relationships with other texts, which is not developed in other methods. From its basic understanding of the notion of discourse, it may be concluded that CDA is open to the broadest range of factors exerting an influence on texts.

From the notion of context, a further difference emerges concerning the assumption about the relationship between language and society. CDA does not take this relationship to be simply deterministic but invokes an idea of mediation. Here there is a difference between the approaches to discourse described above: Norman Fairclough defines the relationship in accordance with Halliday's multifunctional linguistic theory[1] and the concept of orders of discourse according to Foucault, while Ruth Wodak, like Teun van Dijk, introduces a sociocognitive level. This kind of mediation between language and society is absent from ethnomethodological text analysis.

A further distinguishing feature of the different methods is the incorporation of linguistic categories into their analyses. In principle we may assume that categories such as deixis and pronouns can be analysed in each of the methods (including, therefore, content analysis or grounded theory), but that they are crucial for only a few. Examples of such genuine 'linguistic' methods are functional pragmatics and CDA. In functional pragmatics, linguistic categories are found in the so-called linguistic surface, while CDA speaks of *form* and *texture* at the textual level (Fairclough) or of *forms of linguistic realization* (Wodak). Conversation analysis, on the other hand, rejects such premature categorizations and generalizations, and attributes no prior significance to linguistic categories. CDA, therefore, as a linguistic method, distinguishes itself by virtue of the meaning of linguistic features from all other more sociologically inclined methods of text analysis.

A further distinguishing feature of methods of text analysis is found in their analytical procedure. Both Fairclough and Wodak see their procedure as a hermeneutic process; the same is true of functional pragmatics. The sequential procedure of conversation analysis is different from both. Through their interdisciplinary procedure and their description of the object of investigation from widely differing perspectives, as well as their continuous feedback between analysis and data collection, the two methods of critical discourse analysis meet the requirements of grounded theory.

If a crude distinction has to be made between 'text-extending' and 'text-reducing' methods of analysis, then CDA, on account of its concentration on very clear formal properties and the associated compression of texts during analysis, may be characterized as 'text-reducing'. In this sense it contrasts with the 'text-expanding' distinction theory and objective hermeneutics (Oevermann et al. 1979). The distinction theory method may be distinguished from CDA by virtue of the fact that it allows for no experimental variation of a text.

11.10 LITERATURE

Fairclough, Norman (1989), *Language and Power*, London: Longman.

After defining such central concepts as ideology, power, text and discourse, Norman Fairclough describes his method of critical discourse analysis and applies this in Chapter 7 to the political discourse of Margaret Thatcher.

Fairclough, Norman (1995b), *Critical Discourse Analysis. The Critical Study of Language*, London: Longman.

This book is a collection of essays which the author wrote between 1983 and 1992, and it gives an overview of the author's approach and his further development. The themes of language and power, ideology and language, and sociocultural change are of central importance.

Wodak, R., Nowak, P., Pelikan, J., Gruber, H., de Cillia, R. & Mitten, R. (1990), *'Wir sind alle unschuldige Täter': Diskurs-historische Studien zum Nachkriegsantisemitismus*, Frankfurt: Suhrkamp.

The discourse-historical method is applied to anti-semitic discourse using data from settings with differing degrees of public accessibility. The analysis concentrates particularly on justification discourse.

Wodak, Ruth (1996), *Disorders of Discourse*, London: Longman.

This is a collection of previous critical discourse studies by the author on communication in organizations, with a general introduction to critical discourse analysis. The principles of CDA are illustrated by means of examples from medical, educational, media and therapeutic communication.

11.11 SECONDARY LITERATURE

11.11.1 Handbooks

In linguistic handbooks, except in the *Handbook of Pragmatics* (Verschueren, et al. 1995), there are no special entries on critical discourse analysis. Critical approaches normally receive a brief mention as new developments within discourse analysis.

Wodak, Ruth (1995), 'Critical linguistics and critical discourse analysis', in Jef Verschueren, Jan-Ola Östman & Jan Blommaert (eds), *Handbook of Pragmatics. Manual*, Amsterdam: Benjamins, 204–10.

11.11.2 Other presentations of methods and coursebooks

Discourse & Society 4 (2), 1993, is a special number on critical discourse analysis. It contains theoretical and methodological essays (by Gunther Kress, Theo van Leeuwen and Teun van Dijk), as well as empirical analyses by Norman Fairclough, and Ruth Wodak and Bernd Matouschek (see 11.11.3).

Fowler, Roger (1991), 'Critical linguistics', in Kirsten Malmkjaer (ed.), *The Linguistics Encyclopedia*, London: Routledge, 89–93.

This is a presentation of general features of critical linguistics, which are also valid for critical discourse analysis, together with the main characteristics of their scientific tradition. By concentrating on Halliday's functional approach, the author gives a close description of an important fundamental of Fairclough's discourse analysis. These presentations provide a framework for the approaches described here.

11.11.3 Typical applications

In principle all the studies mentioned in 11.10 (above) contain examples of applications of the various methods. Additional examples may be found in the following works:

> Fairclough, Norman (1993), 'Critical discourse analysis and the marketization of public discourse: the universities', *Discourse & Society*, 4 (2): 133–68.

Norman Fairclough analyses the discursive aspects of marketing in public discourse with the example of texts from higher education (job advertisements, CVs, etc.).

> Fairclough, Norman (1995a), *Media Discourse*, London: Arnold.

This is a portrayal of the relationship between the modification of discursive practices in the media, and larger social and cultural changes. With a series of examples Fairclough illustrates the tension between public and private domains, information and entertainment.

> Lutz, Benedikt & Wodak, Ruth (1987), *Information für Informierte. Linguistische Studien zu Verständlichkeit und Verstehen von Hörfunknachrichten*, Wien: Akademie der Wissenschaften.

This contains an elaboration of the socio-psychological theory of text comprehension which is applied to news broadcast texts.

"THEY THINK A BOWL OF ALPHABET-SOUP WILL GIVE THEM ALL THAT DATA THEY NEED TO STUDY TEENAGE-DISCOURSE"

Matouschek, B., Wodak, R., & Januschek, F. (1995), *Notwendige Maßnahmen gegen Fremde? Genese und Formen von rassistischen Diskursen der Differenz*, Wien: Passagen.

The investigation of Austrian discourse towards migrants from Eastern European states since 1989 shows the subtle forms of the discourse of prejudice, together with setting and context-specific differences.

NOTE

1   Michael A. K. Halliday developed, in the 1960s, a model of descriptive grammar which interprets the grammar of a language as a system of systems, and symbolizes it as a network system. The network indicates the combinatory possibilities of units of the descriptive level, so that every linguistic unit can be explained as a subsystem of choices. A simplified network for the English sentence would first distinguish a choice between *imperative* and *indicative*. For indicative there would be a choice between *interrogative* and *declarative*, and so on (Malmkjaer 1991c: 448). Halliday views grammar as functionally organized, where 'function' is understood as a reply to the general question 'why is language as it is?' (Halliday 1970: 141). 'The particular form taken by the grammatical system of a language is closely related to the social and personal needs that language is required to serve' (Halliday 1970: 142). Halliday attempts to link language function with linguistic structure by relating the networks of choices to the three metafunctions: the *ideational, interpersonal* and *textual* functions. For a more precise account the original literature should be consulted (Halliday 1970, 1985).

CHAPTER 12

FUNCTIONAL PRAGMATICS

12.1 THEORETICAL ORIGINS

The most general and probably the most valid short description may be derived from the characterization which functional pragmatics gives itself. Unlike other pragmatic approaches, functional pragmatics is derived neither from Morris's semiotic conception, nor from Carnap's logical idea of a linguistic *pragmatics*. It comes rather from the ideas which developed in the 1970s in Dieter Wunderlich's research group (see Wunderlich 1972) of an action-centred pragmatics based on the work of Bühler. The notion of pragmatics is based on an integration of semiotic and logical ideas, a critical view of speech act theory and the analysis of deixis, together with Bühler's applications. Functional pragmatics is therefore organized in accordance with the action-centred understanding of the term. This implies that pragmatic aspects are not simply added to non-pragmatically understood linguistic forms, but that questions are asked about the action bases of the use of a linguistic system and the linguistic system itself (see Ehlich & Rehbein 1986: 46f., Ehlich 1993, 1991: 131f.). In this way functional pragmatics also sees itself as a reaction to the additive process of 'loss-compensation' in linguistics, which manifests itself in the coining of such terms as *pragmalinguistics*, *sociolinguistics* or *psycholinguistics*. Instead of adding what is missing to the 'core' of linguistics, as in these examples, functional pragmatics concerns itself with a fully performative theory of language and its modes of use. *Functional* implies that it has to do with the functions of linguistic forms.

Functional pragmatics is an approach which, based on a specific *theory* of action, has developed its own analytical instruments. Rehbein describes one detailed and frequently used instrument of functional pragmatics – the linguistic pattern – and comes to the conclusion that 'the theory equipped with this kind of conceptual and methodical equipment (i.e. pattern analysis) is known as functional *pragmatics*' (Rehbein 1988: 1183). Whether a school of functional pragmatics has already developed is a question which recent studies leave unanswered. Brünner & Graefen (1994b: 9) speak only of a 'specific mode of analysis', unified by a 'shared interest in a fundamental renewal of scientific procedures in linguistics, and by criticism of a common research practice that has led to serious empirical and analytical shortcomings and distortions' (Brünner & Graefen 1994b: 9f).

Functional pragmatics was developed and elaborated primarily by Konrad Ehlich and Jochen Rehbein. A detailed presentation of its theoretical bases is in Rehbein's (1977) doctoral dissertation. A frequently quoted analytical example is Ehlich & Rehbein's 'Restaurant'. Here the authors show for the first time that, in communicative acts, speakers refer to socially elaborated communicative forms which are determined by purposes. Further theoretical developments, using concrete empirical analyses, may be found in Ehlich & Rehbein (1979, 1986). Functional pragmatic analyses of institutional communication have been published in Redder (1983) and examples of recent applications are in Brünner (1994).

12.2 BASIC THEORETICAL ASSUMPTIONS

The point of departure is a view of language based on a performative theory: 'Language is an object of use, with words one can do something' (Ehlich & Rehbein 1972: 209). Further theoretical development is based on criticism of Searle and Austin, whose approaches – from a functional pragmatic point of view – do not lead to a systematic theory of speech as action, but which again are limited to a theory of language as system (Ehlich & Rehbein 1972: 210). In concrete terms this criticism of the limitations of speech act theory applies to the sentence level, which is felt to be responsible for the inadequate treatment of addressees or hearers. This sentence-based analysis of the felicity of speech acts leads to the creation of a concept of perlocutionary act, which Ehlich calls the 'infelicitous member of the categories of speech act theory' (Ehlich 1991: 130). From this criticism of speech act theory there developed, in the work of Wunderlich (1972), a social conception of language which incorporates speakers and hearers equally by means of the concept of 'speech actions'. This is fundamental to functional pragmatics: through the distinction which is made between 'speech actions' and 'speech acts', functional pragmatics distances itself from speech act theory.

Speech acts are speaker-oriented and concentrate on individual sentences; *speech actions* are actions fulfilled by means of language and have the status of socially agreed obligatory forms (Ehlich 1972). They are intended to handle the complex structures of interactions between speakers and hearers. Speech actions have three constituent acts: (a) utterance, (b) propositional act and (c) illocutionary act. Speech actions can be linked to each other as a chain or speech-action-sequence (Brünner & Graefen 1994b: 11). The notion of *perlocutionary act* is criticized as a fundamentally false categorization. In its place the category of *purpose* is seen as central. 'The interaction between speaker and hearer, as a truly mutual action and sequence of actions between two or more participants, culminates in the *purpose of the linguistic action* (or purpose of the sequence of linguistic actions)' (Ehlich 1991: 131).

The analytical definition of purpose, therefore, takes on a central role in the reconstruction of linguistic action. The *purpose* (after Rehbein 1977: 135f.) is distinguished from the *goal*: a single actor aims at a goal, and in the pursuit and realization of goals actors use socially agreed patterns which belong to purposes. The transformation of individual goals into socially developed purposes takes place via the 'stages of the action process'.

Purpose is central for the reconstruction of linguistic action in that the functional analysis of linguistic action implies a back-channelling from the action to the purposes which govern it. 'A functional analysis can only be achieved if one can discover the forces and structures which underlie social life. It is only from them that an explanation of surface phenomena can be developed' (Ehlich & Rehbein 1972: 215). Here the strict methodological separation of *surface* (the single special case) and *structure* (a socially agreed form) is already addressed. This is characteristic of the most prominent functional-pragmatic instrument – the linguistic *pattern*.

A functional analysis therefore implies the discovery of those forces and structures which permit the explanation of surface phenomena. With the idea of pattern a category was developed to handle this separation of linguistic surface and deep structure. Ehlich defines patterns as 'organizational forms of linguistic action' and 'depictions of social circumstances in linguistic form' which provide the standardized versions of recurrent constellations of reality. Patterns are therefore deep structure categories, the realization of which is achieved by the linguistic surface (Ehlich 1991: 132). In its definitions of patterns, functional pragmatics sets itself apart from the popular use of the word 'pattern'.

Of particular importance is the knowledge of actions or patterns which Ehlich and Rehbein presuppose, in order to be able to assume standardized processing of recurrent purposes of action (Ehlich & Rehbein 1986: 136f.). Individuals actualize, in interactions, their general knowledge of actions – that is to say their knowledge of forms used to process purposes – and behave with reference to previous experience and taking prognoses into account. Patterns of action are the ensembles of activities and activity sequences which are thereby constituted.

Rehbein sees every action as embedded in action spaces, or socially structured settings:

> an action space is not only a visible place. It also includes a specific definable ensemble of preconditions which are crystallized by the total social structure and its reproduction, and which occur specifically in those actions that take place in the particular action space. The 'preconditions', for their part, are independent of the specific action space, so that they can, to a certain extent, be analysed as independent entities. (Rehbein 1977: 12)

In concrete terms the mediation of language and society takes place through institutions (Ehlich 1991: 136f., Ehlich & Rehbein 1986: 136f.): institutions are seen as complex structure-contexts within which actors organize themselves to process action purposes.

> Institutions characterize a large part of how and where we act linguistically. Institutions are, in Althusser's words, 'social machines' for the processing of social

> purposes. In that sense they are themselves mediators of the general aim of a society towards concrete social action, that is to say, the action of social participants. (Ehlich 1991: 136)

In consequence, this means that institutions provide 'standardized ways of dealing with recurrent constellations' (Ehlich & Rehbein 1986: 5). A functional pragmatic analysis of linguistic action, therefore, often refers to action within institutions.

The social determination of human behaviour assumed by functional pragmatics implies a need for social analysis. For Ehlich & Rehbein (1972) this means the analysis of the 'basic relationships of the different cultural and social phenomena in production activity and their organization in particular production relationships' (Ehlich & Rehbein 1972: 216). In the work of Ehlich & Rehbein this social analysis is traced back to Hegel and Marx.

The basic assumption of the purposive nature of language – ('acoustic production does not occur for its own sake, but underlies purposes that cannot be immediately recognized from their perceptible form' (Ehlich & Rehbein 1986: 134)) – is not only related to socially developed purposes, but also to intra-linguistic purposes. Ehlich is critical of the fact that in additive pragmatics this purposive character of linguistic structure is often disregarded (Ehlich 1994: 68). Under the heading of *procedures*, functional pragmatics understands types of linguistic action in which mental activities of speakers and hearers are considered in their relation to one another. The procedural types also differ according to these underlying purposes of action. Ehlich adopts Bühler's idea of 'field' when he allocates procedural types to those fields which make available the corresponding means of linguistic expression. He thereby extends Bühler's distinction between symbolic and deictic fields by adding fields of *prompting*, *toning* and *operation*. The relationship between fields, procedures and the action purposes realized by speakers and hearers is summarized in Table 12.1 (see Ehlich 1994: 73, 1991: 139, 1979).

Through transpositions of fields, linguistic units may be used for different procedural types (Ehlich 1994: 75f.). Units traditionally classified as pronouns are found on the one hand in the deictic field (demonstrative pronouns) and on the other hand in the operation field (interrogative and relative pronouns). Nouns and verbs are allocated mostly to the symbol field. Interjections are located in the prompting field.

Table 12.1   Purpose of action, procedures and fields

Purpose of Action	Procedure	Field
S communicates to H the attitudes of S in relation to X, Y	pictorial/ expressive	Toning field
S intervenes directly in the action or attitudinal structure of H	expeditive	Prompting field
S draws the attention of H to an Object X in the demonstration space common to S and H	deictic	Deictic field
S indicates an Object X, a fact Y, . . . for H	appellative/ symbolic	Symbol field
S enables H to process the linguistic action elements of S	operative	Operation field

Typological differences between languages are seen very clearly in the field of toning, for which German or English – in contrast to certain African languages – have very few words available. They rely instead on highly developed intonational means of expression (Redder 1994: 240). Table 12.2 gives a summary of the functional pragmatic method. The examples show that functional pragmatics uses the category of procedures to account for the transmediation of linguistic action and linguistic forms.

The fundamental purposive character of linguistic action leads functional pragmatics to the development of an analytical instrument – the *pattern* – for the mediation of language and society. In its procedural and pattern analysis it endeavours to remove traditional dichotomies such as form and function, or even grammar and pragmatics.

Table 12.2   Summary of the functional pragmatic method

Instruments	Purpose	Transmediation of	Relation to linguistic actions	Example
Procedures	Language-internal	Linguistic action and linguistic form	Procedures are the smallest units of linguistic action	I, here, now = deictic procedure
Patterns	Language-external	Linguistic action and social form	Patterns are potentials for action that have surface realizations through one or more linguistic actions	Task setting, task fulfilment, effective reasoning

12.3 OBJECTIVES OF THE METHOD

Konrad Ehlich and Jochen Rehbein see the goals of linguistic pragmatics in an action theory of language. This is required:

> to take account of the complex features of such action as a component of reality, to acknowledge this, in its complexity and in its contexts, as an analytical object, to recognize the place value, for the social action of co-operating actors, of all specific social activities, and to determine their internal and external formal features. (Ehlich & Rehbein 1986: 5)

> The aim of investigating social reality is the conceptual reconstruction of concrete events. It is only when such a reconstruction has been achieved that we can recognize the blind context which is concealed below the surface of linguistic action (as if behind the backs of the social actors). (Ehlich & Rehbein 1986: 176)

'Concrete' means observable phenomena such as communication in the classroom, in a restaurant, and so on. The authors achieve the reconstruction of these surface phenomena with reference to the conformities that determine and underlie a text – the so-called deep structure. The place value of a reconstructed complete context is allotted to the results of the analysis 'in anticipation' (that is 'as far as is compatible with the state of the analysis', Ehlich & Rehbein 1986: 176).

A functional pragmatic analysis of linguistic action seeks to reconstruct the purposes for which the action was undertaken by the actors; these include both the language-external purposes of the society and the language-internal purposes of the linguistic structure. The aim is to relate 'internal relationships' (Ehlich & Rehbein 1986: 177) to observable phenomena. This facilitates insight into the conditions of normal actions, and is said to create for the actors a set of circumstances where they no longer have to reproduce blindly the normal 'system of the self-evident' (Ehlich & Rehbein 1986: 178).

To illustrate the practical significance of this awareness of the internal organization of actions on classroom reality, Ehlich & Rehbein list four different factors (1986: 178f.). First, one's own actions no longer have to be carried out blindly, and contradictions no longer have to remain misunderstood. Secondly, actors can see what communicative changes are made possible by changes in institutional circumstances. Thirdly, actors learn what short-term changes are possible through adoption of the experiences of others and through individual corrections. Finally, it is also possible to recognize where all changes will necessarily remain unsuccessful because of some general weakness in the institution.

Functional pragmatics pursues these goals in the analysis of texts and discourses, and here a systematic distinction, founded on action theory, is made between discourse and text (cf. Brünner & Graefen 1994b: 7–8, Ehlich 1991: 136).

Discourse is a specific combination of linguistic action: 'I understand discourses as sequences of patterns constituted through the context of purposes. These are manifested on the linguistic surface as a sequence of linguistic actions' (Ehlich 1991: 135). Discourses are characteristically oral, but this feature, for instance in the example of communication via computers, does not have to be present. A precondition for discourse is that speakers and hearers must be present simultaneously.

Text, like discourse, is the realization and concretization of linguistic action, but differs from discourse by virtue of its distinguishing feature of the 'extended' speech situation. 'This extension of speech action implies that the fundamental category of "speech situation" is transcended in itself. The extension of the speech action arises from a specific area of purposes, namely that of transmission' (Ehlich 1991: 136). This means that linguistic action is separate from the receptive action of readers or hearers. The written mode is not an essential feature of this transmission.

12.4 OUTLINE OF THE METHOD

12.4.1 Procedure in pattern analysis

Pattern analysis is an important instrument of functional pragmatics that is applied in varying social circumstances. The research process is described as a totality of research stages, without, however, determining what the individual research stages should consist of. Ehlich & Rehbein (1986: 176) even assert that any pre-determination of individual research stages would amount to a ban on creative thinking and would hinder the research process. An important feature of the functional-pragmatic research process is the anticipation of the total context for the observable phenomenon by means of the analytical goal of reconstructing reality (Ehlich & Rehbein 1986: 176f.). This implies a quite specific mode of operation, by means of which functional pragmatics is distinguished from other analytical methods.

> The individual results of the research process should always be related back to the reality which is under analysis, by virtue of the fact that such results both modify the overall understanding of the material and thereby extend it. The research process does not, therefore, operate in a *linear way*), nor is it simply recursive, because if it were regulated in this way the application of any new insights would be lost'. (Ehlich & Rehbein 1986: 177; emphasis in original)

In this way functional pragmatics rejects naïve modes of operation and defines itself as accommodating, hermeneutic and integrative. This can be reconstructed by means of the example of the analytical components of pattern analysis. The individual points should not be understood as constituting a structural succession, but rather as an integrative process corresponding to the hermeneutic requirement postulated above:

(1)   Description of the total context, as for instance in a specific institution (for example school, restaurant). The aim is to discover the central structures (Ehlich & Rehbein 1972).
(2)   The search for recurrent interchangeable elements (such as the D-element in clarification; see Figure 12.1).
(3)   The classification of these interchangeable elements according to place of occurrence and procedures (for example 'hm' as a self-sufficient procedure, or the distinction between operative and deictic procedures).
(4)   The search for places where this interchangeable element recurs in a similar context.
(5)   The identification of a pattern.
(6)   The discovery of – often very slight – differences from similar patterns.

12.4.2 The reasoning pattern

Ehlich & Rehbein (1986) analyse, in the context of the classroom, a range of patterns such as task-setting, task-fulfilment, problem-solving, lecturing and reasoning. The reasoning pattern can be used to reconstruct the functional-pragmatic method of analysis, and theoretical assumptions such as the distinction between surface and deep structure may be illustrated.

The action pattern of effective reasoning comes into operation when, in the system of action, some defect arises or is suspected which must be removed if the communication is to continue successfully. At least two persons must, therefore, be involved in the communication. The speaker presumes or recognizes some defect in the interlocutor and realizes the effective reasoning pattern with the purpose of removing this defect. The purpose of the effective reasoning pattern is to bring about some change in the hearer's knowledge that is essential for successful continuation of the communication. According to whether or not this purpose is achieved, Ehlich & Rehbein (1986: 95) distinguish between *reasoning* and *effective reasoning*.

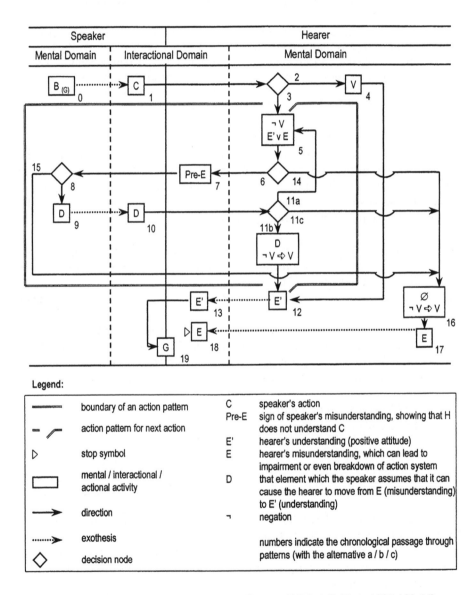

FIGURE 12.1   Effective reasoning pattern (Source: Ehlich & Rehbein 1986: 100, 16)

The typical course of action of the affective reasoning pattern, according to Ehlich & Rehbein (see Figure 12.1), may be subdivided as follows:

(a)   The speaker S has performed action C.
(b)   S knows through some signal of misunderstanding on the part of hearer H, that H does not understand C. This signal of misunderstanding is represented as Pre-E.
(c1) (i) S knows that H will adopt towards C either a positive attitude E' (understanding) or a negative attitude E.
       (ii) The negative attitude E includes an impairment (up to some break-off point) of the action system of S and H.
       (iii) The positive E' of H to C includes the continuation of the action system.
(c2) S desires a continuation of the action system of S and H.
(d)   S must therefore influence H to transform the alternative into E'.
(e)   S therefore looks for the element of D of which it is assumed that it will bring about, in H, the transformation of the alternative into E'.
(f)   S *exothesises* D: *exothesis* is understood as the unmodified representation of mental element in the interaction space of S and H (Ehlich & Rehbein 1986: 98).

This is the ideal course of the pattern. Patterns, however, are not realized as rigid linear sequences. The deep structure described here is represented in quite different ways on the linguistic surface. H may, for instance, realize Pre-E in a question which simultaneously incorporates the request for clarification. Instead of asking explicitly 'what did you do?', H may also indicate misunderstanding by some appropriate mime or gesture. Even when no indication of misunderstanding is given on the part of the hearer, a clarification pattern is conceivable if S is personally aware that a particular action is potentially problematic and interprets it as requiring clarification.

The possible variants of the pattern at the deep structure level are symbolized as decision-making nodes. It is quite conceivable that S is not interested in a prolongation of the action system. Then the search for, and verbalization of, the D-element will be omitted and H will be left in a condition of not understanding. It is equally possible that D is unable to bring the hearer from the condition of not understanding to that of understanding. In this case the effective reasoning pattern may be prematurely abandoned, without having achieved its purpose. The effective reasoning pattern may, however, be given another attempt: H expresses lack of understanding in a pre-E, S decides to look for a D-element capable of bringing H to the condition of understanding and exothesises this. If H is thereby enabled to attain the necessary piece of knowledge, he or she will exothesise a condition of understanding and thus quit the effective reasoning pattern. In principle, recursion during reasoning is possible an infinite number of times.

The two core elements of the effective reasoning pattern are: C – the action itself which is not understood by H; and D – the element which is introduced by the speaker to put the hearer into the condition of understanding. Proceeding from C, Ehlich & Rehbein distinguish a number of types of effective reasoning pattern: in action clarification C is a previous action of S. Intention reasonings are said to occur when, instead of C, a Pre-F is realized – that is the exothesis of some future action. If instead of C the speaker addresses a request for a future action to the hearer, Ehlich & Rehbein call this *obligatory clarification*. In cognitive reasoning, instead of C, the speaker utters a statement or an assertion.

As a variant of action-reasoning a justification pattern may be understood. Here too there may be a past or future action of the speaker at the outset, but this must address the hearer's integrity zone to bring the justification pattern into action (Ehlich & Rehbein 1986: 119). This is used by the speaker to raise serious questions about the continuation of the action system. Ehlich & Rehbein frequently present patterns in diagrammatic form (Ehlich & Rehbein 1986: 100), as we have already seen for the effective reasoning pattern (see Figure 12.1).

With the identification of patterns, functional pragmatics is able to analyse speech actions in detail. Since the mode of operation should be understood as a hermeneutic process, the results must always be related back to the total context. The example given of the effective reasoning pattern comes from the context of classroom communication. Ehlich & Rehbein exemplify this with the realization of an action-reasoning, in a classroom context, in the sentence: 'I'll write the sentence up again so that it will be quicker'. Institutional communication in the classroom is obligatory communication in a socially secured communication space. Understanding on the part of the pupils is obligatory, and therefore does not have to be justified by reasoning. For pupils this obligatory communication means that they will attempt to break out of the action system. To prevent precisely this risk of obligatory communication, the teacher, in the example quoted, changes his action strategy and tries to reinstate the co-operation of the pupils by means of a process of understanding. He realizes this through a reasoning pattern which, in the example given, puts the communication type 'good relations' before institutional communication.

12.5 QUALITY CRITERIA

The classical quality criteria are not discussed in functional pragmatics, but this does not mean that a functional-pragmatic analysis does not have to meet such criteria. From the requirements that a functional-pragmatic analysis seeks to fulfil, specific quality criteria may be derived – even though they are not described as such. In every sense the category of purpose is central, in both intra-linguistic and extra-linguistic respects. Whether or not the purposes identified in the analysis reconstruct the concrete reality can only be clarified by textual comparison. If patterns or procedures do occur in other contexts beyond the immediate text, this becomes the criterion for demonstrating the validity of the underlying purposes that are employed to process patterns or procedures.

Furthermore, we may take as quality criteria: (a) the systematic involvement of the linguistic surface of discourse, in accordance with the requirements of empiricism, (b) its reflective quality, and (c) criticisms. Functional pragmatics does not simply adopt everyday categories, but scrutinizes them and critically examines their analytic potential in order to redefine its frontiers (Ehlich 1991: 142).

The functional-pragmatic quality criteria lead to the research goal of the conceptual reconstruction of concrete phenomena. This explains why Popper's requirement of setting up and falsifying hypotheses cannot be applied in functional pragmatics, since each individual case is of interest as a reconstruction task and not for purposes of falsification.

12.6 AREAS OF APPLICATION AND PRECONDITIONS

A precondition for analysis is the transcription of authentic texts using the authors' own system of transcription, '*Halbinterpretative Arbeitstranskription*' (HIAT) or 'semi-interpretative working transcription' (Ehlich & Rehbein 1976).[1] HIAT is the most widely used system of transcription in German-speaking countries. Two computerized versions are available: HIAT-DOS for PC and SyncWriter for Macintosh.

Potential areas of application, in line with the basic theoretical assumptions and the procedure and pattern instruments, are: the social use of language in the case of pattern analysis, and linguistic structure in the case of procedures. For procedures there have been grammatical analyses (for example Redder 1984), and investigations of deixis (Ehlich 1979), of the field of operation (Redder 1990), or of the toning field (Redder 1994). Of even greater importance than these are the analyses of patterns. The works of Ehlich & Rehbein provided the starting point (Ehlich 1984, Rehbein 1984, Ehlich & Rehbein 1986) and laid the foundations for an important area of applications, namely the study of language in institutions. As examples of this we may mention concrete professional practice in the field of medicine (Menz 1991), in law courts (Koerfer 1994), in sales talk (Brünner 1994), and in teacher–learner discourse (Becker-Mrotzek 1994, Friedrich 1994, Koole & ten Thije 1994).

Functional pragmatics sees itself as applied discourse research and seeks explanations and – wherever possible – the improvement of social practice through scientific means (Brünner & Becker-Mrotzek 1992). The achievements of pattern analysis (Ehlich & Rehbein 1986: 163–4) are in reconstructing the contexts of action purposes, of actual instances of actions, and also of the underlying knowledge that promotes action without working at the conscious level. An example of this is the practical relevance of the analysis of classroom communication (Ehlich & Rehbein 1986: 178).

12.7 SIMILARITIES AND DIFFERENCES IN COMPARISON WITH OTHER METHODS

There are parallels between critical discourse analysis and functional pragmatics which have already been addressed (see Chapter 11). These are connected with the practical relevance of its results, its hermeneutic procedures, the importance it attaches to precise transcription, and the theoretical connection, through some mediation, which is assumed to exist between language and society.

Differences from other methods can be determined quite simply from one essential feature of functional pragmatics, namely the theoretical elaboration of *purpose* as the central concept at both intra-linguistic and extra-linguistic levels. In terms of the relation between language and social structures, this means that in reconstructing underlying purposes by pattern analysis, functional pragmatics adheres to a strict methodological distinction between *linguistic surface* (the isolated special case) and *structure* (the socially elaborated general form; see also Rehbein 1988: 1183). This gives rise to similarities with those methods which similarly distinguish two levels of texts: objective hermeneutics accepts a level of latent meaning; narrative semiotics, like functional pragmatics, makes an explicit distinction between surface and deep structure. Of course, the deep structure level in narrative semiotics, unlike that in functional pragmatics, does not refer to social forms but to the level of base norms, values and attitudes (Greimas & Rastier 1968, Fiol 1990: 380).

For intra-linguistic purposes instruments are available, in the shape of linguistic procedures, which – in contrast to conversation analysis – imply a preoccupation with linguistic categories (such as rhetorical devices). Moreover, the purposefulness of linguistic action puts form and function, as dialectic determinants, into a new perspective. In this way functional pragmatics becomes open not only to discourse and text analysis, but also to grammatical analysis, and distances itself from all other methods (Redder 1994: 239).

12.8 LITERATURE

Brünner, Gisela & Graefen, Gabriele (eds) (1994a), *Texte und Diskurse. Methoden und Forschungsergebnisse der Funktionalen Pragmatik*, Opladen: Westdeutscher Verlag.

Ehlich, Konrad & Rehbein, Jochen (1986*)*, *Muster und Institution. Untersuchungen zur schulischen Kommunikation*, Tübingen: Narr.

Wunderlich, Dieter (ed.) (1972), *Linguistische Pragmatik*, Frankfurt: Athenäum.

Rehbein, Jochen (1977), *Komplexes Handeln. Elemente der Handlungstheorie der Sprache*, Stuttgart: Metzler.

Rehbein, Jochen (ed.) (1997), *Funktionale Pragmatik im Spektrum*, Opladen: Westdeutscher Verlag.

This book provides not only a collection of essays but, for the first time, a bibliography and a systematic register of the subject areas of functional-pragmatic analyses.

12.9 SECONDARY LITERATURE

12.9.1 Handbooks

Functional pragmatics has not been accepted in the literature in English. For this reason one will look in vain for entries on functional pragmatics in English handbooks or accounts of methods. The method has so far been applied and developed by its representatives mostly in German-speaking countries, but has hardly been noticed by proponents of other approaches.

Ehlich, Konrad (1986/1996), 'Funktional-pragmatische Kommunikationsanalyse: Ziele und Verfahren', in Ludger Hoffmann (ed.) *Sprachwissenschaft. Ein Reader*, Berlin: de Gruyter.

Rehbein, Jochen (1988), 'Ausgewählte Aspekte der Pragmatik', in Ulrich Ammon, Norbert Dittmar & Klaus Mattheier (eds), *Soziolinguistik: ein internationales Handbuch zur Wissenschaft von Sprache und Gesellschaft*, vol. 2, Berlin: de Gruyter, 1181–95.

Rehbein provides an overview of the development of pragmatics since Searle and Austin, and concentrates in particular on papers by German-speaking authors. He also gives a more extensive presentation of pattern analysis.

12.9.2 Other methodological presentations

Schlobinski, Peter (1996), *Empirische Sprachwissenschaft*, Opladen: Westdeutscher Verlag, 179–208.

Schlobinski does mention the linguistic action pattern in his chapter on discourse analysis, and gives an example of speech action analysis; however, he presents this without any systematic reference to the functional-pragmatic method and its theoretical background.

12.9.3 Sample applications

The following two books contain the best-known (Ehlich & Rehbein 1986) and the most recent (Brünner & Graefen 1994a) applications of functional-pragmatic methods.

Ehlich, Konrad & Rehbein, Jochen (1986), *Muster und Institution. Untersuchungen zur schulischen Kommunikation*, Tübingen: Narr.

Brünner, Gisela & Graefen, Gabriele (eds) (1994a), *Texte und Diskurse. Methoden und Forschungsergebnisse der Funktionalen Pragmatik*, Opladen: Westdeutscher Verlag.

In their introduction Brünner & Graefen define functional pragmatics, although not all of the contributions belong to functional pragmatics. As examples of applications of the functional-pragmatic method, the following are of particular interest: Konrad Ehlich develops a 'functional etymology' on the basis of his 'field theory' (1994: 68–82), Angelika Redder investigates depiction procedures in common stories (1994: 238–64), and Georg Friedrich investigates classroom language with visually impaired pupils (1994: 374–85).

NOTE

1 The 'musical score' method of writing makes it possible to note in parallel the simultaneous speech of several speakers. In principle punctuation marks correspond to those of conventional orthography, but the full stop has a special function of indicating pauses. Several full stops indicate a longer pause. Interruptions are represented by a slash. Unintelligible passages are simply placed between brackets, while comments are placed in double brackets, e.g. '((clicking of fingers))'.

CHAPTER 13

DISTINCTION THEORY TEXT ANALYSIS

The 'Distinction Theory' approach (DTA) to text analysis was developed by Titsher and Meyer in the course of a research project entitled *Diplomacy and Language*. It is based, on the one hand, on Niklas Luhmann's (1984, 1995) theoretical assumptions and, on the other hand, on the receptions that he inspired of George Spencer Brown's distinction calculus (1979, see also Baecker 1993a, 1993b). The concept of distinction, or differential organization, of signs has a tradition both in semiotics and in structuralism (see, for instance, the presentation in Titzmann 1977: 12ff.). The notion of markedness (that is, *marked* versus *unmarked*) was taken up in linguistics by Linda Waugh and may be traced back to Nikolaj Trubetzkoy and Roman Jakobson (Waugh 1982: 299).

Niklas Luhmann's communication theory, on which DTA is based, implies a departure from current models of communication. The focus is no longer on the transmission metaphor (communication as transfer of information within the feedback control system of sender and receiver) but on the selectivity of communication. It is understood as a three-stage selection process, consisting of the components of *information, utterance* and *understanding*. Information is manifest as a selection from a (known or unknown) repertoire of possible themes: that is to say, a difference which makes a difference. Next, someone must select a behaviour that imparts the information: the second selection from the broad spectrum of possible utterance forms. The third selection, of understanding, brings about a change of state in the receiver, distinguishes between information and utterance, and selects one of many possibilities. Communication therefore means the synthesis of selectivity of the information itself, the selectivity of utterance and the expectation of success, the expectation of a choice of connection. Without understanding there is no communication, and this change of state in the receiving system relates to an observation of the difference between information and utterance. This difference is observed, expected, and underlies the ensuing behaviour – the reaction to the utterance.

Communication is therefore seen as a three-term unit: as a synthesis of the selections made as for information, utterance and understanding (see Luhmann 1984: 193ff.). Any communicative content may be devoted to one theme or to another, is imparted in a particular way, but could also be imparted differently or not at all. It is understood or misunderstood, although it could equally be overlooked or not noticed. Communication is successful when its selective content – information – is adopted as constituting the premises for subsequent selections: that is, when a connection is made and the selectivity is thereby strengthened (see Luhmann 1981: 26). Communication is therefore not concerned with 'consistency, justifiability, truth or rationality but with connectivity, and this must engender communication beyond the preparedness of individuals to understand, since communication relates only to communication. . . . Communication itself creates all meanings that produce resonance in communication and that are communicated' (Bardmann 1994: 106). Luhmann (1984: 196) bases himself initially on Karl Bühler's 'Organon model' (see Bühler 1965: 24ff.), which makes distinctions between the representative, expressive and appellative functions of language, but subsequently avoids Bühler's action theory approach (see Bardmann 1994: 103).

DTA analyses the utterance components of communication, that is, the only observable part of the process. In this it makes it a rule that all observation is based on distinctions: 'draw a distinction' is the instruction that, according to Spencer Brown (1979), comes at the beginning of every discovery. The instruction to 'draw a distinction' has three components: (a) drawing a boundary; (b) marking of one side; and (c) naming a side. This gives rise to a *form*, by which Spencer Brown understands a space divided by distinction. This form may again be distinguished from other forms, which are called *marked*. The name of the form then characterizes the *identity* of the distinction.

By means of naming, the direction is indicated. In this process, coming from outside, the border is crossed and one side is emphasized (see Figure 13.1). *Information* thus means to bring into form, to distinguish an inside from an outside, and to mark the inside. In-formation causes a distinction in unmarked data and always depends on an operation of the observer, who draws a border, marks one side and thereby crosses this border from outside in an inward direction. This operation requires time and is irreversible.

An example will serve to illustrate Figure 13.1: if a text producer observes the commitment of a fellow worker, he or she first draws a border (1), marks one side (2) and calls it *involvement* [3]. The alternative, the outside {3} is seldom explicitly named. If the text producer (or text observer) does this he or she could, for instance, distinguish this personal involvement from constant personal qualities, skills and knowledge of the fellow worker. The distinction between [3] 'involvement' and {3} 'skill' constitutes *Form I* which is now distinguished, by the text observers, from other possible distinctions (4). Form I is then named (5); the *identity* of the first distinction – that is, what is shared

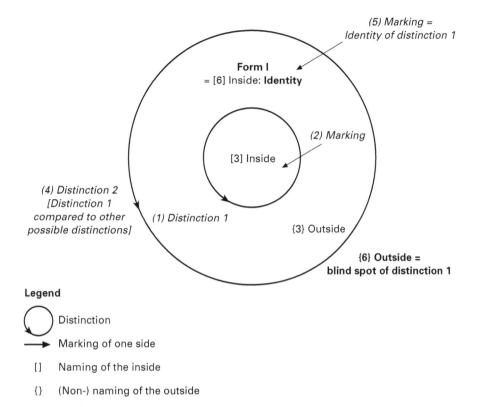

FIGURE 13.1   The operation of distinction

between involvement and skill – is called [6]: for instance 'personal achievement factors'. When observations are carried out using this form (identity), the outside at [6] cannot be seen: the text producer is blind to this. The text observer, however, can now name this outside {6}, the blind spot of the text producer: for example 'organizational and structural achievement factors'. To sum up: if someone observes fellow workers using the involvement/skill distinction and uses it to explain their achievement, he or she remains blind to the structural conditions of the organization. No other distinction (such as 'promotion/ reward') is possible at the same time as the involvement/skill distinction: this is only possible later.

Communication draws distinctions, and DTA seeks to reconstruct the distinctions in utterances and, from this, the only visible aspect of perceptual frameworks. George A. Kelly, in his 'Psychology of Personal Constructs', also stresses the differential character of perceptual frameworks: 'The person's choice of an aspect determines both what shall be considered similar and what shall be considered contrasting' (Kelly 1955: 59). For example, the concept of masculinity depends on the associated concept of femininity, and only the two together produce the basis for a construct (see Kelly 1955: 60). Kelly recommends to psychotherapists a mode of procedure which is not dissimilar to our method: 'The therapist's task was to find the implied contrast which she was unable to put into words' (Kelly 1955: 62).

13.3 GOALS OF THE METHOD

DTA seeks an answer to three questions: (a) What information can be extracted from the messages of a text? (b) What perceptual framework may be deduced from a text? (c) What blind spots do speakers have in their current observations?

13.4 OUTLINE OF THE METHOD

13.4.1 Macro design

The procedure followed in DTA can be represented as shown in Figure 13.2. When the texts in question have been selected and identified the analysis may be subdivided into the following phases:

1   The analysis of explicit distinctions. In this stage the concepts named in the text are extracted and opposites to them are formulated. These differential pairs are then analysed.
2   The analysis of implicit distinctions. This consists of the search for unnamed oppositions to those places in the text which are considered to be important.
3   Comparison of the explicit and implicit distinctions.
4   Further analyses deriving from these stages (optional).
5   Summary.

13.4.2 Micro design

Functional syntactic units are the basic unit of analysis in DTA and in this 'constituent grammar' is referred to (see Figure 13.3). Here, irrespective of the concrete research question, a selection can be made. For example, a distinction may be made between content and interactive passages in texts.

In the analyses of both explicit and implicit distinctions, it is a matter of naming distinctions in order to characterize both sides of the form. First the analyst asks what are the analytical units according to which explicit conceptual contrasts are named; secondly, what is the clear opposing concept to those units of analysis that are not explicitly contrasted by the speaker. If both sides of the form are named, the following questions are dealt with:

- How can the form (that is, identity) of the individual (explicit and implicit) distinctions be named?

- What are the (possible) blind spots in the distinction?

- Do the forms and blind spots have any common features, and can any repetitions be determined?

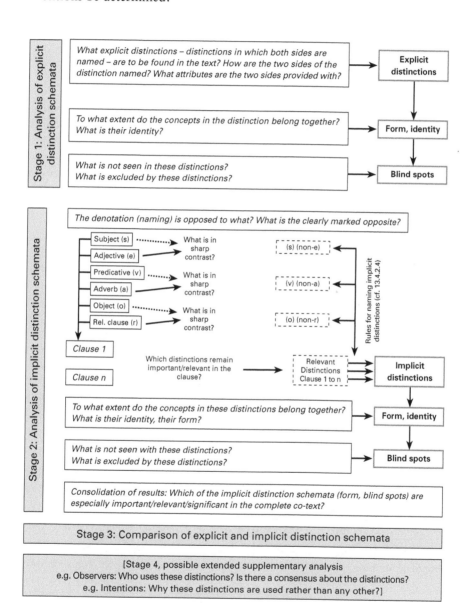

FIGURE 13.2   Flowchart of DTA

13.4.2.1 Clues for the definition of explicit distinctions

First the analyst must extract all the concepts and characterizations to which explicit opposites are formulated in the text. These distinctions are to do with the semantic level, and in most cases lexical and grammatical indicators for them can be found. For example:

- adversative and concessive prepositions – against, opposite, in spite of, irrespective of;

- adversative conjunctions – whilst, whereas, but, only, yet, however;

- alternative conjunctions – or, or else;

- adversative connectors or participial constructions (for example, whilst it was fine yesterday it is raining today; yesterday it was fine but today it is raining).

Very occasionally explicit distinctions remain unmarked lexically. Such cases require a semantic-pragmatic approach which also refers to cotextual and contextual information. These are used, for example, to identify (unmarked) oppositions within the framework of rhetorical figures of speech.

13.4.2.2 Units of analysis

The starting point for DTA is grammatical sentences. To characterize opposing concepts, however, it is not individual words but sentence constituents that are examined (see Figure 13.3). Constituent grammar divides sentences into phrases, and classifies them according to their syntactic function as verb, noun and prepositional phrases. These individual constituents (noun phrases, verb phrases, prepositional phrases) consist of words which are grammatically and semantically closely interrelated. As functional syntactic units they specify and carry the meanings of the concepts. The first task is therefore to break down the individual sentences into their constituents. Consequently we are no longer, strictly speaking, looking for 'opposing concepts' but 'opposing phrases'.[1]

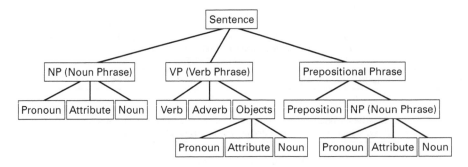

FIGURE 13.3   Constituent structure of a sentence (see Macheiner 1991: 27)

13.4.2.3 The selection of units of analysis

The units of analysis are therefore sentence constituents. If the focus is on the communicative content, the analysis of organizing and metacommunicative passages of the conversation may be omitted. In this case verbs of feeling and thinking that fulfil parenthetic functions (such as moderation or reinforcement) may be excluded. The background to this procedure is the idea that such passages have the effect of establishing interactional relationships, in the same way as modal verbs: in using them the speaker defines his relationship to the listeners or to the theme. If this aspect is of central importance, the analysis concentrates on precisely these phrases.

For phrases that serve to illustrate those that have already been analysed, concrete oppositions are sought. Examples, it is believed, repeat in a paraphrased form information that has already been imparted, and they confirm the distinctions. Here, however, an additional question may also be asked: why is this particular example selected rather than some other?

13.4.2.4 Rules for the naming of implicit distinctions

To facilitate the characterization of the other side of a form whose marked side represents the unit of analysis, a number of rules may be formulated.

- *Rule 1*   Name the opposing concept to main verbs and nouns. In general it is the verb in verb phrases – and the noun in noun phrases – that serves as the starting point in the search for opposing concepts.[2] This general rule 1 is always valid when none of the special rules 3–7 are applicable.

- *Rule 2*   Name the opposing concept to the preposition. In prepositional phrases the first step (before analysis of the embedded noun phrase) is to find, where possible, an opposing preposition.
  Example: after completion – before completion.

- *Rule 3*   Name the opposing modal verb. With verb phrases that contain a modal verb, opposing concepts to the modal verb itself must be found. This does not apply when the focus is on the relation-forming function of the modal verb, for instance when requirements or demands of the listener are moderated or reinforced.
  Example: they can't listen – they mustn't listen.

- *Rule 4*   Name the opposing voice. In verb phrases the active and passive voices provide additional clues: the possible counterpart can always be found in the other voice. This often implies looking for synonymous verbs, which may, however, be antonymous in terms of their meaning in the particular voice.
  Example: the prospect of an increased budget was offered to us – we demanded a higher budget.

- *Rule 5*   Name the opposing concept to the pronoun. In noun phrases the search for opposing concepts can also be directed towards demonstrative

pronouns, if from the context an opposing side is recognizable that is excluded by the use of a pronoun.
Example: this project – other projects; that particular different project (often connected with intonation, see rules 6 and 7, but then not: the matter in hand).

- *Rule 6* Name the opposing concept to adverbs and attributes. In verb phrases it is adverbs and adverbial constructions, and in noun phrases it is attributes and relative clauses, that serve as the starting point since they specify the meaning of the characterization. To name the opposing concept these specifying components are invoked.
  Examples:
  expensive computer programs – cheap computer programs (but not: hardware);
  capable workers – incompetent/unwilling workers;
  to do something quickly – to do something slowly.
  In composites it is often illuminating to look for opposing concepts to the individual components.

- *Rule 7* Name the opposing concept to the stressed concept. In oral texts that have been precisely transcribed in respect of para-verbal and supraseg-mental phenomena (hesitations, modulations, intonation patterns), such phenomena are only considered if a specification can thereby be achieved that runs counter to the previous rules. Intonation is particularly helpful in the search for opposing concepts. This rule also follows the discoveries made in intonation research (see Jacobs 1988).
  Examples:
  this SUCCESSFUL meeting – a failed meeting (rule 6 applies here);
  the successful MEETING – the work in progress (rule 7 applies here).

- *Rule 8* Reformulate negations positively. Negated phrases can be turned into their opposites by positive formulation: negating words (not, nothing, never, nowhere) are eliminated or replaced by antonyms.

- Competition between Rules   These rules are ordered according to their speci-ficity: rule 1 is the most general and rule 7 the most specific. If the rules come into competition with one another – that is to say, if several rules are applica-ble to a particular phrase – it is then assumed that the specific rules contribute more than the general rules to the discovery of the unnamed counter-concept. In noun phrases, therefore, negation (rule 8) precedes intonation (rule 7), attribute (rule 6), pronoun (rule 5) and noun (rule 1).
  In verb phrases negation (rule 8) again precedes intonation (rule 7), adverb or adverbial constructions (rule 6), voice (rule 4), modal verb (rule 3) and verb (rule 1).
  In prepositional phrases rule 2 should be considered first and only then should the embedded noun or verb phrases be analysed.

In applying DTA all plausible counter-concepts should first be established. In the course of further analysis of the text, particular differential pairs will then become more probable and others may be discarded.

13.4.2.5 The reconstruction of significant distinctions
In order to select from the large number of distinctions which are implicitly conveyed in texts the ones which are of special significance in the analysed extract, the following questions should be asked after the distinctions have been reconstructed:

- Is the distinction new or has it already occurred in the same (or a slightly modified) form?

- What earlier distinction was confirmed by this?

- What earlier distinction seems improbable because of this? Must it be reformulated?

By repetition a distinction is confirmed and condensed. On the one hand the repetition of naming is equivalent to naming;[3] on the other hand, repetition is of course an act in its own right that confirms the previously made distinction.

> According to the direction of reading two acts are condensed into one or one act is extended and confirmed through a first and second execution. In one direction it is found that an identity arises from a condensation of a majority of operations. In the other direction it is found that confirmation is a second operation and that it requires a different situation. (Luhmann 1990b: 22)

In any case it seems plausible that confirmed distinctions of this sort are particularly relevant for the reconstruction of perceptual schemata of a textual message.

A different starting-point for the meaning of distinctions is found in the constituent structure or syntactic construction of sentences. In most languages there is a 'normal' sentence structure in which the subject (noun) is in initial position, followed by the verb (verb phrase) and the objects or prepositional phrases. In German, for example, the location of the finite verb, in particular, is fixed, but apart from that departures from the 'normal' structure may be made. This is usually related, however, to a meaning shift (see Höhle 1982, Cinque 1993). Here is an example from German:

Karl hat dem Kind das Buch geschenkt.

[Karl has to the child the book given]

This is the normal sentence structure and it is not obvious from the sentence itself what information is new or of especial importance. If the order of elements is changed, however, to

Dem Kind hat Karl das Buch geschenkt

[To the child has Karl the book given]

the object 'Kind' becomes particularly prominent. Further variants are conceivable, each of which carry a specific narrowing of the information content. This is where DTA begins: deviations from the normal structure have a similar function to intonation. They mark new or particularly significant points of information in the sentence.

13.4.2.6 The naming of forms and blind spots

In naming forms it is a matter of identity: the common denominator of the concepts on both sides of the distinction.[4] The form can be named only by a second order observer, who observes again the distinction made by the first order observer in contrast to other possible distinctions. Every form relates to typical 'blind spots', which does not mean only the totality of other possible forms. In identifying blind spots, as in labelling opposing concepts, it is a matter of the 'other' side, and in this case the side that has been omitted through the use of a form.

It is above all from the cotext that an analysis recognizes which blind spot is especially 'typical'. Blind spots may be found throughout a text. If, for instance, the speaker who refers to the assistant (as distinct from boss) observes, a few sentences before and afterwards, 'payment' as a form, then this will probably not be the blind spot in the hierarchy. According to the cotext, other omissions – such as motivation or competence, career rules and so on – are thinkable.

13.5 PRECONDITIONS AND AREAS OF APPLICATION AND QUALITY CRITERIA

DTA may be characterized as a heuristic method. A set of questions informs the observation of the text, and with the help of this investigative strategy the text is varied using clearly defined rules. The text observer's interpretative scope is limited by the close relationship between variations and the phrases (characterizations) or syntagmatic locations in the text. It is therefore replicable and controllable for other observers of the analysis.

In principle DTA may be applied to all possible texts. If all the phases are gone through, of course, the demands of the analysis are such that very large quantities are not manageable. It is possible to imagine an 'abbreviated' version that deals only with explicit distinctions. Then only manifest and open perceptual schemata will be investigated. A precondition for DTA is a knowledge of the concepts that occur in the texts and the meaning attached to them in context. In this sense DTA does not explicitly provide contextual information, but it does count on appropriate background knowledge on the part of the analyst. The questions that must be clarified before implementation of the method do not differ from the usual preparatory activities for any text analysis: What text is selected? To answer what research questions? For the stronger 'interpretative' component – the naming of forms and blind spots – analysis by a team is recommended.

The extent to which the results of DTA text observation meet conventional quality criteria can only be vaguely predicted. Validity is probably influenced quite strongly by the context of the text's origin (see also Leithäuser et al. 1977: 128ff.): Is it a question of 'typical' or everyday situations (external validity)? How is the reactivity of the collection to be evaluated (internal validity)? To what extent are perceptual schemata truly collected with the phrases, counter-phrases, forms and blind spots (construct validity)? Reliability, in the sense of similar replicability of the analysis, is probably possible in only a limited sense. The results, however, must be intelligible and plausible, and 'intersubjectivity' must be guaranteed by a detailed explanation of rules.

13.6 SIMILARITIES AND DIFFERENCES IN COMPARISON TO OTHER METHODS

How is a method that relies on differences to be distinguished from other methods? Our approach must now at least become clearly reflexive: we are dealing with differences from other (selected) methods of text analysis, and the differences that we find here all have their specific blind spots. Even beyond the distinction between qualitative and quantitative methods that is often blind to the necessary interplay between these two research strategies, there are forms of distinction that are applicable here.

Kleining (1994: 118) distinguishes in this way between subject- and object-oriented methods: subject-oriented methods tend to use introspective procedures that require an interpretative talent from the investigating subject; object-oriented procedures are more strongly exploratory or heuristic, with the accent on discovery rather than on meaning. DTA is 'object-oriented': it concentrates on the text and not on the meaning capacity of the analyst. Through its detailed prescription of sequence and rules, but also through its preoccupation with distinctive pairs rather than with conceptual content, DTA assists in maintaining distance from a text, and thereby involves little 'interpretative' empathy. DTA is therefore not a 'Kunstlehre', unlike objective hermeneutics, for example (see Oevermann et al. 1979).

It also makes a difference whether methods of text analysis have an explicit theoretical foundation. The questions asked by DTA are theoretically founded to the extent that they follow the constructivist distinction theory and are thus indebted to a specific epistemological concept. In this DTA differs from other heuristic procedures that approach texts with 'content' questions. As an important consequence of the theoretical commitment of DTA, it follows that the consciousness of the text producer, as a closed system, is in principle 'incomprehensible'. It is therefore impossible to reconstruct those purposes, intentions and strategies that were pursued by the performers of speech actions in the way which these are postulated by other approaches to text analysis (see Ehlich & Rehbein 1986: 5, Projektteam 1989: 93).

Methods of text analysis can also be differentiated with regard to their instruments and rules: Are the instruments standardized or 'frameable'? How precisely and clearly formulated are the rules that determine the sequence and inform the analysis? With its table for the analysis of differential pairs, constructed according to four dimensions, DTA provides – compared to other 'qualitative' methods – a relatively standardized instrument. The sequencing and analytical rules of DTA are relatively precisely and clearly defined – at least in comparison to more strongly interpretative methods. The latter are in this respect problematic from the following point of view: 'What . . . consciousnesses do with texts is, with some exceptions, unpredictable, since texts do not "penetrate the consciousness", but only form stimuli for self-organizing cognitive operations' (Schmidt 1992: 311). These cognitive operations of the text observer are disciplined in DTA by the limitation of the questions, and by the restrictive investigative strategies, in that they incorporate in the interpretation an organizational schema and certain stabilization patterns.

Finally a crude distinction may be made between 'text-expanding' and 'text-reducing' methods of analysis. While, in the first of these, additional text is produced through particular procedures on the basis of the source materials, the latter methods attempt – particularly through the use of schemata of categories – to condense the texts. DTA is text-expanding. Before results are achieved, counter-phrases, identities and blind spots must be produced in addition to the units of analysis. In this respect DTA is similar to objective hermeneutics (Oevermann et al. 1979).

DTA differs from ethnographic and grounded theory oriented methods in respect of the following points: it proceeds from questions based on epistemological theory (perceptual schemata) rather than from a list of sensible and possible but theoretically unsubstantiated questions (see Hammersley & Atkinson 1995: 173). It has available clear sequencing and analytical rules instead of coding procedures and rules (see, for example, Strauss 1987: 55ff.). It attaches less importance to contextual information. The methods resemble one another with regard to the value of the text itself, which is always of central importance (object orientation).

DTA has the same focus as MCD analysis: both seek to reconstruct a perceptual apparatus. Through its notion of the blind spot, however, DTA concentrates more strongly on the latent area.

Narrative methods of analysis are also oriented towards distinctions, even if the temporal components (before/after) are foregrounded. Narration is mostly related to a unique event and a complication in the course of events. The narrative genre is governed by a temporal principle of ordering. If one compares DTA with narrative semiotics, for example, both methods are concerned with observation of the latent; and even in Greimas (1983: 18ff.), opposition relationships as depicted in the semiotic square, play a central role. Unlike narrative semiotics, DTA undertakes no prior categorizations. The time-axis is in the background.

NOTES

1 Experimental pragmatic arguments also support this mode of procedure. The naming of opposing concepts for every single word in a text and the resulting problems of selection would restrict the applicability of the method to very short texts.

2 For this process a dictionary of antonyms is a useful tool.

3 $\rceil\rceil = \rceil$. 'Condensation' (Spencer Brown 1979: 5).

4 Here a parallel is made with the 'collections' of membership categorization device analysis (see Sacks 1972a, 1972b). If, for instance, *boss* and *assistant* are differentiated, the organizational hierarchy is the form of the differentiation.

CHAPTER 14

Objective hermeneutics belongs to the group of reconstructive procedures that are characterized by the notion of discovering latent structures. Without relying on any scientific epistemology of its own, it rather works on the basis of everyday understanding and refines this by means of a clearly motivated and explicit set of rules. In its historical development it 'grew from being an empirical procedure derived from research practice, and is in that sense based on the experiences of such research practice and on their reconstruction' (Bohnsack 1991: 69).

The development of objective hermeneutics as a method of text analysis was accompanied by a need for the development of a new methodology for the social sciences. This need has its origin in the extension of the research domain of sociology into areas that are attributed to the existence of a social subconscious. As hermeneutics, the method thereby transcends that boundary imposed on the classical variant, because the latter is trapped in the world of the individual and his or her intentions.

In addition to this 'looking behind the scenes' objective hermeneutics is characterized above all by a comparatively explicit determination of principles and procedures that analysts must follow.

14.1 THEORETICAL ORIGINS

The procedures used in objective hermeneutics were developed in the context of an investigation of the socialization of children in families, in order to be able to interpret records of family-internal interaction. The deciding moment for this study was the question of how children can participate in the social world of the family even though they first have to acquire the necessary competences for this. The classical subjectivist learning theories of Ericson, Mead and Piaget could provide no adequate answers to this, and so the method was developed by falling back on the theories described below.

From hermeneutics the method borrowed the notion that all understanding is conditioned by the prior knowledge of the interpreter and that it is extended through interpretation and thereby creates new conditions for understanding (*hermeneutic circle*). Looked at in this way one could take the sequential analytical procedure as a special case of the hermeneutic circle.

The concept of the subconscious was borrowed from Freudian psycho-analysis and extended into the social subconscious. This applies to those parts of meaning structures that are not realized by participants, even though they exert influence as unrecognized conditions or unintended consequences of an action. The reference to Freud, however, should only be understood as a struc-tural analogy to illustrate the model and not as a transfer of the concept of drive into the realm of interactions (Oevermann et al. 1979: 368).

Like the critical theory of Horkheimer and Adorno, objective hermeneutics rejects all those models that seek to understand texts using a preordained system of categories. It also adopts the claim of the enlightenment which would show, in this case on a linguistic level, how action is constrained by dogmas, myths and ideologies.

14.2 BASIC THEORETICAL ASSUMPTIONS

In objective hermeneutics a particular view emerges of the relationship between individual and society that maintains an equal distance from two opposite poles: a subjectivist position on the one hand and a social-theoretical objectiv-ity on the other. These two perspectives are not seen as contradictions but as a dualism contributing to a plausible description of interactive human behaviour. The tension between individual autonomy and the determined nature of society is maintained. The freely acting subject is investigated within the constraints of both his or her personal biography and prevailing social structures.

This model has consequences for the definition of text. The significance of text-producers as psychologically observable individuals disappears.

> Interactive texts constitute, on the basis of reconstructable rules, objective mean-ing structures, and these objective meaning structures represent the latent meaning-structures of the interaction itself. It can also be said that a text, once it is produced, constitutes a social reality with its own rules and its own procedures for reconstruction. This reality can be attributed neither to the speaker's disposi-tion for action and attendant psychic circumstances, nor to the internal psychic reality of the recipient. (Oevermann et al. 1979: 379)

Accordingly objective hermeneutics understands meaning as an objective social structure that emerges interactively. This implies that meaning arises in mutual action, but that the contributions of the respective participants in the creation of meaning are inaccessible and therefore outside the interest of the researcher. A level of latent meaning-structures (also known as objective meaning-struc-tures) is postulated as an essential basis for individual intentions. From this arises a further need, to introduce – at least at the descriptive level – a concept of the subconscious. Transferred to the model of psychoanalysis this means that 'from the viewpoint of Objective Hermeneutics the boundary between the conscious and the pre-conscious is decisive, since it coincides with the delimi-tation of what is intentional' (Oevermann et al. 1979: 377). Personality structures, in the view of objective hermeneutics, are not defined as psychological structures but as 'manifestations of social structures' and should be interpreted accordingly (Heinze 1987: 76).

By means of the central notion of latency, account is taken of the fact that social subjects are tied into action contexts and participate in actions whose meaning-structure they can only partially interpret. It is no accident that the starting point for the method comes from research into socialization. This is concerned, among other things, with explaining how children participate actively in meaning-creating actions even though they lack the competence to understand the meaning that is created. An analogous situation arises when we consider the objective hermeneuticist who analyses using the counter-factual construct that assumes a competent speaker. The competent speaker is characterized by a total understanding of created sense-structures. This appeal to a competent speaker in the generic sense – the human as a genus, not as an individual – forms the basis in objective hermeneutics for the use of intuitive assessments of appropriateness in transmitting the latent sense-structures of interactions. On the basis of linguistic competence and competence in norm-governed behaviour that result from belonging to a social community, the interpreter justified the actions of the subjects. In terms of epistemology there is no difference between the analyst and the subject involved in the case under investigation. The analyst has only the advantage of an objective view unencumbered by situational constraints.

14.3 GOALS OF THE METHOD

With the concept of the latent meaning structures objective possibilities of meaning are introduced as real, irrespective of whether or not they are intentionally realized by the participants to the interaction. Objective Hermeneutics means that interpretative procedure that is needed to unlock this reality. (Oevermann et al. 1979: 381)

The goal of this method, therefore, is to render visible objective structures of interactions. The structures are characterized as objective because they operate independently of the subjective intentions of the participants. This motivates the need to extend the field of analytically accessible social reality by a latent but action-determining level.

'Oevermann's goal is truly ambitious. He is looking for a practical research-oriented basis to a social science theory and methodology that, at the same time, extends over the entire field of what humans are able to experience' (Garz & Kraimer 1994: 7). In the words of Oevermann et al. (1979: 353) themselves: 'The claimed general significance of this position for sociological analysis *overall* is reflected in the strong claim that meaning-analysis procedures that follow this model demonstrate the fundamental operation of measurement or of the production of theoretically relevant data in the social sciences.' If like Oevermann et al. (1979: 367) we consider latent meaning-structures to be real, this brings with it a requirement for a general re-orientation in the social sciences that has so far not led to any adequate intelligible methods of data collection. This helps to explain why statements on the concrete goal of the method are normally embedded in the broader context of discussion of the reality of the above-mentioned objective meaning-structures:

> However we may ultimately solve the problem that materializes here of allocating objective meanings to psychic causes, it is in the first instance a matter of proving the existence of two fundamentally different levels of reality. On the one hand, there is the reality of the latent meaning structures of a text that can be reconstructed irrespective of their mental representation on the part of the text producer and text recipient, and that must constitute the starting point for social research, at whatever level of reality. And on the other hand there is the reality of subjectively and intentionally represented meanings in a text on the part of the acting subjects. (Oevermann et al. 1979: 367)

Objective hermeneutics, as a method of text analysis and as a methodology, may be summarized thus: 'it is exclusively a matter of the careful extensive analysis of the objective meaning of interactional texts and of the latent meaning of interactions, and this procedure of reconstructive textual understanding has nothing to do with . . . the understanding of processes within the psyche' (Oevermann et al. 1979: 381).

14.4 OUTLINE OF THE METHOD

14.4.1 Principles and procedures

The method of objective hermeneutics is based on two modes of procedure – sequential analysis and detailed analysis – that are determined by four principles, of which three may subsumed under the heading of *context variation*. The fourth principle, however – the principle of the sequential mode of procedure – will be discussed under the heading *procedures*.

14.4.1.1 *Basic concepts*
Context variation   In thought experiments, context variation means the attempt to put the meaning unit to be analysed into all conceivable contexts, in order to be able to reconstruct, through the resultant differences in meaning, the latent meaning-structures and also the concrete conditions of the action.

External and internal context   Oevermann makes a strict distinction between external and internal context since they play a different role in the analysis. By 'external context' he refers to 'information on the case or the reported event that are not contained in the report or text which has to be reconstructed' (Oevermann 1996: 101) – in other words, the factual pragmatic conditions that determine the text from the outside and limit the range of interpretative possibilities. In respect of this external context Oevermann

(1996: 100) insists that 'a knowledge of the actual context of the utterance may only be used if all the readings compatible with the text to be interpreted have really been explicated as fully as possible'. 'Internal context', on the other hand, refers to the cumulative information that is derived from the sequential analysis. This type of context may well be, and indeed should be, invoked for the exclusion of some of the resultant readings. This means that only the first place in a sequence is analysed independently of internal and external context.

Readings 'We consider the relationship between utterance and a contextual condition that pragmatically realizes the utterance to be a reading' (Oevermann et al. 1979: 415). That is to say, a reading includes a textual segment and the possible pragmatic framework that relates to it. The production of readings is the central operation conducted by objective hermeneutics in its sequential analysis procedure, based on the model of latent meaning-structures (see Oevermann 1996: 93).

The principle of extensive interpretation In this respect *extensiveness of analysis* plays an essential role. Oevermann et al. characterize this as follows:

> This means going against the everyday practice of understanding motives in that the intention of an action partner should not be revealed as accurately and quickly as possible, but on the contrary as fully as possible. This involves that all presuppositions in the text should be included as explicitly as possible, including the most 'improbable' readings or those that – in the light of prior knowledge of the case – may be totally excluded. (1979: 393)

It is therefore crucial that at the beginning of an interpretation as many readings of a text as possible are made explicit and then investigated in the course of the detailed analysis (at level 6 of the framework of categories designed by Oevermann et al. 1979: 395ff., see also section 14.4.3.), in order to establish which may be excluded on grounds of the actual interaction and which may be upheld. In general even the most improbable readings should be preserved until the appearance of an explicit contradiction.

The principle of complete interpretation This principle is rooted in the assumption that everything that is said has more sense than is actively perceived. Therefore everything that can in some way be determined should be incorporated into the analysis. This implies that 'every particle, every legible, audible, visible, tangible (ultimately even tastable or smellable) element no matter how small and inconspicuous must be explicitly interpreted for its motivation and must be fitted into the context of the whole' (Oevermann 1996: 112). For pragmatic reasons, however, audiovisual material is normally dispensed with in favour of transcribed material, although due consideration is given to striking intonation patterns, speech rhythms and similar events.

The principle of economical use of individual hypotheses (economy rule) This rule means that, in the sense of the greatest possible contextual variation, everything that could restrict the multiplicity of readings is omitted. This particularly affects the external context (see above, and Oevermann 1996: 99), but also so-called individual hypotheses, since one of the basic assumptions of this method is that psychology and other features specific to an individual are the consequence of social phenomena (Heinze 1987: 79).

14.4.1.2 Procedures

Sequential analysis   The sequential-analytical mode of procedure is of fundamental importance in the methodology of objective hermeneutics. It consists of breaking down the text or material selected for analysis into smaller units and then interpreting them in sequence. The meaning possibilities which are thereby achieved are progressively more restricted during the progress of the analysis until the structure of a particular case is clear. 'In this the individuality of a case becomes apparent. It appears during the sequential analysis as a successively constructed internal context' (Oevermann et al. 1979: 426). Oevermann et al. explain further:

> In the course of sequential analysis, what we refer to as the internal context of an interactive text is constituted with successively increasing conciseness. In contrast to the external contextual conditions that may be further subdivided into those which remain unaltered, and those which modify themselves for the course of the entire scene, the internal context is a result of the interpretation of the scene's text, and is traceable only through this text. (1979: 422)

Detailed analysis   Breaking down the text into separate sequences is a precondition for the detailed analysis, in the course of which there is an extensive interpretative procedure, beginning with the smallest meaning units. Here, as many meaning-bearing contexts as possible are constructed for each of these smallest units. Through the sequence of units, the number of possible contexts (or readings) reduces itself during the course of the analysis; in an ideal case, the number of possibles will be reduced to a single context and in this way the case to be analysed may be clearly outlined. Characteristically, and in accordance with the underlying principle of the greatest possible contextual variation, for this purpose no advance knowledge of the case that would preclude particular readings is considered in the analysis.

Through the analysis a real process of selectivity and exclusions of options is reconstructed. This procedure is different from the everyday mode of interpretation in that the analysts dedicate more time to it and attempt to take cognisance of the options that are really possible.

14.4.2 Selection of material and units of analysis

For objective hermeneutics, interaction sequences, such as family conversations or public speeches, come into play as primary sources of data.

> The true object of the procedures of Objective Hermeneutics are records of real, symbolically transmitted social actions or interactions, be they written, acoustic, visual, combined in a variety of media or recordable in other ways. The precise

material form of the record is, for the interpretative procedures of Objective
Hermeneutics, a purely contingent technical circumstance, since its interpretabil-
ity, irrespective of its material form, is bound up in principle with the condition of
the linguistic realizability or paraphrasability of interactive meanings. (Oevermann
et al. 1979: 378)

Here it is mostly a question of transcripts that derive from tape-recorded interactions. The procedure has already also been applied to both sound and
pictures of TV broadcasts, to written passages, and – in contradiction of the
principle of linguistic realization – to film posters and photographs (Garz &
Kraimer 1994). With such static pictorial materials it has, of course, proved
very difficult to realize the sequencing.

On the basis of the theoretical assumption that the entire case structure is
reproduced in each individual unit of interaction, it is not necessary to analyse
the complete case-record but only an extract (or 'scene') from it; this must
lead, however, to a consistent case-hypothesis. The development of such a
hypothesis imposes a minimum length requirement on the extract. For the
opening phase of an extract it is true to say that in interaction systems involving a history (for example families) this is of no particular significance. It is only
in newly emerging systems (such as therapeutic 'first contacts') that initial
sequences are important, since the beginning has a particular impact on the subsequent development. 'We are aware, therefore, that in a trivial sense in the
analysis of interactions with no previous history, the true beginning – the opening sequence in Schegloff's terms – must also form the beginning of the
interaction scene to be analysed' (Oevermann et al. 1979: 434). Otherwise, the
extract is selected purely at random. The results from this first extract may then
be compared with the analysis of further extracts that should ideally be in
some reconstructable relationship with the first one, to compensate for matters
of situation-specific chance. The procedure does not, however, prescribe a minimum number of extracts to be analysed.

The principle of sequential analysis requires that the extract be broken
down into individual meaning units, in order to create the precondition for
analysis of the internal context that must be considered in the production of
readings. The size of such sequences is not laid down in the procedure. In
practice it is decided in such a way as to give the interpreters the impression
that they are gaining new information about the structure through this new
sequence. But since – on the basis of the principle of complete interpretation –
nothing happens by chance for objective hermeneutics and everything is seen
as structurally motivated, these meaning units are normally very short, particularly in an initial phase: sometimes, indeed, they consist merely of
'throat-clearing'. Here is an example of the development of such boundaries:
/up to /now /nobody has /told me, /Mr. Ambassador/, . . . those /categorized
/under D/ and who of course are qualified academic translators/. As already
indicated, the units – particularly at the beginning – are very short and often
only conform to a grammatical patterning into (partial) sentences towards the
end of an extract.

With objective hermeneutics, in the form of sequential detailed analysis, the interpreter has available a concrete instrument with which to approach a text: there is a framework consisting of eight analytical levels. Although Ulrich Oevermann, in recent years, has distanced himself firmly from this framework, its practicability as an introduction to objective hermeneutic interpretation – particularly for beginners – remains uncontested.

With regard to the status and function of this framework, Oevermann et al. (1979: 394) state: 'It is no more than a frame for an exclusively qualitative descriptive reconstruction of the actual utterances, a kind of "check list" for interpreters that should require them to question their material in sufficient detail'.

As a result of this there is nothing to prevent a different weighting being given to the individual levels of the analysis or their conversion into concrete steps in the research. Even if these levels are not to be understood as a rigid classification framework, they remain sufficiently precise in their formulation to be valid as rules in the sense used here. In Table 14.1 we set out the eight levels of Oevermann et al. (1979) in comparison with the concrete reformulations which we applied in our own empirical work. For this truncated presentation we employ the version of the levels as summarized by Schuster (1994: 108–111), who preserves Oevermann's original wording. Subsequently we shall address the problem of the compatibility of the original with our reformulation, and draw attention to possible differences.

Levels 1, 2 and 4 of Oevermann et al. correspond to the concrete formulations with the same numbers. As may be seen in Table 14.1, point 3 of our reformulation covers, in broad outline, several levels – namely 3, 5 and 7. In this case the following restrictions apply to any comparison:

1 The subdivision of point 3 in our concrete realization entails that the italicized sections of the left-hand column can only be understood in a conditional way as counters to the levels given in the right-hand column.
2 The question of summarizing lines of interpretation and evaluating alternative readings against each other (which occurs under level 7 in Oevermann et al.) is not treated separately at any point in our reformulation. We have considered this aspect of interpretative work as a single entity which is inherent in the sequential analytical procedure and therefore permanently present. Accordingly there is little or no correspondence in the case of level 6 of the right-hand column.

On the matter of the compatibility of levels 0 and 5, it must be borne in mind that the numbering in both the left-hand and right-hand columns represents a non-obligatory but partially required ordering of the individual stages in an investigation. The identification of a new meaning unit, therefore, marks the beginning of an interpretative cycle. The primary importance of this step in the sequential analytical mode lies in its experimental aspect. In the fifth stage of

Table 14.1   Interpretative levels of OH and concrete analytical questions

Five concrete research steps[2]	Eight levels of interpretation[3]
1 How can the meaning unit be transformed in the understanding of the investigator? How can the unit normally be understood, what meaning would a 'normal' reader/listener attribute to it? How can the statement be paraphrased (rewritten, freely transformed, clarified)?	**Level 1** Paraphrasing of all meanings of a unit according to the wording of the accompanying verbalization.
2 What does the person speaking wish to present or evoke in a listener through this statement, and what could be his/her intentions? If one takes on the role of the actor: what meaning could the unit have for this person? What intention is probably being pursued? What would be an acceptable interpretation for this person?	**Level 2** Explication of the intention of the interacting subject.
3 (1) What hidden factors could underlie the unit and what could be the objective consequences for modes of action and thought or for the system? How else could the text be read – from the viewpoint of a non-participant third person? What is the result of reading with different emphases?	**Level 3** Explication of the objective motives of the unit and of the objective consequences: i.e. objective changes in the systemic conditions within the framework of the interactive process.
3 (2) What do the following mean? The grammatical form used (active, passive, conditional, etc.)? The themes and (groups of) persons mentioned? The linguistic peculiarities (slips, breakdowns, use and misuse of words)? The self-evident and generalized matters that occur? What might the meaning of the unit relate to?	**Level 5** Characterization of the linguistic features of the unit: identification of distinctive features at the syntactic, semantic and pragmatic levels.
3 (3) What else might the statement mean in different social circumstances?	**Level 7** Explication of general relations and structures, particularly to do with socialization theory.
4 What role distribution arises from the unit? What relations and attributions to persons are given (even when not directly named) or could be involved in the text? What can be said (in interviews) about the relationship between interviewer and interviewee?	**Level 4** Explication of the function of the unit in the distribution of interactive roles.
5 What options are available for the next meaning unit? How will it go on? What arguments can be expected? What are important connection points in the text?	**Level 0** Explication of the context immediately preceding an interactive unit and the systemic condition of the unit in question.
	Level 6 Extrapolation of the interpretation of the unit on to recurrent communicative figures: relational aspects or personality features that transcend the situation.

our reformulation, therefore, on the basis of a successful interpretation, assumptions are made 'blind' about a plausible continuation of the text and these are subsequently measured against the actual continuation. The procedure in level 0 differs in essence only in the sense that this does not happen 'blind', that is without taking cognisance of the actual continuation of the text.

14.4.4 Readings and interpretations

In relation to the production of readings, the criterion of compatibility is decisive. This requires nothing more than that the investigated utterances are surrounded by contexts in the form of stories that create some meaning. In objective hermeneutics the investigator proceeds on the general assumption that the question of the compatibility of a reading can be clarified unambiguously.

Within the compatible readings the following distinction is made: 'Here there are a) those that are forced by a marking that is readable, visible, perceptible or audible within a text, and b) those that are optionally added by an interpreter and of which it may be said that their assertion may, but does not have to, indicate some fact' (Oevermann 1996: 103). Readings of the second category present a number of unresolvable presumptions about alternative possibilities. What cannot be resolved, however, is unproductive in this form of analysis. Such readings, moreover, have a suggestive potential that distracts the analysis from the more pressing possible meanings of a text and should therefore be avoided.

The productiveness of objective hermeneutic interpretation is crucially dependent on the appropriate use of contextual knowledge. The method (as a *Kunstlehre*) indicates to the analysts how they should use the contextual knowledge that is available to them. In this respect a distinction must be made between the process of 'discovery' and justifying the 'validity' of a reading. The use, therefore, 'of theoretical approaches that are as explicit as possible' (see Oevermann et al. 1979: 392) is seen as highly desirable so long as such theories do not run counter to general everyday knowledge. This applies to the discovery procedure, whereas checking the validity of a reading is determined exclusively by the so-called meaning-generating rules. This means that concrete examples of contexts derived from the readings are used to decide on the possibility of the occurrence of such contexts. If we reduce it to a formula, Oevermann's requirement runs as follows: 'Use everything that is useful or helpful in the discovery of readings that are compatible with a textual extract, and beware of using information about the external context of a recorded event to decide on the validity of readings that are compatible with the text' (Oevermann 1996: 101).

The knowledge we have alluded to about the actual context can only be taken into account after the fullest possible interpretation of a textual sequence. Otherwise access to latent meaning-structures would be rendered impossible by the limitation of compatible readings to those that are in accordance with this contextual knowledge. Any contravention of this would mean, as a consequence, that nothing new could be discovered and that interpretation would become circular.

14.5 QUALITY CRITERIA

Because in objective hermeneutics the latent meaning-structures are revealed as the result of intuitive judgements of appropriateness on the part of the interpreters, some statement must be made about the relationship, within this procedure, between the types of representation developed and the underlying reality. Does it reveal what it intends to reveal? On the basis of an epistemological circular argument it is claimed that it is inconclusive and therefore meaningless. From this Oevermann et al. conclude pragmatically:

> If in a theoretical sense precautions can be taken that help, in a practical way, to guarantee the perfection of this intuitive power of judgement, we no longer need to make explicit the rules that constitute this competence as a theoretical precondition for the validity of an objective hermeneutic interpretation, without thereby limiting the falsifiability of the meaning-reconstructions. (1979: 388)

These precautions follow the three factors that necessarily restrict the everyday understanding of meaning. First there is the time factor, which leads to the requirement for a reduction of time pressure on the part of the interpreters. Then the intuitive power of judgement should not be too 'neurotically restricted' (Oevermann et al. 1979: 393) or neutralized by a group interpretation, when the readings produced in the group should be constantly examined. Finally there is the requirement for the implementation of more than one theoretical approach, in order to avoid everyday characterizations in the interpretation.

As for the effect of the knowledge achieved through objective hermeneutics, particularly in socialization theory, Oevermann et al. (1979: 402) assume 'that the empirical validity of general concepts in socialization theory can be measured by the extent to which individual units of interaction, or a series of such units, may be fitted unambiguously into its general definitions'. Theories and their concepts, in this interpretation, have to prove themselves as suitable in concrete cases of analysis. Oevermann et al. (1979) reject the tolerating of individual cases in which an unambiguous fit is impossible. In their opinion the empirical validity of concepts in a theory affected by this type of incompatibility is called into question.

As an accessible escape route in such a problem situation they propose, with relevant examples, that: (a) the theoretical basis of the faulty concepts should be modified, or the concepts themselves should be redefined; and/or (b) additional validity conditions should be introduced. In this way a strategy is proposed which would free the analyst from having to pursue a scientifically oriented and rigid notion of falsification.

14.6 PRECONDITIONS AND AREAS OF APPLICATION

We have already mentioned, from other viewpoints, particular preconditions which affect the analysts themselves and the use of knowledge in applying the method. To complete the picture we shall now address the question of the necessary quality of the (recorded) material.

As far as areas of application are concerned there are no restrictions, in the sense that objective hermeneutics itself claims that in principle any recordings of social interaction may be used as source material. That is to say, textual and audio and visual material may all be used in addition to various combinations of recorded material. The fundamental requirement of the method in this respect concerns the capability of the data to be put into some sequence, which is harder to contrive with non-sequential visual material (such as photographs).

We must look separately at observations, which Oevermann et al. (1979: 428) require 'must be made as extensively and faithfully to reality as possible, in other words at the level of good quality sound-recordings'. This requirement for 'literal' observation records is understandable if one keeps in mind that data which – as is normal for observation – depend on particular frameworks of categories and meaning patterns impede access to latent meaning-structures.

In spite of this general openness concerning the form of the data material to be analysed, objective hermeneutics makes predominant use of carefully transcribed sound recordings.

14.7 SIMILARITIES AND DIFFERENCES IN COMPARISON WITH OTHER METHODS AND PROCEDURES

Objective hermeneutics is distinguished from other reconstructive procedures primarily through its assumption of latency. This provides the most suitable basis for comparison.

Even if objective hermeneutics does not view subjective intentions purely as a soulless reflection of social structures, it does clearly distinguish itself from social-phenomenologically oriented methods that seek to promote individual meaning patterns as 'structuring, orientational and typification processes' (Matthiesen 1994: 81). In these kinds of analyses objective social structure, in the shape of milieu and environment, is conceptualized as a marginal condition which contrasts strongly with the way in which objective hermeneutics handles it.

Objective Hermeneutics – unlike conventional hermeneutics as developed by Habermas for the social sciences – no longer deals solely with orientations transmitted via the psyche and with the psychically unconscious. Rather it claims to elaborate the socially unconscious – i.e. 'latent' social meaning structures. (Bohnsack 1991: 68)

A further comparative dimension derives from the strict separation of external and internal context, as undertaken by objective hermeneutics. (The basis of this is the sequential analytical procedure and the economy rule.) The 'classical hermeneuticists', in order to discover the meaning of the individual segment, irrespective of its position, invoke information from the complete text and also employ contextual information to a different extent.

As for the directions for (a) the approach to the material to be investigated, and (b) the investigation of the material itself, the method provides highly developed guidelines. The steps to be followed for discovering the latent meaning-structures are therefore laid down for the user. This sets objective hermeneutics apart from all those supposed 'methods' that provide only one prescribed framework – normally from a special perspective – within which the researcher can freely operate. This also means, however, that the operationalization of relevant concepts, that is the approach to the material, depends more or less upon intuition. The intelligibility and comparability of results are burdened by this, even if the freedom of interpretation it allows cannot, a priori, be negatively evaluated. From this comparative viewpoint the ethnomethodologically oriented methods, or those collectively styled 'discourse analysis', may primarily be seen as polar opposites to objective hermeneutics.

When compared to content analysis procedures (such as SYMLOG) which analyse a text with the help of a preordained framework of categories, objective hermeneutics stands out by virtue of its requirement for an analysis in the 'language of the case'. A contravention of this principle would lead to a reconstruction of the preconceived opinions of the interpreters rather than a reconstruction of the latent meaning.

14.8 LITERATURE

Oevermann, Ulrich, Allert, T., Konau, E. & Krambeck, J. (1979), 'Die Methodologie einer "objektiven Hermeneutik" und ihre allgemeine forschungslogische Bedeutung in den Sozialwissenschaften, in Hans-Georg Soeffner (ed.), *Interpretative Verfahren in den Sozial- und Textwissenschaften*. Stuttgart: Metzler, 352–434.

Oevermann, Ulrich, Allert, T., Konau, E. & Krambeck, J. (1983), 'Die Methodologie der objektiven Hermeneutik', in Peter Zedler & Heinz Moser (eds), *Aspekte qualitativer Sozialforschung. Studien zu Aktionsforschung, empirischer Hermeneutik und reflexiver Sozialtechnologie*. Opladen: Westdeutscher Verlag, 95–123.

Oevermann, Ulrich (1993), 'Die objektive Hermeneutik als unverzichtbare methodologische Grundlage für die Analyse von Subjektivität. Zugleich eine Kritik der Tiefenhermeneutik', in Thomas Jung & Stefan Müller-Doohm (eds), *'Wirklichkeit' im Deutungsprozeß. Verstehen in den Kultur- und Sozialwissenschaften*. Frankfurt: Suhrkamp, 106–89.

Oevermann, Ulrich (1983), 'Zur Sache. Die Bedeutung von Adornos methodolo-gischem Selbstverständnis für die Begründung einer materialen soziologischen Strukturanalyse', in Ludwig von Friedeburg & Jürgen Habermas (eds), *Adorno Konferenz 1983*. Frankfurt: Suhrkamp, 234–89.

14.9 SECONDARY LITERATURE

14.9.1 Handbooks

Lamnek, Siegfried (1989), *Qualitative Sozialforschung*, vol. 2: Methoden und Techniken. München: Psychologie-Verlags-Union, 213–32.

Heckmann, Friedrich (1992), 'Interpretationsregeln zur Auswertung qualitativer Interviews und sozialwissenschaftlich relevanter "Texte". Anwendungen der Hermeneutik für die empirische Sozialforschung', in Jürgen H. P. Hoffmeyer-Zlotnik (ed.), *Analyse verbaler Daten*. Opladen: Westdeutscher Verlag, 142–67.

Reichertz, Jo (1995), 'Die objektive Hermeneutik – Darstellung und Kritik', in Eckhard König & Peter Zedler (eds), *Bilanz qualitativer Forschung*, vol. II: Methoden. Weinheim: Deutscher Studienverlag, 379–423.

14.9.2 Other presentations of method

Bohnsack, Ralf (1991), *Rekonstruktive Sozialforschung. Einführung in Methodologie und Praxis qualitativer Forschung*. Opladen: Leske, 66–81.

Garz, Detlef & Kraimer, Klaus (eds) (1994), *Die Welt als Text. Theorie, Kritik und Praxis der objektiven Hermeneutik*. Frankfurt: Suhrkamp.

Heinze, Thomas (1987), *Qualitative Sozialforschung: Erfahrungen, Probleme und Perspektiven*. Opladen: Westdeutscher Verlag, 75–96.

Schuster, Gudrun (1994), 'Die objektive Hermeneutik nach Oevermann', in Arbeitskreis Qualitative Sozialforschung (ed.), *Verführung zum qualitativen Forschen*. Wien: WUV-Universitätsverlag, 101–15.

14.9.3 Sample applications

Hildenbrand, Bruno & Jahn, Walter (1988), '"Gemeinsames Erzählen" und Prozesse der Wirklichkeitskonstruktion in familiengeschichtlichen Gesprächen', *Zeitschrift für Soziologie*, 17: 203–17.

Mathes, Rainer (1992), 'Hermeneutisch-klassifikatorische Inhaltsanalyse von Leitfadengesprächen. Über das Verhältnis von quantitativen und qualitativen Verfahren der Textanalyse und die Möglichkeit ihrer Kombination', in Jürgen H. P. Hoffmeyer-Zlotnik (ed.), *Analyse verbaler Daten*. Opladen: Westdeutscher Verlag, 402–24.

Oevermann, Ulrich (1996), 'Becketts "Endspiel" als Prüfstein hermeneutischer Methodologie. Eine Interpretation mit den Verfahren der objektiven Hermeneutik (Oder: Ein objektiv-hermeneutisches Exerzitium)', in Hans-Dieter König (ed.), *Neue Versuche, Becketts Endspiel zu verstehen. Sozialwissenschaftliches Interpretieren nach Adorno.* Frankfurt: Suhrkamp, 93–249.

"DO YOU THINK THE TRANSCRIPTION NEEDS TO BE SO PRECISE IF WE'RE GOING TO SELECT OUR TEXTS IN THIS WAY?"

NOTES

1 This chapter is based on a German paper written by Karl Berger, Thomas Gamperl and Gisela Hagmair.
2 This framework of concrete research steps was developed by Stefan Titscher.
3 Oevermann et al. (1979: 395–402) in the summary given in Schuster (1994: 108–11).

PART THREE

Overview and Comparison

CHAPTER 15

BIBLIOMETRIC SURVEY: THE PROMINENCE OF METHODS OF TEXT ANALYSIS[1]

How can we assess whether the methods of text analysis presented in this book are in widespread use? Which methods are particularly popular, and which have only a shadowy existence in the family of social research methods? To provide answers to questions such as these it is appropriate to conduct a bibliometric investigation. For this purpose the following procedure was adopted:

1   As a first step the diffusion of literature which established a particular method was investigated on the basis of frequency of citation and measured with the help of the CD-ROM SSCI database (Social Sciences Citation Index, see also SSCI 1994, Garfield 1991a, 1991b).
2   To check the results of step 1, a second bibliometric investigation was carried out using four different databases of social science literature. Here the search was based not on citations from the relevant literature but on keywords.
3   As a third step, an attempt was made to measure degrees of proximity between methods bibliometrically through networks of citations: what relations exist between individual methods? How often, in scientific publications, are citations drawn from two or more different works which are basic to the methods in question?

The first two steps both yield one-dimensional indicators. Two-dimensional indicators are calculated by a comparison of citation and keyword investigations and by the analysis of networks (see van Raan 1994: 501).

15.1 FREQUENCY OF CITATION: THE PROMINENCE OF PUBLICATIONS

The first step in the bibliometric process consists of a quantitative analysis of the reception of those works (and their authors) which are either constitutive for a particular method or which are essential to it.[2] This was carried out for each of the years from 1991 to 1998. In addition a selection was made from the source materials. Then a search strategy was agreed and stored, and finally the SSCI was searched.

It is therefore a matter of extracting the frequency of citation. The quality of citation – to what extent and in what form the relevant literature is quoted – cannot be shown on the basis of the SSCI. Citations are therefore counted irrespective of whether they are short references, criticisms or applications. Although it is possible in principle with the SSCI, our analysis makes no explicit identification of self-citations; nor does it uncover citation 'cartels'. Citation references are taken as an indicator of the reputation of a method of text analysis or of its authors. Despite all the weaknesses of such analyses, scholars will in future have to submit to these evaluation processes to an increasing extent. It is hoped that the following presentation will show that such findings should be interpreted with great caution (see also Schoepflin, 1993, van Raan 1994, Winterhager 1994, Stock 1995). The significance of the SSCI is restricted in two general ways:

- The SSCI is a database with a marked dominance of Anglo-American publications. German and French sources are only represented as a minority. For instance, the total of German-language journals in the SSCI is 50 (of a worldwide total of 1,500; see Winterhager 1994: 545). Whether and to what extent Anglo-American publications are *over-represented* cannot be determined because of a lack of information about the basic totals or the actual impact of different languages in the scientific community.

- The SSCI is a pure journal database. In the social sciences, unlike the natural sciences, monographs and collections of papers still play a considerable role: in the German language SOLIS database (*Sozialwissenschaftliches Literaturinformationssytem*, dealt with in 15.2 below) only 42% of all entries are from journals, 32% are contributions in collections, and 26% are monographs (see Winterhager 1994: 544f.). In the SSCI analysis, therefore, almost 60% of the relevant entries are lost. On the other hand it may be supposed that, in the social sciences, not only is more being published in journals, but relevant publications are also appearing there to an increasing extent. Because of the peer-review process involved, greater prestige is attached to this form of publication.

We assume that for every method of text analysis there are literary sources which are of central importance to the method, and written by authors occupied in some way with this method who ought to be quoted. The extent to which a method appears in the SSCI can then be calculated by asking in how many documents one of the basic sources of a particular method is cited.[3]

As far as the selection of sources is concerned, there are differences between the methods with regard to quantity. With most methods the question of sources is clear, because these methods are presented in only a small number of basic publications. In this respect there are difficulties with only three methods:

- In the case of *content analysis*, because of its age and long establishment, it is not to be expected that there will be any marked diffusion of the original literature (for example Lasswell 1946). In addition, because of its great diversity, it is difficult to select representative works. A strict selection was undertaken, however, by looking for citations of the monographs of Berelson (1952) and Holsti (1969). Accordingly, it might be the case that this method has a tendency to under-representation in our results. This is especially likely since the explicit sources for open, non-standardized or 'qualitative' content analysis are only from German-speaking countries.

- The *membership categorization device* (MCD) analysis used by ethnomethodology – although it can be traced back to a single author, Harvey Sacks – turns up in a whole range of publications in which it is rarely the only theme of the publication. Because four such publications were incorporated in the search strategy, it may be presumed that MCD analysis has a tendency to be overvalued.

- Much the same may be said of the text analysis adaptation of the *SYMLOG* framework. With this – at least in the case of the SSCI – citations concerning the (principal) aspect of the method (group theory, the observation of interactions) cannot be excluded.

In a more general sense, the distorting effect of the SSCI's makeup cannot be ignored; German and French publications have a smaller chance of being cited in the predominantly Anglo-American journals of the SSCI. This affects narrative semiotics, qualitative content analysis, Ruth Wodak's CDA, functional pragmatics, and objective hermeneutics.

Not least to measure the extent of these distortions, the second stage of the bibliometric analysis extracted the frequency with which the various methods were mentioned in four content-oriented databases (see 15.2 below).

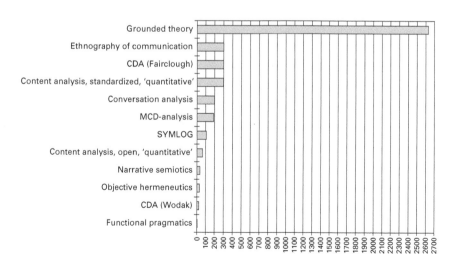

FIGURE 15.1   Absolute frequencies of method literature citations
(Source: SSCI 1991–98)

In all, 4,134 citations for the selected method literature were found for the years 1991 to 1998. (For 1998, only the period from January to August was included.) If the total of citations is compared, there is a clear top position for literature dealing with grounded theory. (see Figure 15.1): the three grounded theory publications that were examined achieve 2,622 citations. This is more than eight times as many as the literature for the next following method, ethnography of communication with 298 citations. After these methods the upper middle range consists of Fairclough's CDA (291 citations), classical content analysis (289 citations), conversation analysis (196) and MCD (182 citations). The lower middle range includes SYMLOG (103 citations, concerning all applications), Mayring's qualitative content analysis (65 citations), narrative semiotics (34 citations) and objective hermeneutics (29 citations). Just behind these comes Wodak's CDA (21 citations). By far the smallest number of citations is for functional pragmatics (4).

Between 1991 and 1998 there is a definite increase in the overall number of references to text analysis literature. If the frequencies for the individual years are compared, the following tendencies are seen for the most prominent methods (see Table 15.1):

- Citations from the literature of grounded theory show a strong growth from 1991 to 1998. (1998 includes only the period from January to August.)

- For citations from ethnography of communication and classical content analysis there is no clear trend; they appear to be developing in a stable fashion.

- Fairclough's CDA shows a striking increase in the numbers of citations.

- In both ethnomethodological conversation analysis and in MCD there has been, in recent years, a distinct increase in the number of references.

Table 15.1   Absolute annual frequencies of method literature citations

No	Method of text analysis	91	92	93	94	95	96	97	98[4]	Total
1	Content analysis (standardized)	38	26	38	40	31	35	50	31	289
2	Content analysis open ('qualitative')	2	3	13	5	13	9	15	5	65
3	Grounded theory	187	196	257	280	377	443	472	410	2622
4	Ethnography of communication	36	48	46	32	39	32	39	26	298
5	MCD-analysis	10	12	10	21	22	32	39	36	182
6	Conversation analysis	23	23	16	25	19	34	35	21	196
7	Narrative semiotics	7	4	2	4	3	4	6	4	34
8	SYMLOG	22	11	12	19	11	11	11	6	103
9	CDA (Fairclough)	9	4	21	31	42	65	68	51	291
10	CDA (Wodak)	3	2	3	1	5	3	3	1	21
11	Functional pragmatics	0	3	0	0	0	0	0	1	4
12	Objective hermeneutics	4	3	7	5	2	5	2	1	29
	Total	341	335	425	463	564	673	740	593	4134

Source: Based on SSCI 1991–98.

For other methods the frequency of citations for individual years is too small to determine definite trends.

It seems inappropriate to relate the dominant position of citations from works by Glaser and Strauss directly to the degree of diffusion of their method. This is not only in view of the limitations formulated above, that the SSCI research makes no claims about the quality of citations. Lee and Fielding (1996, 3.1) observe, first, that a reference to grounded theory guarantees a high degree of recognition for one's own work; and, secondly, that 'a detailed examination of work claiming the label [grounded theory] may deviate sharply from what Glaser and Strauss had in mind. Evidently the Grounded Theory works of Anselm Strauss, Barney Glaser and Juliet Corbin function as a powerful attractor within so-called "Qualitative Social Research".'

15.2 FREQUENCY OF KEYWORDS: THE PROMINENCE OF METHODS

The results of the keyword research into the 15 methods[5] in the WISO-Social Science database (FORIS, SOLIS), in Sociofile, Psyndex, and the MLA International Bibliography appear in Figure 15.2.[6] It must be noted here that the keywords *Inhaltsanalyse* and *content analysis* achieved by far the highest scores, with over 12,000 instances (not included in Figure 15.2). The research in this area had to be limited by the additional targets *qualitative, standardized* or *quantitative, non-standardized*, and *open*.

During the search process we tried first to find the keywords in specific fields (descriptor, subject, title), but this achieved only a small success rate. Only the WISO-databases contain a special field of method. Within this field only a few keywords are used, and of our methods only *Inhaltsanalyse* (content analysis) is included. In the end, therefore, we conducted a 'free text investigation', where the search for method keywords was not restricted to the fields included in particular databases.

In this research there is a marked dominance of open and standardized content analysis and conversation analysis (see Figure 15.2). Grounded theory is strongly represented, although clearly less so than in the citation analysis. It was also surprising that objective hermeneutics occupied fifth position, and was mentioned in almost 220 data entries. Altogether three clusters of methods may be distinguished (see also Table 15.2):

● very strongly represented are the standardized and open variants of content analysis, conversation analysis and grounded theory;

● a middle position, from the point of view of prominence, is occupied by objective hermeneutics, ethnography of communication, other types of ethnographically oriented text analysis and (all types of) critical discourse analysis;

● no impact was made by the two concrete variants of CDA focused on here; functional pragmatics and MCD analysis.

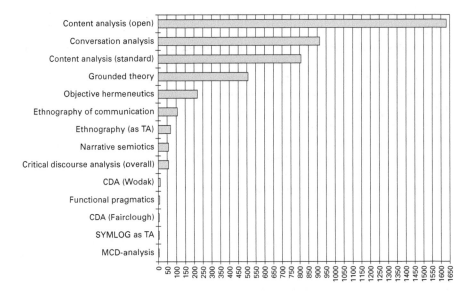

FIGURE 15.2   Search results from the databases of WISO-Social Science, Psyndex,
Sociofile and MLA International Bibliography

Table 15.2   Results from the Psyndex, Sociofile, WISO-Social Science and MLA International
Bibliography

Method of text analysis	Psyndex	Sociofile	WISO	MLA	Total
Content analysis (overall)	1,181	3,244	7,778	80	12,283
Content analysis (open/unstandardized)	287	278	1055	1	1.621
Conversation analysis	83	357	71	402	913
Content analysis (standardized)	166	176	458	5	805
Grounded theory	43	335	122	4	504
Objective hermeneutics	78	24	115	0	217
Ethnography of communication	5	46	17	38	106
Ethnography (as text analysis)	4	42	16	7	69
Narrative semiotics	1	13	4	40	58
Critical discourse analysis (overall)	0	22	4	29	55
CDA (Wodak)	2	0	8	1	11
Functional pragmatics	2	1	5	2	10
CDA (Fairclough)	0	2	0	5	7
MCD-analysis	0	3	0	0	3
SYMLOG as TA	2	0	1	0	3
Total of Documents	1,854	4,543	9,654	614	16,665

As for the specialist focus of the individual databases, there are evident differences between linguistic and non-linguistic methods. For example, content
analysis is comparatively poorly represented in the linguistic MLA International
Bibliography, whereas conversation analysis owes its prominence to precisely
this database. The other linguistic methods (ethnography of communication,

narrative semiotics, CDA) are much more strongly represented in the MLA. In the MLA there are comparatively few occurrences for the selected methods. The richest source, in this respect, is the WISO-Social Science database (cf. Table 15.2).

Table 15.3   Deviations between the SSCI citation analysis and the keyword research (relative frequency in SSCI research minus relative frequency in keyword research)

Method of text analysis	Share SSCI-Research	Share WISO/Sociofile/Psyndex/MLA-Research	Deviation
Content analysis (standardized)	6.99%	18.91%	−11.91%
Content analysis (open/unstandardized)	1.57%	38.07%	−36.50%
Grounded theory	63.43%	11.84%	51.59%
Ethnography of communication	7.21%	2.49%	4.72%
MCD-analysis	4.40%	0.07%	4.33%
Conversation analysis	4.74%	21.44%	−16.70%
Narrative semiotics	0.82%	1.36%	−0.54%
SYMLOG as TA	2.49%	0.07%	2.42%
CDA (Fairclough)	7.04%	0.16%	6.87%
CDA (Wodak)	0.51%	0.26%	0.25%
Functional pragmatics	0.10%	0.23%	−0.14%
Objective hermeneutics	0.70%	5.10%	−4.39%

The result of the keyword analysis shows considerable deviations from the citation analysis presented in 15.1 (above), and this is summarized in Table 15.3. If our findings are to be trusted, then grounded theory is clearly 'overquoted'. In more than 63% of all SSCI data sets that were found the basic works of Barney Glaser and Anselm Strauss were quoted, whereas relevant keywords were only found in approximately 12% of all the text analysis data sets. This could be due to the prominence of the authors or to the fact that the works in question are particularly referred to in general methodological contexts.

In contrast, a significant degree of 'under-citation' (see Ming-Yulh 1995: 334) is found for content analysis and conversation analysis. Standardized content analysis is no longer covered by the selected works (Berelson 1952, Holsti 1969). This is even more so for open content analysis, for which an extended reference was found only for German-speaking countries in Mayring (1988). For conversation analysis, too, the quantity of sources now seems much more extensive than was suggested by our SSCI research.

The 'over-citation' of Dell Hymes's ethnography of communication and Norman Fairclough's CDA is probably due to the prominence of the authors. That of SYMLOG and MCD analysis may also be readily explained: in the case of SYMLOG the keyword research was narrowed down to its application in text analysis, and this reduced its share of findings from around 2.5% to 0.07%. With MCD analysis, many citations were probably related to other aspects of the works of Sacks.

15.3 CITATION NETWORKS: LINKS BETWEEN METHODS

Behind the search for citation networks there is the question of links between the 12 methods of text and analysis, where this is operationalized by using the frequency of citations of different method-sources with a single item. Here too it must be remembered that a bibliometric link in no way signifies similarity of content or the adoption of concepts. On the contrary, it may be a manifestation of some contradiction or distinction between two methods. From many possible ways of operationalizing networks of methods, we concentrate on the following: in some independent scholarly source A, which belongs neither to the basic literature of Method 1 nor to that of Method 2, there is a citation of both a passage fundamental for Method 1 and a passage fundamental for Method 2.

Out of a total of 4,134 data sets in which literature relevant to the 12 methods is cited, there are only 210 items that cite literature belonging to more than a single method (i.e., *c.* 5%). Accordingly only a very small number of items that discuss and apply methods of text analysis have more than a single method in their 'evoked set'. When methods of text analysis are selected and applied, the choice of the method is apparently very seldom discussed.

The results summarized in Figure 15.3 permit an analysis of networks according to method. This shows that, as expected, the strongest link is between the two ethnomethodological methods, MCD and conversation

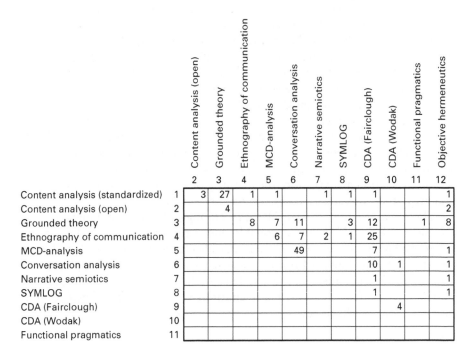

		Content analysis (open) 2	Grounded theory 3	Ethnography of communication 4	MCD-analysis 5	Conversation analysis 6	Narrative semiotics 7	SYMLOG 8	CDA (Fairclough) 9	CDA (Wodak) 10	Functional pragmatics 11	Objective hermeneutics 12
Content analysis (standardized)	1	3	27	1	1			1	1	1			1
Content analysis (open)	2		4										2
Grounded theory	3			8		7	11		3	12		1	8
Ethnography of communication	4				6		7	2	1	25			
MCD-analysis	5					49				7			1
Conversation analysis	6									10	1		1
Narrative semiotics	7									1			1
SYMLOG	8									1			1
CDA (Fairclough)	9										4		
CDA (Wodak)	10												
Functional pragmatics	11												

FIGURE 15.3   Totals of networks according to method in the years 1991–1998

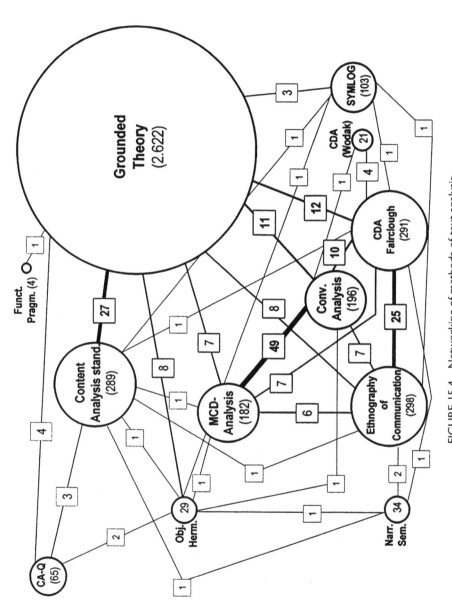

FIGURE 15.4   Networking of methods of text analysis
(circles represent the frequency of citation per method; thickness of lines the frequency of the link)

analysis (49 locations). Strong connections (≥ 20 locations) are also found between Fairclough's CDA and Hymes's ethnography of communication (that is, two linguistic methods), and between content analysis and grounded theory.

Grounded theory displays the highest degree of 'centralization', which is hardly surprising in view of its absolute impact. It is linked with very many other methods, and particularly clearly with content analysis, objective hermeneutics, conversation analysis and ethnography of communication. The latter comes closest to the centrality of grounded theory. In addition to the links already mentioned, there is also a clear similarity of references between grounded theory and both Fairclough's CDA and conversation analysis. If these networks are compared with the overall frequency of citation, however, it becomes clear that the share of multiple-method-citation is lowest (*c.* 3%) in those items which cite grounded theory. This share is highest in conversation analysis (*c.* 40%) and MCD analysis (*c.* 39%), not least because of reciprocal referencing. A high proportion of multiple-method-references is also found in those articles that cite Fairclough's CDA.

The proximity between methods, operationalized on the basis of the frequency of items that cite basic literature from more than one method sample, can also be represented graphically as a network (see Figure 15.4). Here too we may see the dominant position of grounded theory, the relationship between the linguistic methods (CDA, conversation analysis, ethnography of communication) and the peripheral position of functional pragmatics.

What is striking about these results is not only the central position of grounded theory and ethnography of communication, but also the relatively weak networking of classical content analysis. This seems to have a strong link only to grounded theory, but the latter distinguishes itself quite clearly from content analysis.

Items which cite literature from more than two methods are distinctly uncommon. In the period from 1991 to 1998 there are, in the SSCI, only nine scientific articles which fulfil this criterion:

- Two items cite literature from grounded theory, MCD and conversation analysis.

- Two items refer to MCD and conversation analysis and also Fairclough's CDA.

- The five remaining instances of multiple citation relate to the following triads:
  (a) grounded theory – ethnography of communication – CDA (Fairclough)
  (b) ethnography of communication – MCD analysis – conversation analysis
  (c) standardized content analysis – grounded theory – SYMLOG
  (d) grounded theory – SYMLOG – objective hermeneutics
  (e) standardized content theory – grounded theory – MCD analysis.

Since scientific work devoted to a more comprehensive comparison could not be found, it may be supposed that methodological comparison has hitherto been generally rather unusual in the field of text analysis.

NOTES

1   The bibliometric investigation was undertaken with the collaboration of Sybille Krausler. We are grateful for the support of the Social Science Information Unit (SOWIS) of the Library at the Vienna University of Economics and Business Administration, and in particular Bettina Schmeikal and Georg Fessler.

2   There are in all 12 methods, but in content analysis two variants, and in critical discourse analysis two distinct methods are examined.

3   A list of all publications from which citations are derived is in the Appendix.

4   January to August 1998.

5   A list of the keywords which were looked for is in the Appendix. The names of methods occupy a central place, since several methods have more than one name. Finally titles were extracted which refer to central and distinctive concepts for the method in question (e.g. *open coding* in grounded theory, *linguistic procedures* in functional pragmatics, *turn-taking* in conversation analysis).

6   The databases cover differing periods of publication, but the main focus for each of them is the period between 1980 and 1998.

CHAPTER 16

COMPARISON OF METHODS OF TEXT ANALYSIS

In Part 2 (Chapters 5–14) we presented 12 methods of text analysis:

1   Content Analysis
2   Grounded Theory
3   Ethnographic Text Analysis, and Ethnography of Speaking
4   Ethnomethodological MCD Analysis
5   Ethnomethodological Conversation Analysis
6   Narrative Semiotics
7   SYMLOG as a method of Text Analysis
8   Critical Discourse Analysis (CDA) according to Norman Fairclough
9   Critical Discourse Analysis (CDA): the discourse-historical method of Ruth Wodak
10 Functional Pragmatics
11 Differential Text Analysis
12 Objective Hermeneutics

The linguistic methods (particularly 5, 8, 9, 10) were selected because they are very different in their respective theoretical backgrounds and their understanding of context. In addition it was thought desirable to present other methods, not solely those from the Anglo-American world. The other eight methods provide a cross-section in respect of their prominence, theoretical background and development.

Two of the methods presented occupy a special place: both content analysis and grounded theory are less concerned with concrete methods of text analysis than with (rival) research programmes. While classical content analysis postulates the rules of a deductive-quantitative research tradition (see for instance Berelson 1952), the grounded theory of Barney Glaser and Anselm Strauss was developed in the course of a critical treatment of precisely this tradition – a criticism, that is, of the 'deductive formulation of theories before contact is made with the object of empirical study' (Kelle 1994: 283). Content analysis requires the operationalization of theoretical concepts before the analysis of texts, while grounded theory develops its theoretical concepts during the empirical analysis.

It was quite difficult to identify criteria for comparing and distinguishing the 12 methods. Very few criteria could be found that seemed to be applicable to all the selected methods. In what follows, six points will be discussed that may stimulate a more precise comparison of methods.

16.1 ON THE DIFFERENTIATION OF LINGUISTIC AND NON-LINGUISTIC METHODS

Linguistic methods analyse coherence and cohesion as well as the relationship between these two 'textual criteria' (see Chapter 2, 2.3), while non-linguistic methods normally only analyse coherence. Cohesion in this respect refers to the components of the textual surface, i.e. its textual-syntactic connectedness. Coherence (Textual Semantics) constitutes the meaning of the text. The systematic analysis of the relationship between these two dimensions is confined to linguistic methods, whereas the non-linguistic methods place a great emphasis on coherence. Only rarely (for example in the rules of DTA, see Chapter 13) do they also deal with aspects of cohesion.

In this sense, of the methods we have presented, the following may be characterized unequivocally as linguistic: the versions of CDA discussed here (Fairclough, Wodak) and functional pragmatics. Moreover, all three of these methods, on the basis of the great significance attributed to text-external factors, may be classified as types of discourse analysis (see the distinction between text analysis and discourse analysis in Chapter 2, 2.2).

MCD analysis, ethnomethodological conversation analysis, ethnography of communication and narrative semiotics are very difficult to classify. Even though cohesive elements play an important role for them, they do not regard a systematic analysis of the cohesion–coherence relationship as obligatory.

Non-linguistic methods, according to this criterion, are objective hermeneutics, DTA, SYMLOG and a substantial proportion of the familiar applications of content analysis and grounded theory.

16.2 ON THE RULE-GOVERNED NATURE OF MODES OF OPERATION

Social research methods can incorporate procedures, instruments and rules (see Chapter 1). The 12 methods of text analysis are distinct from one another with regard to the degree of development of these components and, consequently, offer users differing degrees of freedom; for recipients, therefore, replicability is made correspondingly easier or more difficult.

For content analysis the literature contains numerous procedures. Instruments (for example schemata of categories) are not explicitly foreordained, but have to be developed for each undertaking. Content analysis does formulate general rules (for example for sampling, for improving intra- and inter-coder reliability, for guaranteeing inference), but concrete rules for its main area of interest, for the allocation of units of analysis to categories, must again be developed anew for each application. In grounded theory there are a number of different coding procedures and a series of rules (that is for open and axial coding), for the writing of memos. As for instruments, a number of computer programs have been developed in recent years (for example NUDIST, Atlas/ti).

In ethnography of communication there are neither procedures nor instruments and very few rules. MCD analysis and ethnomethodological conversation analysis do formulate some rules, but provide no procedures and instruments. Narrative semiotics formulates rules for the analysis of narrative structures (*actants*, isotopes) and of deep structure (the semiotic square), and makes crude instruments (schemata of categories) available for this purpose. For applications involving group analysis SYMLOG provides a series of procedures and instruments. For applications to text analysis, instruments were also drawn up (schemata of categories, SYMLOG Atlas) and rules were formulated. For CDA Fairclough provides no kinds of procedures, rules or instruments, while in Wodak's version there are a number of instruments and few rules. Functional pragmatics offers two instruments for text analysis (pattern, procedure).

Objective hermeneutics makes use of highly developed procedures (detailed analysis, sequential analysis) and proposals for rules. DTA formulates a series of heuristic rules for the discovery of explicit and implicit differences.

16.3 ON THE AREA OF APPLICATION OF THE METHODS

The methods of text analysis display different areas of potential application: certain methods may be applied to all types of text, while others foresee some limitations.

Content analysis and grounded theory, as research programmes, anticipate almost no restrictions in their area of application. The two versions of CDA, objective hermeneutics and ethnography of communication, likewise foresee no restriction. The situation with narrative semiotics is different, and its applicability – as the name suggests – is confined to textual varieties of an essentially narrative character. The ethnomethodological methods, MCD and conversation analysis, are particularly suited to the analysis of spoken material and the latter also presupposes turn-taking. Functional pragmatics also prefers oral communication and its application is indeed restricted to dialogue texts (even if the addressees are only implicitly present).

In this brief outline we have ignored the distinction between linguistic and non-linguistic texts, and the great differences in the respective definitions of text and content. In addition it may be supposed that MCD analysis, narrative semiotics, DTA, the variants of CDA and functional pragmatics are suited primarily to linguistic texts. Conversation analysis, apart from linguistic texts, can also process pictorial material such as video-recordings of conversations. Similarly, in content analysis, grounded theory, ethnography of communication and objective hermeneutics, an application to non-linguistic texts or systems of signs is both plausible and possible.

16.4 ON THE TYPES OF QUESTIONS IN THE DIFFERENT METHODS: CONFIRMATORY AND EXPLORATORY FOCUS

With regard to the types of questions used by the different methods of text analysis, we may distinguish three categories of methods:

(a) Content analysis and grounded theory prescribe no explicit questions. But if these research programmes are pursued it is indispensable that concrete questions will be formulated. In content analysis they are a precondition for the development of a schema of categories. Grounded theory proceeds on the basis of general and abstract research questions which become increasingly detailed and concrete on the basis of the material under investigation.

(b) A number of methods, such as ethnography of communication (speaking grid) and SYMLOG, formulate in advance precise content-related questions. Other methods require this at least for partial components, as CDA does for textual cohesion and narrative semiotics for the narrative structure of texts. In narrative semiotics (deep structure) and CDA, the search for latency phenomena plays an important role (as in type (c), below). Since this search is based upon concrete research questions, however, it is better to treat these methods as examples of type (b).

(c) A third group of methods formulates general, abstract research questions: DTA and objective hermeneutics are examples of methods that seek above all to capture latency phenomena and to enquire about perceptual frameworks or the latent sense of texts. Likewise, in MCD analysis, conversation analysis and functional pragmatics the principal focus is on latent sense or latent structure.

Concrete questions about content imply certain assumptions about the subject of study, they systematize this (for instance in the form of categories), and they require and stimulate hypotheses. The variables to be investigated are already contained in the question or may be derived from it. The results of the analysis then allow the investigators (if they are interested in quantification) to make statements about the distribution of these variables. This strategy constitutes a confirmatory research goal. Assumptions and hypotheses about the subject of study may be rejected or provisionally confirmed.

More general or abstract questions about underlying structure, latent content, or the perceptual schemata which are reproduced in texts, normally lead to an expansion of the text. It is only this expanded material that constitutes the basis for conclusions and results.

All methods that have precise questions about content and a confirmatory focus make use of rules and also, to a certain extent, of instruments which operationalize the variables to be investigated. These aids are partly prepared in advance but partly have to be developed for a specific application in order to guarantee the comprehensibility of the analysis. The analysis of textual cohesion, which plays a part in all linguistic methods, indicates at least a partially confirmatory focus: syntax and grammar provide the schemata of categories and specify the variables to be investigated. Methods with a more exploratory focus often make use of heuristic rules or procedures: DTA, therefore, formulates a series of discovery rules; objective hermeneutics does not formulate any direct heuristic rules but makes suggestions as to how the process of hypothesis-generation within the research team should be represented.

16.5 KARL WEICK'S 'RESEARCH CLOCK' (1979)

At some distance from traditional epistemological categories the organizational theorist Karl Weick (1979: 36ff.) outlines the model of a 'research clock' (see Figure 16.1) which will be used here to provide an unconventional perspective on the comparison of methods. Weick is guided by Thorngate's (1976) postulate of appropriate complexity, according to which a theory of social behaviour cannot be at the same time general, accurate and simple. The picture of a clock (with two hands) is intended to demonstrate that only two of the three possible criteria can be fulfilled simultaneously.

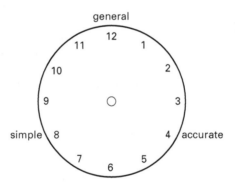

FIGURE 16.1   The research clock (Source: Weick 1979: 36ff.)

- The *simplicity* of methods is primarily specified by the preconditions of the application. A method becomes simpler to the extent to which its theoretical bases and the procedures, instruments and rules it employs become less complex.

- The *accuracy* of a method derives from a combination of three aspects and becomes greater (a) the more textual dimensions are being analysed (cohesion/coherence, latent/manifest textual structures); (b) the smaller the unit of analysis is; and (c) the more variables there are and the more accurate their operationalizations.

- The *generality* of a method refers here particularly to the breadth of the theoretical content and the conclusions that are attainable using it. The breadth of the application to particular varieties of text or episodes (for example turn-taking) seems to us to be of lesser importance in meeting this criterion. Both aspects should of course be considered from the point of view of their empirical generalizability (cf. Chapter 3), and this depends in every specific application on the selection and quantity of texts included in the analysis.

In order to locate the individual methods on the research clock we have referred above all to the self-presentations of methods in the primary and secondary sources (see the *outlines of methods* in Part 2).

Since both content analysis and grounded theory are research programmes, their location with regard to generality, accuracy and simplicity will depend on the particular application. The following tendencies may, however, be noted:

- *Content analysis*, for most applications discussed in the literature, may be classified as comparatively simple. Its accuracy is dependent on the choice of the unit of analysis and the preciseness of the schema of categories. As far as its area of potential use is concerned, content analysis may be given the label 'general', but this can seldom be said of particular procedures or the breadth of its results because, in most cases, rather precise and narrow research questions are pursued. On the other hand, if one follows the rules and procedures of inductive statistics, generalizations about underlying totalities may be made using the results of content analysis. However, most content analysis undertakings can at best be evaluated as simple and accurate.

- Text analysis methods based on *grounded theory* tend to be simple, because they normally dispense with theoretical preconditions and because their rules are formulated simply and clearly. Grounded theory is general in respect of its possible applications and guarantees a certain empirical generalizability by means of theoretical sampling (Strauss 1987: 10ff.). But since it was set up for the precise purpose of providing a counter-position to 'general' theories, the breadth of its results and conclusions is restricted but still accurate. For the restricted subject of study as many different variables as possible have to be analysed, by relying on different units of analysis (from word-fragment to whole text). In general GT methods may therefore be assessed as simple and accurate.

Using the criteria of the 'research clock' it becomes clear, therefore, that content analysis and grounded theory – research programmes that are seen as very different and mostly as polar opposites – do not differ very greatly from one another. This may be because of our assessment or because the criteria used are unsuitable. On the other hand it could mean that content analysis and grounded theory are 'empty concepts' to the extent that their characterizations give no guidance on how to proceed and what kind of results should be sought.

- *Ethnography of communication* appears at first glance to be general. It is applicable to widely differing types of text and aims to make far-reaching statements about cultural patterns of social entities. This general applicability is, however, at the cost of accuracy; the speaking grid is merely a rudimentary analytical schema and the speech event a very crude unit of analysis. The simplicity of the method suffers under the influence of the very demanding theoretical concepts (communicative event, communicative competence, and so on).

- Both *ethnomethodological MCD* and *conversation analysis*, however, are simple and accurate methods. The narrow theoretical range, the restricted area of application and the limited empirical generalizability (which would also counter the demand for a 'member'-oriented micro-analysis that always analyses particular communicative situations) – all of these lead to a need to locate these methods at the opposite pole to generality. These methods are accurate mostly because of their micro-analysis units and their differentiated modes of systematization that include multiple variables.

- *Narrative semiotics* may be characterized as accurate particularly because of its detailed analytical framework. To achieve this the biggest sacrifice is simplicity of method in that the semiotic theories which lie behind the instruments are extremely complex. The area of application is limited, and the generalizability of results (deep structure of the narration) is strongly dependent on the analysed text. The lack of an embedded sociological or social-psychological theoretical dimension means more general conclusions can hardly ever be derived from the results.

- *SYMLOG* as a specific content analysis procedure is particularly characterized by simplicity and accuracy. Its theoretical bases are manageable, its rules and instruments are simple and highly suited to a precise operationalization of variables.

- The variants of *critical discourse analysis (CDA)* are – depending on the particular operationalization of the research questions – accurate and general in character. Several textual dimensions are analysed, the units of analysis range from individual words to complete arguments, and the methods are generally applicable. If the theoretical guidelines of CDA are accepted, the results also permit conclusions to be drawn about social structures.

- *Functional pragmatics* also shows itself to be an accurate and general method; in its generality some concessions have to be made on account of restrictions in the area of applications (dialogue texts).

- *Objective hermeneutics* is also located between accuracy and generality, but this method can certainly not be characterized as simple. The detailed proposals for rules, the procedures that guarantee a particularly intensive type of analysis, and the choice of units of analysis (smallest sense units) result in a high degree of accuracy. The unrestricted area of application and the postulated generalizability of results (rooted in socialization theory) testify to a high degree of generality.

- The same may be said of *DTA* that it may also be described as accurate and general, but certainly not as simple. This assessment is based on the unit of analysis (phrases) and the consideration of varying textual dimensions (manifest/latent) as well as the communication theory background of the method.

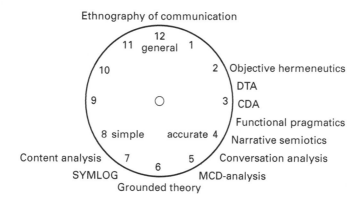

FIGURE 16.2   The methods of text analysis on Weick's research clock

The location of the methods of text analysis on Weick's research clock is summarized in Figure 16.2, where it may be seen that none of the selected methods of text analysis is located between the poles 'general' and 'simple'. This may be explained, on the one hand, by the fact that methods with such a location would be accused of being 'unscientific'. On the other hand it is also connected with the interpretation presented here of simplicity and generality, both of which are strongly related to the theoretical foundation of a particular method. Theories which have broad scope must involve a minimum of distinctive concepts to show relationships between micro-(texts) and macro-phenomena, if they are to underpin the creation of empirical methods.

16.6 EXPLANATIONS AND ATTRIBUTION

Scientific investigation can also be regarded as a socially distinctive system, determined programmatically by theories and methods, which is concerned with finding explanations. Scientists are always observers whose actions are directed at explaining perceived events as the effects of particular causes (see, for instance, Luhmann 1990a). Patterns of explanatory behaviour, in their turn, are the subject of a specific social-psychological theory, known as *attri-*

bution theory (see Heider 1958, Kelley 1967, Herkner 1980, Weiner 1986). Accordingly, methods of text analysis, in so far as they relate to theories, must also give explanations. In most cases they seek to explain the linguistic actions that are manifest in a text by means of psychic and/or social factors. Every method favours particular patterns of explanation that may be located on the well-known attribution schema:

• According to *locus of control* or *system reference*, a distinction may be made between internal and external explanations. A theory that explains individual behaviour through social structures, therefore, has external attribution.

• According to the *stability of causes* a distinction may be made between constant and variable explanations. The factors *intention* and *situation*, therefore, relate to variable, internal or external factors, whereas *structure* and *predisposition* relate to constant factors.

If one employs this schema, the methods of text analysis may be located as shown in Figure 16.3. Content analysis and grounded theory cannot be located because of their character as research programmes. They do not depend on simple (explanatory) theories but rather invoke these according to a particular research question for the purpose of hypothesis formulation (content analysis) or else they only develop the theory in the course of the analytical work (grounded theory). Only concrete applications can be arranged on the attribution schema.[1]

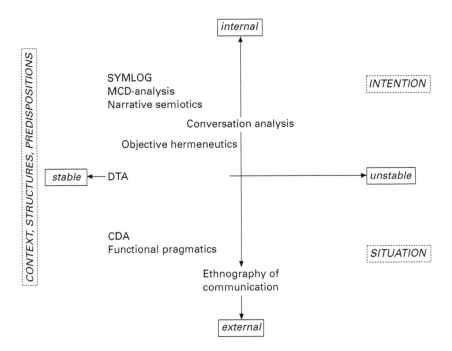

FIGURE 16.3 Attribution tendencies in methods of text analysis

SYMLOG, MCD analysis and narrative semiotics are methods that have a predominantly internal/stable foundation: SYMLOG explains group behaviour with reference to group structures. MCD analysis looks for no explanations of the observational and categorizing devices of members beyond the predispositions produced and reproduced by the members of particular groupings. Narrative semiotics avoids all types of social explanations of narrative structures and of the underlying structures of stories, and so it must be assumed that the narrators are seen as responsible for these.

At the intersection between internal/stable and internal/unstable explanations we find ethnomethodological conversation analysis: with theoretical consistency (for ethnomethodology avoids relying on 'objective' social structures) it also offers no external reasons for perceived interactional structures and processes. In conversation analysis, however, the particular situation, the variable social setting that arises from the interplay of individual interactions, does play a central part.

Objective hermeneutics and DTA are located at the intersection between external and internal (but stable) attribution tendencies: these methods have in common that they refer back to theories, and seek to explain a particular text (albeit from a different viewpoint) through the interplay between psychic and social factors. In this objective hermeneutics, in the form of the concept of *motivation*, also incorporates an internal-variable component.

CDA and functional pragmatics, on the other hand, offer predominantly external/stable patterns of explanation: the circumstance to be explained, the text as a manifestation of speech actions or discourse, is explained through social structures and socio-historic contexts that are often understood as macro-structures.

Ethnography of communication is allocated a middle position here, because although it gives external explanations for individual (speech-)action through cultural patterns, it also allots an explicit and significant role to situational factors.

The crude distribution of the methods of text analysis shown in Figure 16.3 also demonstrates that variable explanations play a subordinate role. This is an expression of one specific feature of any scientific investigation, namely the search for constant (if limited) causes; variable causes, whether they reside in the unstable intentions of speakers or in the variable situational conditions of the environment, do not provide satisfactory scientific explanations. All methods attempt, to a greater or lesser extent, to capture situational factors. As a rule this is mostly in order to establish common features and relate them to constant causes, in spite of these fluctuations. Only conversation analysis and ethnography take explicit account of a greater degree of variability.

But even in those methods which have set themselves the task of looking for stable foundations, this plan is not always consistently adhered to. Particularly where theoretical ideas are borrowed from speech act theory, an internal/variable component is admitted with the category of *intention*. This may be seen, for example, in the version of CDA developed by Wodak: in her theory of text-planning, intentions – together with extra-linguistic factors – play a significant role (Wodak et al. 1990: 47).

NOTE

---

1 In the content analysis procedures of evaluative assertion analysis (EAA) and in SYMLOG a dominant internal/stable attribution tendency might be determined. The examples of applications given in Strauss (1987: 209, for instance) display a mixture of internal and external, stable and unstable explanations.

Abduction (Latin *abducere* – to take away.) Charles S. Pierce (1939–1914) characterized *abduction* as the logic which governs the formation of any hypothesis. Every observation and interpretation is a hypothesis made on the basis of an abduction. As a conscious process, abduction – after deduction and induction – is the third form of logical conclusion ('the art of inference'). Abduction may be characterized as the search for the best explanation for any observed phenomenon that requires explanation: X (for instance the unexpected use of a particular word) is remarkable; A, B, C are possible explanations for this use; B (for instance the social position of the speaker, which distinguishes him from the other interlocutors) seems the most convincing. If B is true, phenomenon X is no longer remarkable; B is therefore accepted as the one hypothesis which can account for the occurrence of X. Abduction is the search for a rule by which particular events may be explained. This form of inferencing is always marked by great uncertainty, but – in contrast to deductive and inductive processes – it provides the only conclusion that can lead to new ideas. To show that a given explanation is a suitable hypothesis with general validity – rather than simply the best account of a single phenomenon – this kind of reasoning requires tests first of induction and then of deduction (to determine its general applicability). Abductive inferencing plays a central role in the formulation of hypotheses and therefore in qualitative social investigation, which is concerned with the development of explanations. (See *deduction, induction.*)

Acceptability While *grammaticality* determines what is structurally possible in a given language, *acceptability* determines which of the structurally possible forms will actually be selected for the fulfilment of a particular function.

Ad hoc sampling This takes place when, for a studied selection, a population is constructed a posteriori. The statements are then valid only for the sample and the constructed totality. Under what circumstances can this be done? In fact, this occurs only when one stumbles across material or is offered (access to) texts which seem so worthy of investigation that one dispenses with all normal criteria for selection. One could then still set up the analysis as a case study, but one would have to go into great detail and resist the temptation to generalize the results.

Assertion In the definition used in functional pragmatic pattern analysis *assertion* means 'statement' or 'claim'. Functional pragmatics makes a distinction between *assertion,* (the introduction of the basic pattern), *request,* the announcement of a future act – and of an already completed act – and on the basis of this distinction subdivides the basic pattern into four main types. An assertion introduces a cognitive reason. The discourse-historical method uses *assertion*, like *predication*, to refer to an explicit attribution of properties and modes of behaviour.

Cluster sampling   This is a form of multi-stage sampling and denotes a procedure in which the sample focuses not on individual elements but on clusters (as subsets of the population). Within these randomly selected clusters all elements must then be investigated. The procedure is admittedly more economical but subject to sampling errors greater than purely random sampling. For example, if one wishes to investigate political speeches, the individual clusters could consist of parliamentary speeches, electoral speeches, the speeches of party officials, etc.

Coding   In text analysis *coding* means that text phenomena are related to individual concepts. That is, a connection is established between concrete text extracts (units of analysis) and certain more abstract categories. In grounded theory coding is the general term for the conceptualization of data. In this theory, coding means that the investigator asks questions about categories and their contexts and offers provisional answers (or hypotheses).

Communicative competence   In the sense of the ethnography of speaking (Dell Hymes) this term refers to all those abilities of speakers which enable them to communicate appropriately in a speech community. This knowledge includes rules of linguistic and sociolinguistic communication, rules of interaction, and also those cultural rules which determine the context and the content of communicative events and processes of interaction. Communicative competence guarantees that what is structurally possible (in a given language), feasible and appropriate to particular situations, functions and contexts will be linked to actually occurring cultural behaviour. (See also *acceptability*, *grammaticality*.)

Constituents   In a Chomskyan type of grammar (or *constituent* grammar) sentences are composed of phrases, which may be sub-categorized, according to syntactic function, into verbal, nominal and prepositional phrases. These phrases are then understood as the central, meaningful components of texts.

Context   In text linguistics *context* means the situational environment (speech situation, setting, attitude, experience, etc.) which is external to the text. In pragmalinguistics the notion of context refers to (a) the linguistic means by which an utterance is localized in a concrete situation, lexical expressions, (b) the linguistic means which make an utterance a text (pronominalization, anaphora, cataphora, theme-rheme, etc.), (c) any non-verbal resources (gestures, facial expressions), and (d) all extralinguistic features of the communicative situation (age, gender, profession, level of education, etc.). The text-linguistic use of the term *context* is more usual.

Concept indicator model   *Concepts* are abstractive terms and labels that are attached to individual events. If such events are attached to individual concepts (or categories), they then function as empirical indicators of the concepts.

Cotext   This term is used to refer to the linguistic environment which precedes or follows a concrete text location. According to Glück (1993) *cotext* denotes the text-internal linguistic context which precedes or follows a text location, as opposed to the text-external situational *context*. Petöfi (1971) uses cotext to refer to the grammatical and semantic representation of the textual surface (textual structure) which achieves a denotative correspondence ('world structure') by means of interpretation.

Deduction (Latin *deducere* – to proceed, to derive from some origin.) A deductive conclusion proceeds from the general to the particular. From a general premise a particular case is inferred. For example, if one assumes that women (as opposed to men) attribute their career more to circumstances than to their own ability, one may expect that, in the analysis of a particular conversation where a woman is talking about her career, this feature will be found. One cannot, on the other hand, be surprised to find this confirmed. The conclusions deriving from deductions are true if the premises are true, and so deductions – provided that the rules of logic are obeyed – offer no new discoveries. They do not extend the knowledge of the investigator. Research which follows the principles of critical rationalism (K. Popper) is basically organized along deductive lines; from theories (systems of general assertions), hypotheses (explanations) are derived whose validity must then be critically tested on specific cases of empirically observed data. This procedure is also characterized as 'rule governed'. Text analysis may be said to follow the deductive principle if schemata of categories are first developed and texts are then examined to determine in what form and with what frequency these theoretical constructs occur. (See *abduction, induction.*)

Deep structure Different methods of text analysis attempt to reconstruct in texts a variously defined *deep structure*. This underlies the idea that in text production a latent meaning is pursued of which the text producer is not always aware. This 'meaning' is variously conceptualized according to different theoretical perspectives. In narrative semiotics it corresponds to 'fundamental values', while in DTA it is a question of latent perception schemata. (Cf. *surface structure.)*

Deictic procedure This term is used in functional pragmatics to refer to that type of linguistic act by which speakers draw the attention of listeners to an object in their common sphere of reference, that is to say, in their speaking situation. Deictic procedures are indicative in meaning.

Deixis Deictic or indexical expressions refer to the extralinguistic reality and acquire their meaning only with reference to the speech situation in which they are uttered. Examples of deictic expressions are personal pronouns (*I, you,* etc.), demonstratives (*this, that* and so on) or adverbs (*here, now*).

Disclaimer Reservations or *disclaimers* weaken speech contributions. They may relate to differing units of communication. '*If you don't mind*', for example, is a disclaimer to the listeners. The disclaimer realized in '*I am not a computer specialist*', on the other hand, relates to the speaker.

Discourse representation This is a term elaborated in the course of historical discourse studies of post-war anti-Semitism (Projektteam 1989, Wodak et al. 1990) to indicate the reproduction of utterances of third parties. This may happen in a number of very different ways: for example in direct or indirect speech. By such devices speakers can express their distance from, or proximity to, the utterance and/or legitimize their own opinion by reference to third parties. Discourse representations are typical of media texts.

Evocations   This refers to that kind of textual allusion which is based less on the reproduction of lexical elements than on special effects. *Evocations* in newspaper articles, for instance, can stimulate associations with other text types such as fairy tales or detective stories.

Exothesis   In functional pragmatics this refers to the verbalization of some mental element such as, for instance, a sign of incomprehension. Speakers may exothesize the mental element 'incomprehension' with the question, '*what does that mean?*'

Grammaticality   This is the central explanatory concept of Chomsky's (1965) mode of linguistic analysis, which is independent of the act of communication. Chomskyan generative grammars are tested by their capacity to generate a set of particular sentences and by the coincidental generation of new sentences. Grammatical competence means the cognitive ability of speakers to produce structurally *correct* or *acceptable* (see *acceptability*) sentences (see also *communicative competence*).

Hermeneutics   This is the art of explaining cultural manifestations, particularly texts, which should ensure the general validity and adequacy of the interpretations and processes of comprehension. Here, in contrast to the (causal) explanations of the natural sciences, it is a question of grasping and producing meaning relations. Human behaviour is always taken to be meaningful. An important element is the hermeneutic circle: the meaning of one part can only be understood in the context of the whole, but this in turn is only accessible from its component parts.

Heuristic   (Greek *heurisko* – find.) This is a collective term for various search and discovery techniques, or for the study of these procedures. *Heuristic* procedures permit the acquisition of knowledge by systematic discovery, in which, of course, (unlike algorithmic procedures) there is no guarantee of any solution. Heuristic procedures, such as experiments in reasoning or incrementalism, normally make use of so-called heuristic principles, such as analogy, abstraction and the set-up of aspiration levels. Heuristic procedures, rules and instruments are used in methods of text analysis to discover new variables and to generate hypotheses.

Induction   (Latin *inducere* – to draw or lead; *inductivus* – suitable as precondition.) Inductive conclusions proceed from individual cases to a generalization. One derives general pronouncements from individual observations, proceeds from data and arrives at hypotheses. This type of procedure is therefore described as 'data-driven'. For example, it is determined in the course of a study that, in a conference, contributions are more often adopted if they contain pictorial expressions. It is then concluded that the prominence of contributions is substantially influenced by the choice of memorable keywords. Such generalizing conclusions are susceptible to error. In a particular case the conclusion could, for instance, be influenced by the fact that other considerations (such as the position of the speakers, the length of contributions, sympathy with the audience, etc.) were not taken into account. Inductive conclusions belong to the permanent repertoire of research techniques, provided the investigator proceeds from samples to the (total) population. Text analyses follow the inductive principle when general categories are distilled from transcripts. One example of this is the open coding of the grounded theory. (See *abduction, deduction.*)

Inference   The statistics of inference are concerned with drawing conclusions for some population from the results of a sample. Conclusions of this kind are only drawn when a sample is representative of an entire population about whom statements may (or should) be made on the basis of sample results.

Isotopy   The concept of isotopy is central to the structural semantics of Algirdas J. Greimas (1983). For him the concept refers to the cluster of redundant semantic categories which underlie discourse. Examples are the isotopy of space and time by means of which the environment of an action and movement are characterized along the time axis. Isotopies indicate iterativity in a syntagmatic chain of classemes and guarantee the homogeneity of the discourse utterance. The concept was borrowed from chemistry.

Metaphor/metaphorical lexeme   A *metaphor* is a linguistic image based on some similarity between two objects or concepts. It is formed through the transference of some word to a counterfactual meaning. An example of a metaphor is 'sharp criticism' (or 'blunt statement'). The term *metaphorical lexeme* refers to individual words which form metaphors.

Modality   This is a semantic-pragmatic category. It indicates the orientation of a speaker to an utterance. *Modality* may be expressed by syntactic means (declarative, interrogative), verb form (active/passive), or by various other linguistic means such as adverbs (*hopefully, fortunately*) or modal verbs (*may, can, must, should*).

Multi-stage sample   This denotes a multiple random sample at different hierarchical levels within a population. If this procedure is selected in preference to a pure random sample, it is normally for economic reasons. For example, one could take a random sample from all the states of the USA. From this sample a number of cities would be selected. A random sample of all the newspapers appearing in those cities would then be taken and, finally, from these newspapers, a random sample of articles would be taken for analysis. The sampling error increases according to the number of stages, but this may be countered by combining this procedure with a *stratified sample*.

Norm respect   This refers to the adherence to generally applicable and binding norms. For the type of organization to be found in our textual examples, *norm respect* is realized in the statement 'Each one of us works with the greatest dedication'.

Phonology   This linguistic sub-discipline investigates the sound system of a given language. Phonology proceeds from the smallest elements of the language that distinguish meaning, the phonemes. The research emphases are different in the various schools of phonology, such as *functional phonology* (Trubetzkoy and the Prague School), *generative phonology* (Chomsky), or *natural phonology* (Dressler).

Predication   This is the process of attributing or denying to the subject of a sentence (things, persons or events) the properties or modes of behaviour which are expressed in the predicate. The discourse-historical method examines *predication*, like *assertion*, as the explicit attribution of properties and modes of behaviour with regard to the categorization and typification of groups.

Quota sampling This mode of sampling attempts, by means of a conscious rather than a random selection, to bring the characteristics of the sample closer to those of the population. This technique is rather controversial but frequently used in public opinion surveys. It predetermines percentages of particular categories or combinations of features (*quotas*) and uses these to control the selection of the subjects of study. There are two preconditions: first, the distribution of the predetermined variables over the whole population must be known; and secondly, the variables must be relevant to the research questions. The investigation is then representative for no more than those predetermined variables.

Random sample A pure random sample requires the availability of a list which indicates all the elements of a total population. Only on this basis (for example by the use of random numbers) can a purely random selection of units of investigation be made. Since it is very unlikely that all the elements of a population can be identified (and even where they can, the researcher rarely has access to the relevant documents), pure random samples are very rare. Linguistic investigations which meet all the necessary criteria are almost never encountered.

Reliability In the classical theory of testing, reliability is one of the central criteria used to indicate the extent to which the results of some measurement (or test) may be trusted. In essence the requirement that a measurement should show the highest possible degree of reliability conveys the idea that the procedure used should measure what it is intended to measure as accurately and constantly as possible, and in a way which may be replicated by other investigators. For instance, in content analysis the measurement of agreement between different coders is often taken as a measure of reliability. Quantitative research has developed a range of checking procedures which often, however, cannot be used in their original form in interpretative research. The reliability of some part of a questionnaire or a test is therefore assessed by repeated application of the test (test-retest method) or by comparing the results of some other equally valid procedure (parallel test). A high degree of reliability is seen as a necessary but not, in itself, sufficient condition for *validity*. (See *validity*.)

Sample This denotes a set of objects of investigation (e.g. persons, objects or events) which are selected according to certain defined criteria (for instance, a set of copies of daily newspapers determined by the use of random numbers) and which are deemed to be representative of some total population. A *sample* must be representative if the results achieved are to be transferable to the whole, that is to say, if conclusions are to be drawn about the facts in question in the relevant population. Samples are normally judged to be representative; the basic types are *random sample, stratified sample, cluster sample* (a survey of a number of 'clusters' selected at random), and *multi-stage sample*.

Sampling error This denotes some deviation between the 'true' value for some variable in the total population and the corresponding value in a sample. It arises through the making of a random sample. For example, if one has quoted an average value for the intelligibility of a series of texts (such as information leaflets for applicants to public authorities), this value will differ from the 'true' rate of intelligibility which could only be calculated if all the relevant texts have actually been evaluated.

Sapir-Whorf hypothesis   The central idea of the hypothesis formulated by Edward Sapir and Benjamin L. Whorf is that a language functions not only as an instrument for the description of experience but also, and more significantly, as a means of defining experience for speakers of that language. In this sense language determines, on the basis of its formal completeness and the unconscious projection of its implicit expectations, the possibilities and the limitations of our experience.

Self-assessment   This refers to the process of attributing to oneself, in a text, certain positive characteristics, as in 'our department is highly skilled in this area'.

Semantics   This term is adopted from Charles W. Morris (1938) who used *semantics* to refer to that sub-discipline of *semiotics* which concerns itself with the relationship between signs and objects. In general terms, and leaving aside the specific differences between the various sub-types of linguistic semantics (such as lexical, sentence or text semantics) and the different approaches (such as structural, generative or interpretative semantics, or stereotypic, instructional and referential semantics), we may describe semantics as the theory and practice of meaning analysis.

Semiotics   Modern *semiotics*, or the theory of signs, derives from the work of Charles S. Pierce, Charles W. Morris and Ferdinand de Saussure. It is concerned with the use of signs, or *semiosis*. It consists of three sub-disciplines: *semantics* (for the relationship between signs and objects), *pragmatics* (for the relationship of sign and interpreter to the subject of investigation) and *syntax* (for the formal relation of signs to each other).

Speech community   Although there is no general agreement in the literature about a definition of speech community, the following criteria – at least in Dell Hymes's 'ethnography of communication' – seem to summarize the concept: (a) common use of language, (b) frequency of interaction of a group, (c) shared rules of speaking and interpreting, (d) shared attitudes and values with regard to linguistic form and usage, and (e) shared socio-cultural assumptions.

Speech act   According to Searle (1969) speech acts are the basic units of human communication. In Searle's extended definition they consist of *locutions* (the articulation of linguistic elements), *propositions* (formulations of the content of an utterance) and *illocutions*, which are the actions performed by speech acts. Various typologies for classifying illocutions have been developed by Austin (1962), Searle (1982) and Wunderlich (1978). To characterize the effect which a speech act has on the listener, the term *perlocution* (Austin 1962) may be added to these three units.

While the act of *utterance* is understood as the physical activity of a person resulting in some phonic or graphic phenomena, a speech act is the 'interpretation of such activity in relation to a particular linguistic system, a particular system of behaviour, and to the social situation in which both speakers and interlocutors find themselves' (Wunderlich 1978: 51). *Speech acts* (or 'acts of speaking') may have the following functions: (a) they replace concrete actions, (b) they prepare for concrete actions, (c) they clarify past concrete actions, (d) they lead to concrete actions, or (e) they establish social facts (Wunderlich 1978: 23). Different orientations in speech act theory (Austin 1962, Searle

1982, Wunderlich 1978) distinguish between the varying functions of speech acts in different ways.

Speech event   Speech events (or communicative events) are the smallest units of analysis in the 'ethnography of communication' (Hymes 1979). A communicative event is defined by a common general goal, a common general theme, and common participants who normally use the same level of language in a common setting and follow the same rules of interaction (Saville-Troike 1989: 27). Hymes (1962: 24f.) gives the following examples of classes of speech event: Sunday morning sermon, inaugural address, pledge of allegiance, heart-to-heart talk, sales talk, talk man-to-man, woman's talk, polite conversation.

Stratified sample   By *stratifying* a sample it is possible to reduce the extent of sampling error. The population is divided, according to variables relevant to the investigation, into a number of sub-groups from which random samples can be taken. These samples are proportional to the distribution of the variables in the total population. One precondition of this procedure is that the investigator knows the characteristics of the population, since only then can he or she classify it according to categories which are relevant to the research.

Superstructure   In Marxist theory this term refers to the totality of political ideas, ideologies, social values and norms. It is essentially determined by the material, economic 'base', however, the circumstances of production, also affect this economic base. For Marxist oriented research, or research showing partial Marxist inspiration, this means that any investigation of everyday circumstances must also take into account the *superstructure* of the relevant historical situation or must, in its interpretation, consider the different forms of social consciousness.

Surface structure   Surface structure refers to the immediately recognizable and easily accessible forms of texts. This means those structures which are regularly investigated in traditional modes of text analysis, that is such manifest phenomena as themes and linguistic realizations. (Cf. *deep structure*.)

Symbolic interactionism   This term was coined by Herbert Blumer to characterize a (microsociological) direction in social research based on the idea that 'significant symbols' (G.H. Mead) form the basis of social connections. The definition of social situations is made possible by the use of meaningful symbols (words, gestures, texts, pictures, pictograms, etc.) which thereby form the basis of all *interactions* (reciprocal acts oriented to one another). Socialization – the process by which an individual comes to terms with his or her environment – is, therefore, the learning of symbols. In sociolinguistics the work of scholars like E. Goffman on *frames* or *impression management* has an important status. Moreover, this approach is one of the theoretical foundations of *grounded theory*, and was also the basis from which *ethnomethodology* (H. Garfinkel) developed. This latter is significant in text analysis, for example in *conversation analysis*.

Validity   In testing theory this denotes one of the central criteria, which give information about the truthfulness of some measurement or test. In essence the requirement that a test shows the highest possible degree of validity implies that the chosen procedure should measure, in accordance with the theoretical concepts, only what one intends or claims to be measuring. Considerations of validity therefore begin with the operationalization of concepts used in research questions and hypotheses. This internal validity must be distinguished from the external form which, in essence, includes the requirement that any results should be valid beyond the immediate sphere of the study. To test different types of validity, a range of classical procedures are available but most of these cannot be used in interpretative types of research. (See *reliability*.)

PUBLICATIONS AND KEYWORDS FOR BIBLIOMETRY

Sources constitutive to the methods	SSCI-Search-Strategy	Keywords
Ethnography of Communication: Gumperz, John J. and Hymes, Dell (eds) (1972), *Directions in Sociolinguistics. The Ethnography of Communication.* New York: Holt, Rinehart and Winston. Hymes, Dell (1979), *Soziolinguistik. Zur Ethnographie der Kommunikation.* ed. by Florian Coulmas. Frankfurt: Suhrkamp. Hymes, Dell (1962), 'The Ethnography of Speaking', in Thomas Gladwin and William C. Sturtevant (eds), *Anthropology and Human Behavior*, pp. 13–53. Hymes, Dell (1970), 'Linguistic Method in Ethnography', in P. Garvin (ed.) *Method and Theory in Linguistics.* The Hague: Mouton, pp. 249–325. Hymes, Dell (1971), , 'Sociolinguistics and the Ethnography of Speaking', in E. Ardener (ed.) *Social Anthropology and Language.* London: Tavistock. Hymes, Dell (1974), *Foundations in Sociolinguistics.* Philadelphia: University of Pennsylvania Press.	Citation: (GUMPERZ-JJ-19*-DIRECTIONS-SOCIOLIN* OR HYMES-D-19*- ETHNOGRAPHY-COMMUNI* OR HYMES-D-19*-SOCIOLINGUISTIC* OR HYMES-D-19*-F*-SOCIOLINGUISTI* OR HYMES-D-19*-DIRECTIONS-SOCIOLIN*)	(Ethnography of Communication) or (Ethnography of Speaking) or (Ethnographie der Kommunikation) or (Ethnographie des Sprechens)
Grounded Theory: Glaser, Barney G. and Strauss, Anselm (1967), *The Discovery of Grounded Theory. Strategies for Qualitative Research.* Chicago, IL: Aldine. Strauss, Anselm (1987) *Qualitative Analysis for Social Scientists.* Cambridge: Cambridge University Press [German: (1976) *Grundlagen qualitativer Sozialforschung.* München: W. Fink (UTB).] Strauss, Anselm and Corbin, Juliet (1990), *Basics of Qualitative Research.* Newbury Park, CA: Sage. [German: (1994) *Grundlagen Qualitativer Sozialforschung.* Weinheim: Psychologie-Verlags-Union, Beltz.]	Citation: (GLASER-BG-19*-DISCOVERY-GROUNDED* OR GLASER-BG-19*-STRATEGIES-QUALITAT* OR STRAUSS-A-19*-QUALITATIVE-ANAL* OR STRAUSS-A-19*-BASICS-QUALITATIV* OR STRAUSS-A-19*-GRUNDLAGEN-QUALITAT*)	(Grounded Theory) or (Open Coding) or (Theoretical Memos)

Sources constitutive to the methods	SSCI-Search-Strategy	Keywords
MCD-Analysis: Sacks, Harvey (1971), 'Das Erzählen von Geschichten innerhalb von Unterhaltungen', in R. Kjolseth and F. Sack (eds) *Zur Soziologie der Sprache.* KZfS 1971, Sonderheft 15, pp. 307–14. Sacks, Harvey (1972a), 'An Initial Investigation of the Usability of Conversational Data for Doing Sociology', in D. Sudnow (ed.) *Studies in Social Interaction.* New York: Free Press, pp. 31-73. Sacks, Harvey (1972b) 'On the Analysability of Stories by Children', in John J. Gumperz and Dell Hymes (eds) *Directions in Sociolinguistics. The Ethnography of Communication.* New York: Holt, Rinehart and Winston. Sacks, Harvey (1974), 'On the Analysability of Stories by Children', in Roy Turner (ed.) *Ethnomethodology.* Harmondsworth: Penguin, pp. 216-32. Sacks, Harvey (1992a, 1992b) *Lectures on Conversation,* edited by Gail Jefferson. Cambridge: Blackwell.	Citation: (SACKS-H-1971-KOLNER-Z-SOZIOLOGI* OR SACKS-H-19*-STUDIES- SOCIAL-INTER* OR SACKS-H-*-LEC*-CON* OR SACKS-H-19*-ETHNOMETHODOLOG* OR SACKS-H-1992-HARVEY-SACKS-LECTUR*)	(Membership Categorization Device) or (MCD) [with restrictions]
Conversation Analysis: Atkinson, J. Maxwell and Heritage, John C. (eds) (1984), *Structures of Social Action. Studies in Conversation Analysis.* Cambridge: Cambidge University Press. Schenkein, Jim (ed.) (1978), *Studies in the Organization of Conversational Interaction.* New York: Academic Press. Sudnow, David (ed.) (1972), *Studies in Social Interaction.* New York: Free Press.	Citation: (ATKINSON-J*-19*-CONVERSATION-ANAL* OR ATKINSON-J*-19*- STRUCTURES-SOCIAL* OR ATKINSON-J*-19*-STUDIES-CONVERSATI* OR SCHENKEIN-J-1978-STUDIES-ORG-CONVERSA* OR SUDNOW-D-1972- STUDIES-SOCIAL-INTE*)	(conversation analysis) or (turn-taking) or (turntaking) or (Konversationsanalyse)

Sources constitutive to the methods	SSCI-Search-Strategy	Keywords
Content Analysis: Berelson, Bernhard (1952), *Content Analysis in Communication Research*. New York: Hafner Holsti, Ole R. (1969), *Content Analysis for the Social Sciences and Humanities*. Reading, MA: Addison-Wesley.	Citation: (BERELSON-B-19*-CONTENT-ANAL-COMMUN* OR BERELSON-B-19*-ANAL- COMMUNICATION-C* OR BERELSON-B-19*-COMMUNICATION-RES* OR HOLSTI-O*-19*-CONTENT-ANAL-S* OR HOLSTI-O*-19*-CONTENT-ANAL- HUM* OR HOLSTI-O*-19*-ANAL-COMMUNICATION-C*)	(Inhaltsanalyse) or (Content Analysis) resp.: (Inhaltsanalyse or Content Analysis) near (quantitati*) [für WISO Soz.Wiss.] (Inhaltsanalyse or Content Analysis) and (quantitati*) [für alle andern Datenbanken]
Qualitative Content Analysis: Mayring, Philip (1988), *Qualitative Inhaltsanalyse. Grundlagen und Techniken*. Weinheim: Deutscher Studienverlag.	Citation: (MAYRING-P*-19* QUALITATIV*-INHAL* OR MAYRING-P*-19*- EINFUHRUNG-QUALITAT*)	((Inhaltsanalyse) or (Content Analysis)) near (qualitati*) [for WISO-Soz.Wiss.] ((Inhaltsanalyse) or (Content Analysis)) and (qualitati*) [für other databases]
Narrative Semiotics: Greimas, Algirdas Julien (1983), *Structural Semantics. An Attempt at a Method*. Lincoln: University of Nebraska Press. [Orig.: (1966) *Sémantique structurale: Recherche de méthode*. Paris: Larousse.]	Citation: (GREIMAS-AJ-19*- SEMANTIQUE-STRUCTURA OR GREIMAS-AJ-19*- STRUCTURAL-SEMANTICS OR GREIMAS-A*-1971-STRUKTURALE-SEMANTIK*)	(Narrative Semiotics) or (Structural Semantics) or (Sémantique structurale)
SYMLOG Bales, Robert F. and Cohen, Stephan P. (1979), *Symlog: A System for the Multiple Level Observation of Groups*. New York: The Free Press. Schneider, Johannes F. (ed.) (1989) *Inhaltsanalyse alltagssprachlicher Beschreibungen sozialer Interaktionen. Beiträge zur SYMLOG-Kodierung von Texten*. Saarbrücken-Scheidt: Dadder.	Citation: (BALES-RF-19*-SYMLOG* OR BALES-RF-1979-SYSTEM-MULTIPLE-LEVE OR SCHNEIDER-JF-1990-INHALTSANALYSE-ALLTA)	(SYMLOG) and ((Textanalyse) or (Text Analysis) (Inhaltsanalyse) or (Content Analysis))

Sources constitutive to the methods	SSCI-Search-Strategy	Keywords
Objective Hermeneutics: Oevermann, Ulrich, Allert, Tilman, Konau, Elisabeth and Krambeck, Jürgen (1979) 'Die Methodologie einer "objektiven Hermeneutik" und ihre allgemeine forschungslogische Bedeutung in den Sozialwissenschaften', in Hans-Georg Soeffner (ed.), *Interpretative Verfahren in den Sozial- und Textwissenschaften.* Stuttgart: Metzler, pp. 352-434.	Citation: (OEVERMANN-U-1979-INTERPRETATIVE-VERFA* OR OEVERMANN-U-1979-METHODOLOGIE-OBJEKTI*)	(Objektive Hermeneutik) or (Sequenzanalyse) or (Objective Hermeneutics)
Functional Pragmatics: Brünner, Gisela and Graefen, Gabriele (eds) (1994a) *Texte und Diskurse. Methoden und Forschungsergebnisse der Funktionalen Pragmatik.* Opladen: Westdeutscher Verlag. Ehlich, Konrad and Rehbein, Jochen (1986) *Muster und Institution. Untersuchungen zur schulischen Kommunikation.* Tübingen: Gunter Narr. Wunderlich, Dieter (ed.) (1972) *Linguistische Pragmatik.* Frankfurt am Main: Athenäum. Rehbein, Jochen (1977) *Komplexes Handeln. Elemente zur Handlungstheorie der Sprache.* Stuttgart: Metzler.	Citation: (EHLICH-K-1986-MUSTER-I-UNTERSUCHUN OR WUNDERLICH-D-1975- LINGUISTISCHE-PRAGMA-P11 OR REHBEIN-J-1977-KOMPLEXES-HANDELN- EL)	(Funktionale Pragmatik) or (linguistische Musteranalyse) or (das sprachliche Muster) or (sprachliche Prozeduren) or (linguistic procedures)
Critical Discourse Analysis (Fairclough): Fairclough, Norman (1989) *Language and Power.* London: Longman. Fairclough, Norman (1992a) *Discourse and Social Change.* Cambridge: Polity Press.	Citation: (FAIRCLOUGH-N*-19*-LANGUAGE-POWER* OR FAIRCLOUGH-N-1989-ANGUAGE-POWER OR FAIRCLOUGH-N-1989-LINGUAGE-POWER OR FAIRCLOUGH-N*-19*-DISCOURSE-SOC*)	[overall for CDA:] (critical discourse analysis) or (Kritische Diskursanalyse) [for Fairclough:] ((critical discourse analysis) or (Kritische Diskursanalyse)) and (Fairclough)
Critical Discourse Analysis (Wodak): Wodak, Ruth, Nowak, Peter, Pelikan, Johanna, Gruber, Helmut, de Cillia, Rudolf and Mitten, Richard (1990) *'Wir sind alle unschuldige Täter!' Diskurshistorische Studien zum Nachkriegsantisemitismus.* Frankfurt: Suhrkamp. Matouschek, Bernd, Wodak, Ruth and Januschek, Franz (1995) *Notwendige Maßnahmen gegen Fremde? Genese und Formen von rassistischen Diskursen der Differenz.* Wien: Passagen.	Citation: (WODAK-R-1990-DISKURSHIST*-S* OR WODAK-R-1990-SIND-ALLE-UNSCHU* OR WODAK-R-1990-WIR-SIND-ALL*-UNS* OR WODAK-R-1990-WIR-SIND-UNSCHULDIGE* OR WODAK-R-19*-DISCOURSE-SOC*)	(diskurshistorische Methode) or (Sozio-Psycholinguistische Theorie der Textplanung) or (SPTT)

BIBLIOGRAPHY

Abraham, Werner (ed.) (1982) *Satzglieder im Deutschen*. Tübingen: Narr.

Agar, Michael (1986) *Speaking of Ethnography*. Qualitative Research Methods Series No. 2. London: Sage.

Alexander, Jeffrey (ed.) (1987) *The Micro-Macro Link*. Berkeley: University of California Press.

Althusser, Louis (1971) *Lenin and Philosophy and Other Essays*. London: New Left Books.

Altmann, Gabriel (1996) 'The nature of linguistic units', *Journal of Quantitative Linguistics*, 3 (1): 1–7.

Altmann, Hans (ed.) (1988) *Intonationsforschung*. Tübingen: Niemeyer.

Ammon, U., Dittmar, N. and Mattheier, K.J. (eds) (1987/1988) *Sociolinguistics*. An International Handbook of the Science of Language and Society, Vols. 1/2. Berlin: de Gruyter.

Arbeitskreis Qualitative Sozialforschung (eds) (1994) *Verführung zum qualitativen Forschen*. Wien: WUV-Universitätsverlag.

Argyris, Chris (1995) 'Interventionen und Führungseffizienz', in Alfred Kieser, Gerhard Reber and Rudolf Wunderer (eds), *Handwörterbuch der Führung*, 2nd edn. Stuttgart: Poeschel, pp. 1253–72.

Atkinson, J. Maxwell (1985) 'Refusing invited applause: preliminary observations from a case study of charismatic oratory', in Teun A. van Dijk (ed.), *Handbook of Discourse Analysis*, Vol. 3: Discourse and Dialogue. London: Academic Press, pp. 161–81.

Atkinson, J. Maxwell and Drew, Paul (1979) *Order in Court. The Organization of Verbal Interaction in Judicial Settings*. London: The MacMillan Press.

Atkinson, J. Maxwell and Heritage, John C. (eds) (1984) *Structures of Social Action Studies in Conversation Analysis*. Cambridge: Cambridge University Press.

Atkinson, Paul and Coffey, Amanda (1997), 'Analysing documentary realities', in David Silverman (ed.), *Qualitative Research*. London: Sage, pp. 45–62.

Atkinson, Paul and Hammersley, Martyn (1994) 'Ethnography and participant observation', in Norman K. Denzin and Yvonna S. Lincoln (eds), *Handbook of Qualitative Research*. Thousand Oak, CA: Sage, pp. 248–61.

Austin, John L. (1962) *How to Do Things with Words*. Oxford. Clarendon Press.

Baecker, Dirk (1992) 'Die Unterscheidung zwischen Kommunikation und Bewußtsein', in Wolfgang Krohn and Günter Küppers (eds), *Emergenz: Die Entstehung von Ordnung, Organisation und Bedeutung*. Frankfurt: Suhrkamp, pp. 217–68.

Baecker, Dirk (ed.) (1993a) *Kalkül der Form*. Frankfurt: Suhrkamp.

Baecker, Dirk (ed.) (1993b) *Probleme der Form*. Frankfurt: Suhrkamp.

Bakhtin, Mikhail M. (1986) *Speech Genres and Other Late Essays*. Austin: University of Texas Press.

Bales, Robert F. (1950) *Interaction Process Analysis*. Cambridge: Addison-Wesley.

Bales, Robert F. (1980) *Symlog Case Study Kit*. New York: The Free Press.

Bales, Robert F. and Cohen, Stephan P. (1979) *Symlog: A System for the Multiple Level*

Observation of Groups. New York: The Free Press.

Bardmann, Theodor (1994) *Wenn aus Arbeit Abfall wird*. Frankfurt: Suhrkamp.

Barton, Allen A. and Lazarsfeld, Paul F. (1979) 'Einige Funktionen von qualitativer Analyse in der Sozialforschung', in Christel Hopf and Elmar Weingarten (eds), *Qualitative Sozialforschung*. Stuttgart: Klett, pp. 41–89.

Baszanger, Isabelle and Dodier, Nicolas (1997), 'Ethnography: relating the part to the whole', in David Silverman (ed.), *Qualitative Research*. London: Sage, 8–23.

Beaugrande, Robert de (1996) *Foundations of a New Theory of Discourse*. London: Longman (in print).

Beaugrande, Robert de and Dressler, Wolfgang U. (1981) *Einführung in die Textlinguistik*. Tübingen: Niemeyer.

Becker-Beck, Ulrich (1989) 'Freie Personenbeschreibung als interaktionsdiagnostische Methode', in Johannes F. Schneider (ed.), *Inhaltsanalyse alltagssprachlicher Beschreibungen sozialer Interaktionen. Beiträge zur SYMLOG-Kodierung von Texten*. Saarbrücken-Scheidt: Dadder, pp. 109–39.

Becker-Mrotzek, Michael (1994) 'Schreiben als Handlung. Das Verfassen von Bedienungsanleitungen', in Gisela Brünner and Gabriele Graefen (eds), *Texte und Diskurse*. Opladen: Westdeutscher Verlag, pp. 158–75.

Bensman, Joseph and Gerver, Israel (1973) 'Vergehen und Bestrafung in der Fabrik: Die Funktion abweichenden Verhaltens für die Aufrechterhaltung des Sozialsystems', in Heinz Steinert (ed.), *Symbolische Interaktion*. Stuttgart: Klett, pp. 126–38.

Berelson, Bernhard (1952) *Content Analysis in Communication Research*. New York: Hafner.

Berger, Peter and Luckmann, Thomas (1967) *The Social Construction of Reality*. New York: Doubleday.

Bergmann, Jörg R. (1981) 'Ethnomethodologische Konversationsanalyse', in Peter Schröder and Hugo Steger (eds), Dialogforschung. Jahrbuch 1980 des Instituts für Deutsche Sprache. Düsseldorf: Schwann, pp. 9–51.

Bergmann, Jörg R. (1994) 'Ethnomethodologische Konversationsanalyse', in Gerd Fritz and Franz Hundsnurscher (eds), *Handbuch der Dialoganalyse*. Tübingen: Niemeyer, pp. 3–16.

Bernstein, Basil (1990) *The Structure of Pedagogic Discourse: Class, Codes and Control*. London: Routledge.

Bilmes, Jack (1993) 'Ethnomethodology, culture and implicature. Toward an empirical pragmatics', *Pragmatics* 3 (4): 387–411.

Blom, Jan-Petter and Gumperz, John J. (1972): 'Social meaning in linguistic structure. code-switching in Norway', in John J. Gumperz and Dell Hymes (eds), *Directions in Sociolinguistics. The Ethnography of Communication*. New York: Rinehart and Winston 407–439

Bloor, Michael (1978) 'On the analysis of observational data: a discussion of the worth and uses of inductive techniques and respondent validation', in *Sociology* 12 (3), pp. 545–557.

Blum-Kulka, Shoshana (1990) 'You don't touch lettuce with your fingers', in *Journal of Pragmatics* 14: 259–288.

Böhm, Andreas (1994) 'Grounded Theory – Wie aus Texten Modelle und Theorie gemacht werden', in Andreas Böhm, Andreas Mengel and Thomas Muhr (eds): *Texte verstehen. Konzepte, Methoden, Werkzeuge. Schriften zur Informationswissenschaft* 14. Konstanz: Universitätsverlag, pp. 121–140.

Bohnsack, Ralf (1991) *Rekonstruktive Sozialforschung. Einführung in Methodologie und Praxis qualitativer Forschung*. Opladen: Leske.

Bortz, Jürgen and Döring, Nicola (1995) *Forschungsmethoden und Evaluation*. 2nd edn.

Berlin: Springer.

Bourdieu, Pierre (1987) [1979] *Die feinen Unterschiede*. Kritik der gesellschaftlichen Urteilskraft. Frankfurt: Suhrkamp [orig.: La distinction. Critique social du jugement. Paris: Les éditions de minuit].

Brown, M.H. and Kreps, G. L. (1993) 'Narrative analysis and organizational development', in S.L. Henderson and G.L. Kreps (eds), *Qualitative Research: Applications in Organizational Communication*. Cresskill, NJ: Hampton Press, pp. 47–62.

Brünner, Gisela (1994) 'Würden Sie von diesem Mann einen Gebrauchtwagen kaufen?' Interaktive Anforderungen und Selbstdarstellung in Verkaufsgesprächen, in Gisela Brünner and Gabriele Graefen (eds), *Texte und Diskurse*. Opladen: Westdeutscher Verlag, pp. 328–50.

Brünner, Gisela and Becker-Mrotzek, Michael (1992) 'Angewandte Gesprächsforschung: Ziele–Methoden–Probleme', in Reinhard Fiehler and Wolfgang Sucharowski (eds), Kommunikationsberatung und Kommunikationstraining. Opladen: Westdeutscher Verlag, pp. 12–23.

Brünner, Gisela and Graefen, Gabriele (eds) (1994a) *Texte und Diskurse. Methoden und Forschungsergebnisse der Funktionalen Pragmatik*. Opladen: Westdeutscher Verlag.

Brünner, Gisela and Graefen, Gabriele (1994b): 'Einleitung: Zur Konzeption der Funktionalen Pragmatik', in Gisela Brünner and Gabriele Graefen (eds), Texte und Diskurse. Opladen: Westdeutscher Verlag, pp. 7–21.

Bühler, Karl (1965) [1934] *Sprachtheorie. Die Darstellungsfunktion der Sprache*. Vol. 2, Stuttgart: Fischer.

Burgoyne, J.G. (1994) 'Stakeholder Analysis', in C. Cassell and G. Symon (eds), *Qualitative Methodes in Organizational Research*. London: Sage, pp. 187–207.

Chomsky, Noam (1965) *Aspects of the Theory of Syntax*. Cambridge: MIT Press.

Cicourel, Aaron V. (1964) *Method and Measurement in Sociology*. Glencoe: The Free Press.

Cicourel, Aaron V. (1992) 'The interpenetration of communicative contexts: examples from medical encounters', in Alexander Duranti and Charles Goodwin (eds), *Rethinking Context*. Cambridge: Cambridge University Press, pp. 291–311.

Cinque, Gugliemo (1993): 'A null theory of phrase and compound stress', *Linguistic Inquiry*, 24: 239–97.

Clark, Herbert H. (1985) 'Language use and language users', in Gardner Lindzey and Elliot Aronson (eds), *The Handbook of Social Psychology*. 3rd edn. Vol. 2: Special Fields and Applications. Research Methods. Reading: Addison-Wesley, pp. 179–231.

Coffey, Amanda, Holbrook, Beverley and Atkinson, Paul (1996): 'Qualitative data analysis: technologies and representations', *Sociological Research Online*, http://www.soc.surrey.ac.uk/socresonline, Vol. 1, No. 1.

Cook, Thomas D. (1993) 'A quasi-sampling theory of the generalization of causal relationships', *New Directions for Program Evaluation*, 57: 39–82.

Corbin, Juliet and Strauss, Anselm (1990) 'Grounded theory research: procedures, canons, and evaluative criteria', *Qualitative Sociology*, 13: 3–21.

Coulmas, Florian (1979) 'Einleitung: Sprache und Kultur', in Dell Hymes, *Soziolinguistik*. Frankfurt: Suhrkamp, pp. 7–25.

Coulmas, Florian (ed.) (1997) *The Handbook of Sociolinguistics*. Oxford: Blackwell.

Danielson, W.A. and Lasorsa, D.L. (1997) 'Perceptions of social change: 100 years of front-page content in the *New York Times* and the *Los Angeles Times*', in C.W. Roberts (ed.), *Text Analysis for the Social Sciences*. Mahwah, NJ: Lawrence Erlbaum, pp. 103–115.

de Sola Pool, Ithiel (ed.) (1959) *Trends in Content Analysis*. Urbana: University of

Illinois Press.

Demirovic, Alex (1992) 'Vom Vorurteil zum Neorassismus': Das Objekt 'Rassismus' in Ideologiekritik und Ideologietheorie, in Institut für Sozialforschung (eds), *Aspekte der Fremdenfeindlichkeit.* Frankfurt: Campus, pp. 21–54.

Denzin, Norman (1970) *The Research Act in Sociology.* London: Butterworth.

Denzin, Norman K. and Lincoln, Yvonna S. (eds) (1994) *Handbook of Qualitative Research.* Thousand Oaks: Sage.

Devereux, G. (1976) *Dreams in Greek Tragedy. An Ethno-Psycho-Analytical Study.* Oxford: Blackwell

Dewey, John (1937) *Logic. The Theory of Inquiry.* New York: Wiley.

Dressler, Wolfgang U. (1989) *Semiotische Parameter einer textlinguistischen Natürlichkeitstheorie.* Wien: Österreichische Akademie der Wissenschaften.

Drew, Paul and Heritage, John (eds) (1992) *Talk at Work. Interaction in Institutional Settings.* Cambridge: Cambridge University Press.

Duranti, Allessandro and Goodwin, Charles (eds) (1992) *Rethinking Context. Language as an Interactive Phenomenon.* Cambridge: Cambridge University Press.

Eco, Umberto (1991) *Einführung in die Semiotik.* 7th edn.. München: Fink UTB.

Ehlich, Konrad (1972) 'Thesen zur Sprechakttheorie', in Dieter Wunderlich (ed.), *Linguistische Pragmatik.* Frankfurt: Athenäum, pp. 122–126.

Ehlich, Konrad (1979) *Verwendungen der Deixis beim sprachlichen Handeln.* Frankfurt: Lang.

Ehlich, Konrad (ed.) (1984) *Erzählen in der Schule.* Tübingen: Narr.

Ehlich, Konrad (1986/1996) 'Funktional-pragmatische Kommunikationsanalyse': Ziele und Verfahren, in Ludger Hoffmann (ed.), *Sprachwissenschaft. Ein Reader.* Berlin: de Gruyter.

Ehlich, Konrad (1991) 'Funktional-pragmatische Kommunikationsanalyse. Ziele und Verfahren', in Dieter Flader (ed.), *Verbale Interaktion. Studien zur Empirie und Methodologie der Pragmatik.* Stuttgart: Metzler, pp. 127–43.

Ehlich, Konrad (1993) 'Diskursanalyse', in Helmut Glück (1993), *Metzler-Lexikon Sprache.* Stuttgart: Metzler, pp. 145–6.

Ehlich, Konrad (ed.) (1994) *Diskursanalyse in Europa.* Frankfurt: Lang.

Ehlich, Konrad and Rehbein, Jochen (1972) 'Zur Konstitution pragmatischer Einheiten in einer Institution: Das Speiserestaurant' in D. Wunderlich (ed.), *Linguistische Pragmatik.* Frankfurt: Athenäum, pp. 209–54.

Ehlich, Konrad and Rehbein, Jochen (1976) 'Halbinterpretative Arbeitstranskriptionen (HIAT)', *Linguistische Berichte,* 45: 21–41.

Ehlich, Konrad and Rehbein, Jochen (1979) 'Sprachliche Handlungsmuster', in Hans-Georg Soeffner (ed.), *Interpretative Verfahren in den Sozial- und Textwissenschaften.* Stuttgart: Metzler, pp. 243–74.

Ehlich, Konrad and Rehbein, Jochen (1986) *Muster und Institution. Untersuchungen zur schulischen Kommunikation.* Tübingen: Narr.

Eisler, Rudolf (ed.) (1927) *Wörterbuch der philosophischen Begriffe.* Berlin: Mittler.

Fairclough, Norman (1989) *Language and power.* London: Longman.

Fairclough, Norman (1992a) *Discourse and Social Change.* Cambridge: Polity Press.

Fairclough, Norman (1992b) 'Discourse and text: linguistic and intertextual analysis within discourse analysis', *Discourse & Society,* 3: 193–219.

Fairclough, Norman (1993) 'Critical discourse analysis and the marketization of public discourse: the universities', *Discourse & Society,* 4 (2): 133–68.

Fairclough, Norman (1994) 'Conversationalization of public discourse and the authority of the consumer', in K. Russel, N. Whiteley and N. Abercrombie (eds), *The Authority of the Consumer.* London: Routledge, pp. 253–68.

Fairclough, Norman (1995a) *Media Discourse*. London and New York: Arnold.

Fairclough, Norman (1995b) *Critical Discourse Analysis. The Critical Study of Language*. London and New York: Longman.

Fairclough, Norman (1996) 'A reply to Henry Widdowson's discourse analysis: a critical view', *Language & Literature*, 5: 1–8.

Fairclough, Norman and Wodak, Ruth (1997) 'Critical discourse analysis: an overview', in Teun van Dijk (ed.), *Discourse and Interaction*. London: Sage, pp. 67–97.

Fetterman, David M. (1989) *Ethnography Step by Step*. Newbury Park, CA: Sage.

Fiehler, Reinhard and Sucharowski, Wolfgang (eds) (1992) *Kommunikationsberatung und Kommunikationstraining. Anwendungsfelder der Diskursforschung*. Opladen: Westdeutscher Verlag.

Fielding, Nigel G. and Fielding, Jane L. (1986) *Linking Data*. Qualitative Research Methods Series No. 4. London: Sage.

Fiol, C. Marlene (1990) 'Narrative semiotics: theory, procedure and illustration', in Anne Sigismund Huff (ed.), *Mapping Strategic Thought*, Chichester: Wiley, pp. 377–402.

Firestone, W.A. (1993) 'Alternative arguments for generalizing from data as applied to qualitative research', *Educational Researcher*, 22: 16–23.

Firth, Alan (1995) 'Ethnomethodology', in J. Verschueren, Jan-Ola Östman and J. Blommaert (eds), *Handbook of Pragmatics. Manual*. Amsterdam: Benjamins, pp. 269–78.

Fitch, Kristine L. and Philipsen, Gerry (1995) 'Ethnography of speaking', in J. Verschueren, Jan-Ola Östman and J. Blommaert (eds), *Handbook of Pragmatics. Manual*. Amsterdam: Benjamins, pp. 263–9.

Flader, Dieter (eds) (1991) *Verbale Interaktion. Studien zur Empirie und Methodologie der Pragmatik*. Stuttgart: Metzler.

Flader, Dieter and von Trotha, Thilo (1988) 'Über den geheimen Positivismus und andere Eigentümlichkeiten der ethnomethodologischen Konversationsanalyse', *Zeitschrift für Sprachwissenschaft*, 7 (1): 92–115.

Flick, Uwe, Kardorff, Ernst v., Keupp, Heiner, Rosenstiel, Lutz v. and Wolff, Stephan (eds) (1991) *Handbuch Qualitative Sozialforschung*. München: Psychologie-Verlags-Union.

Forster, Nick (1994) 'The analysis of company documentation', in C. Cassell and G. Symon (eds), *Qualitative Methods in Organizational Research*. London: Sage, pp. 147–66.

Foucault, Michel (1972) *The Archaeology of Knowledge and the Discourse on Language*, trans. A.M. Sheridan. London: Tavistock.

Foucault, Michel (1981) *History of Sexuality*, Vol. I. Harmondsworth: Penguin.

Foucault, Michel (1990) [1972] *Archäologie des Wissens*. Frankfurt: Fischer. [English: *The Archaeology of Knowledge and the Discourse on Language*. New York: Random House.]

Foucault, Michel (1993) [1971] *Die Ordnung des Diskurses*. Frankfurt: Fischer. [Orig.: *L'ordre du discours*. Paris: Gallimard.]

Fowler, Roger (1991) 'Critical linguistics', in Kirsten Malmkjaer (ed.), *The Linguistic Encyclopedia*. London: Routledge, pp. 89–93.

Fowler, Roger, Hodge, Bob, Kress, Gunther and Trew, Tony (eds) (1979) *Language and Control*. London: Routledge & Kegan Paul.

Friedrich, Georg (1994) 'Zur Funktionalen Pragmatik der Kommunikation im Unterricht sehgeschädigter Schüler', in G. Brünner and G. Graefen (eds), *Texte und Diskurse*. Opladen: Westdeutscher Verlag, pp. 374–85.

Fritz, Gerd and Hundsnurscher, Franz (eds) (1994) *Handbuch der Dialoganalyse*. Tübingen: Niemeyer.

Garfield, Eugene (1991a) 'How to use the Social Sciences Citation Index® (SSCI®)', in *SSCI® Social Sciences Index® (ed.): Guide and Lists of Source Publications*. Philadelphia, PA: Institute for Scientific Information Inc.®, pp. 45–52.

Garfield, Eugene (1991b) 'The Citation Index as a search tool', in *SSCI® Social Sciences Index® (ed.): Guide and Lists of Source Publications*. Philadelphia, PA: Institute for Scientific Information Inc.®, pp. 24–44.

Garfinkel, Harold (1952) *The perception of the other: A study in social order*. Ph.D. dissertation. Harvard University, MA.

Garfinkel, Harold (1967) *Studies in Ethnomethodology*. Englewood Cliffs, NJ: Prentice Hall.

Garfinkel, Harold (1972) 'Studies of the routine grounds of everyday activities', in D. Sudnow (ed.), *Studies in Social Interaction*. New York: The Free Press, pp. 1–30.

Garfinkel, Harold (1974) 'On the origins of the term "ethnomethodology"', in R. Turner (ed.), *Ethnomethodology*. Harmondsworth: Penguin, pp. 15–18.

Garz, Detlef and Kraimer, Klaus (eds) (1994) *Die Welt als Text. Theorie, Kritik und Praxis der objektiven Hermeneutik*. Frankfurt: Suhrkamp.

Geertz, Clifford (1973) *The Interpretation of Cultures*. New York: Basic Books.

Geertz, Clifford (1987) *Dichte Beschreibung. Beiträge zum Verstehen kultureller Systeme*. Frankfurt: Suhrkamp.

Gerbner, George, Holsti, Ole, Krippendorff, Klaus, Paisley, William J. and Stone, Philip J. (eds) (1969) *The Analysis of Communication Content. Development in Scientific Theories and Computer Techniques*. New York: Wiley.

Giles, Howard and Robinson, William P. (eds) (1990) *Handbook of Language and Social Psychology*. New York: Wiley.

Girnth, Heiko (1996) 'Texte im politischen Diskurs. Muttersprache', 106 (1): 66–80.

Glaser, Barney G. (1978) *Theoretical Sensitivity*. Mill Valley, CA: Sociology Press.

Glaser, Barney G. (1992) *Emergence vs. Forcing. Advances in the Methodology of Grounded Theory*. Mill Valley, CA: Sociology Press.

Glaser, Barney G. and Strauss, Anselm L. (1965) *Awareness of Dying*. Chicago, IL: Aldine.

Glaser, Barney G. and Strauss, Anselm L. (1967) *The Discovery of Grounded Theory. Strategies for Qualitative Research*. Chicago, IL: Aldine.

Glaser, Barney G. and Strauss, Anselm L. (1968) *Time for Dying*. Chicago, IL: Aldine.

Glück, Helmut (1993) *Metzler-Lexikon Sprache*. Stuttgart: Metzler.

Goffman, Erving (1974) *Frame Analysis*. New York: Harper & Row.

Goffman, Erving (1981) *Forms of Talk*. Oxford: Blackwell.

Goode, W.J. and Hatt, P.K. (1952) *Methods in Social Research*. New York: McGraw-Hill.

Gramsci, Antonio (1971) *Selections from the Prison Notebooks*. London: Lawrence & Wishart.

Gramsci, Antonio (1983) *Marxismus und Kultur. Ideologie, Alltag, Literatur*. Hamburg: VSA.

Greimas, Algirdas J. (1974) 'Die Isotopie der Rede', in W. Kallmeyer, W. Klein, R. Meyer-Hermann, K. Netzer and H.-J. Siebert (eds), *Lektürekolleg zur Textlinguistik*. Frankfurt: Athenäum, pp. 126–52.

Greimas, Algirdas J. (1983) [1966] *Structural Semantics. An Attempt at a Method*. Lincoln: University of Nebraska Press. [Orig.: *Sémantique structurale. Recherche de méthode*. Paris: Larousse.]

Greimas, Algirdas J. (1987) *On Meaning. Selected Writings in Semiotic Theory*. London: Frances Pinter.

Greimas, Algirdas J. and Rastier, Francois (1968) The Interaction of Semiotic Constraints. Yale French Studies: Game, Play and Literature. New Haven, CT: Eastern Press.

Grice, H. Paul (1975) 'Logic and conversation', in P. Cole and J.L. Morgan (eds), *Syntax and Semantics*, Vol. 3: Speech Acts. New York: Academic Press, pp. 41–58.

Gruber, Helmut (1996) *Streitgespräche. Zur Pragmatik einer Diskursform.* Opladen: Westdeutscher Verlag.

Gülich, Elisabeth and Kotschi, Thomas (1987) 'Reformulierungshandlungen als Mittel der Textkonstitution. Untersuchungen zu französischen Texten aus mündlicher Kommunikation', in W. Motsch (ed.), *Satz, Text, sprachliche Handlung.* Berlin: Akademie Verlag, pp. 199–261.

Gülich, Elisabeth and Quasthoff, Uta M. (1985) 'Narrative analysis', in Teun A. van Dijk (ed.), *Handbook of Discourse Analysis*, Vol. 2: Dimensions of Discourse. London: Academic Press, pp. 169–97.

Gumperz, John J. (1982) *Discourse Strategies.* Cambridge: Cambridge University Press.

Gumperz, John J. and Levinson, Stephen, C. (eds) (1996) *Rethinking Linguistic Relativity.* Cambridge: Cambridge University Press.

Gumperz, John J. and Hymes, Dell (eds) (1964) 'The Ethnography of Communication', *American Anthropologist*, 66 (6).

Gumperz, John J. and Hymes, Dell (eds) (1972) *Directions in Sociolinguistics. The Ethnography of Communication.* New York: Holt, Rinehart and Winston.

Habermas, Jürgen (1970) *Zur Logik der Sozialwissenschaften.* Frankfurt: Suhrkamp.

Habermas, Jürgen (1971) *Erkenntnis und Interesse.* Frankfurt: Suhrkamp.

Hakim, C. (1992) *Research Design. Strategies and Choices in the Design of Social Research.* London and New York: Routledge, pp. 61–74.

Halliday, Michael A.K. (1970) 'Language structure and language function', in John Lyons (ed.), *New Horizons in Linguistics.* Harmondsworth: Penguin, pp. 140–65.

Halliday, Michael A.K. (1973) *Explorations in the Functions of Language.* London: Arnold.

Halliday, Michael A.K. (1978) *Language as Social Semiotic.* London: Arnold.

Halliday, Michael A.K. (1985) *An Introduction to Functional Grammar,* 2nd edn 1994. London: Arnold.

Halliday, Michael A.K. and Hasan, Raquiah (1976) *Cohesion in English.* London: Arnold.

Hammersley, Martyn (1992) *What's Wrong with Ethnography. Methodological Explanations.* London: Routledge.

Hammersley, Martyn and Atkinson, Paul (1995) *Ethnography. Principles in Practice,* 2nd edn. London: Routledge.

Hare, A. Paul and Naveh, David (1986) 'Conformity and creativity: Camp David, 1978', *Small-Group-Behavior*, 17 (3): 243–68.

Hartley, J.F. (1994) 'Case studies in organizational research', in C. Caselle and G. Symon (eds), *Qualitative Methods in Organizational Research.* London: Sage, pp. 208–29.

Heckmann, Friedrich (1992) 'Interpretationsregeln zur Auswertung qualitativer Interviews und sozialwissenschaftlich relevanter "Texte". Anwendungen der Hermeneutik für die empirische Sozialforschung', in Jürgen H. P. Hoffmeyer-Zlotnik (ed.), *Analyse verbaler Daten.* Opladen: Westdeutscher Verlag, pp. 142–67.

Heider, Fritz (1958) *The Psychology of Interpersonal Relations.* New York: Wiley.

Heinemann, Wolfang and Viehweger, Dieter (1991) *Textlinguistik: eine Einführung.* Tübingen: Niemeyer.

Heinze, Thomas (1987) *Qualitative Sozialforschung: Erfahrungen, Probleme und Perspektiven.* Opladen: Westdeutscher Verlag.

Helm, June (ed.) (1967) 'Essays on the verbal and visual arts'. Proceedings of the 1966 Annual Spring Meeting of the American Ethnological Society. Seattle: University of Washington Press for the American Ethnological Society.

Hempel, Carl G. (1952) *Fundamentals in Concept Formation in Empirical Science*. Chicago, IL: University of Chicago Press.

Heritage, John (1984) *Garfinkel and Ethnomethodology*. Cambridge: Polity Press.

Heritage, John (1985) 'Analysing news interviews: aspects of the production of talk for an overhearing audience', in Teun A. van Dijk (ed.), *Handbook of Discourse Analysis*, Vol. 3: Discourse and Dialogue. London: Academic Press, pp. 95–131.

Herkner, Werner (1974) 'Inhaltsanalyse', in Jürgen von Koolwijk and Maria Wieken-Mayser (eds), *Techniken der empirischen Sozialforschung*, München: Oldenbourg, vol. 3. pp.158–91.

Herkner, Werner (eds) (1980) *Attribution. Psychologie der Kausalität*. Bern: Huber.

Hildenbrand, Bruno and Jahn, Walter (1988) '"Gemeinsames Erzählen" und Prozesse der Wirklichkeitskonstruktion in familiengeschichtlichen Gesprächen', *Zeitschrift für Soziologie*, 17: 203–17.

Hoefert, Hans Wolfgang and Klotter, Christoph (eds) (1994) *Neue Wege der Psychologie. Eine Wissenschaft in der Veränderung*. Heidelberg: Asanger.

Hoffmann, Ludger (ed.) (1996) *Sprachwissenschaft. Ein Reader*. Berlin: de Gruyter.

Hoffmeyer-Zlotnik, Jürgen H.P. (ed.) (1992) *Analyse verbaler Daten*. Opladen: Westdeutscher Verlag.

Höhle, Tilman (1982) 'Explikationen für "normale Betonung" und "normale Wortstellung"', in W. Abraham (ed.), *Satzglieder im Deutschen*. Tübingen: Narr, pp. 75–153.

Holstein, James A. and Gubrium, Jaber F. (1994) 'Phenomenology, ethnomethodology, and interpretive practice', in Norman K. Denzin and Yvonna S. Lincoln (eds), *Handbook of Qualitative Research*. Thousand Oak, CA: Sage, pp. 262–72.

Holsti, Ole R. (1968) 'Content analysis', in G. Lindzey and E. Aronson (eds), *The Handbook of Social Psychology*, 2nd edn, Vol. 2: Research Methods. Reading: Addison-Wesley, pp. 596–692.

Holsti, Ole R. (1969) *Content Analysis for the Social Sciences and Humanities*. Reading: Addison-Wesley.

Hopf, Christel (1979) 'Soziologie und qualitative Sozialforschung', in Ch. Hopf and E. Weingarten (eds), *Qualitative Sozialforschung*. Stuttgart: Klett-Cotta, pp. 11–37.

Huff, Anne Sigismund (ed.) (1990) *Mapping Strategic Thought*. Chichester: Wiley.

Hughes, Everett C. (1993) *The Sociological Eye*, 2nd edn. New Brunswick, NJ: Transaction Books.

Hutchby, Ian and Drew, Paul (1995) 'Conversation analysis', in J. Verschueren, J.-O. Östman and J. Blommaert (eds), *Handbook of Pragmatics. Manual*. Amsterdam: Benjamins, pp. 182–9.

Hymes, Dell (1962), 'The ethnography of speaking', in Thomas Gladwin and William C. Sturtevant (eds), *Anthropology and Human Behavior*. Washington, DC: Anthropolological Society of Washington. pp. 13–53.

Hymes, Dell (1970), 'Linguistic method in ethnography', in P. Garvin (ed.), *Method and Theory in Linguistics*. The Hague: Mouton, pp. 249–325.

Hymes, Dell (1971), 'Sociolinguistics and the Ethnography of Speaking', in E. Ardener (ed.), *Social Anthropology and Language*. London: Tavistock.

Hymes, Dell (1972), 'Models of interaction of language and social life', in John J. Gumperz and Dell Hymes (eds), *Directions in Sociolinguistics. The Ethnography of Communication*. New York: Holt, Rinehart and Winston, pp. 35–71.

Hymes, Dell (1974), *Foundations in Sociolinguistics*, Philadelphia: University of Pennsylvania Press.

Hymes, Dell (1976), 'The state of the art in linguistic anthropology', in Anthony F.C. Wallace (ed.), *Perspectives on Anthropology*. Washington: American Anthropological

Association.

Hymes, Dell (1979) *Soziolinguistik. Zur Ethnographie der Kommunikation*, ed. by Florian Coulmas. Frankfurt: Suhrkamp.

Iedema, Richard and Wodak, Ruth (1999) special issue 'Discourse in organizations', *Discourse and Society*, 10 (1).

Iedema, Rick and Wodak, Ruth (1999) 'Introduction: organizational discourses and practices', *Discourse & Society*, 10 (1): 5–20.

Ihwe, Jens (ed.) (1971) *Literaturwissenschaft und Linguistik. Ergebnisse und Perspektiven*. Bad Homburg v. d. H.: Gehlen, pp. 173–212.

Institut für Sozialforschung (eds) (1992) *Aspekte der Fremdenfeindlichkeit*. Frankfurt: Campus.

Jacobs, Joachim (1988) 'Fokus-Hintergrund-Gliederung und Grammatik', in H. Altmann (ed.), *Intonationsforschung*. Tübingen: Niemeyer, pp. 89–134.

Jäger, Siegfried (1993) *Kritische Diskursanalyse. Eine Einführung*. Duisburg: Diss.

Jakobson, Roman (1960) 'Concluding statement: linguistics and poetics', in T.A. Sebeok (ed.), *Style in Language*. Cambridge, MA: John Wiley and MIT Press.

Jefferson, Gail (1972) 'Side sequences', in D. Sudnow (ed.), *Studies in Social Interaction*. New York: The Free Press, pp. 294–338.

Jung, Thomas and Müller-Doohm, Stefan (eds) (1993) *'Wirklichkeit' im Deutungsprozeß. Verstehen in den Kultur- und Sozialwissenschaften*. Frankfurt: Suhrkamp.

Kallmeyer, Werner (1988) 'Konversationsanalytische Beschreibung', in U. Ammon, N. Dittmar and K. Mattheier (eds), *Sociolinguistics*. Berlin and New York: de Gruyter, pp. 1095–108.

Kallmeyer, Werner and Schütze, Fritz (1976) 'Konversationsanalyse', *Studium Linguistik* 1: 1–28.

Kallmeyer, Werner, Klein, Wolfgang, Meyer-Hermann, Reinhard, Netzer, Klaus and Siebert, Hans-Jürgen (eds) (1974) *Lektürekolleg zur Textlinguistik*. Frankfurt: Athenäum.

Kant, Immanuel (1974) [1781] *Kritik der reinen Vernunft*. Frankfurt: Suhrkamp.

Kearny, M.H., Murphy, S., Irwin, K. and Rosenbaum, M. (1995) 'Salvaging self: a grounded theory of pregnancy on crack cocaine', *Nursing Research*, 44: 208–13.

Keat, Russel, Whiteley, Nigel and Abercrombie, Nicholas (eds) (1994) *The Authority of the Consumer*. London: Routledge.

Kelle, Udo (1994) *Empirisch begründete Theoriebildung. Zur Logik und Methodologie interpretativer Sozialforschung*. Weinheim: Deutscher Studienverlag.

Kelley, Harold H. (1967) 'Attribution theory in social psychology', in D. Levine (ed.), *Nebraska Symposium on Motivation*. Lincoln: University of Nebraska Press, pp. 192–238.

Kelly, George A. (1955) 'The Psychology of Personal Constructs' Vol. 1. *A Theory of Personality*. New York: Norton.

Kenny, Anthony (1974) *Wittgenstein*. Frankfurt: Suhrkamp.

Keppler, A. (1994) *Tischgespräche. Über Formen kommunikativer Vergemeinschaftung am Beispiel der Konversation in Familien*. Frankfurt a. M.: Suhrkamp.

Kieser, Alfred, Reber, Gerhard and Wunderer, Rudolf (eds) (1995) *Handwörterbuch der Führung*, 2nd edn. Stuttgart: Poeschel.

Kintsch, Walter and van Dijk, Teun A. (1983) *Strategies of Discourse Comprehension*. New York: Academic Press.

Kleining, Gerhard (1994) 'Qualitativ heuristische Sozialforschung', *Schriften zur Theorie und Praxis*. Hamburg-Harvestehude: Fechner (printed in 2nd edn, 1995).

Kluckhohn, C. (1944) *Navaho Witchcraft*. Boston, MA: Beacon Press.

Knauth, Bettina, Kroner, Wolfgang and Wolff, Stephan (1990/91) 'Konversationsanalyse von Texten', *Angewandte Sozialforschung*, 16 (1–2): 31–43.

Koerfer, Armin (1994) 'Interkulturelle Kommunikation vor Gericht. Verständigungsprobleme beim fremdsprachlichen Handeln in einer kommunikationsintensiven Institution', in G. Brünner and G. Graefen (eds), *Texte und Diskurse*. Opladen: Westdeutscher Verlag, pp. 351–73.

König, Eckhard and Zedler, Peter (eds) (1995) *Bilanz qualitativer Forschung*, Vol. 2: Methoden. Weinheim: Deutscher Studienverlag.

König, Hans-Dieter (ed.) (1996) *Neue Versuche, Becketts Endspiel zu verstehen. Sozialwissenschaftliches Interpretieren nach Adorno*. Frankfurt: Suhrkamp.

König, René (ed.) (1974) *Handbuch der empirischen Sozialforschung*, Vol. 4: Komplexe Forschungsansätze. Stuttgart: Enke.

Koole, Tom and ten Thije, Jan (1994) 'Der interkulturelle Diskurs von Teambesprechungen. Zu einer Pragmatik der Mehrsprachigkeit', in G. Brünner and G. Graefen (eds), *Texte und Diskurse*. Opladen: Westdeutscher Verlag, pp. 412–34.

Koolwijk, Jürgen von and Wieken-Mayser, Maria (eds) (1974) *Techniken der empirischen Sozialforschung*, Vol. 3: München: Oldenbourg.

Kotthoff, Helga (1996) *Spaß verstehen. Zur Pragmatik von konversationellem Humor*. Wien: Habilitationsschrift, Universität Wien.

Kracauer, Siegfried (1952) 'The challenge of qualitative content analysis', *Public Opinion Quarterly*, 16: 631–42.

Kress, Gunther (1993) 'Against arbitrariness: the social production of the sign', *Discourse & Society*, 4 (2): 169–93.

Kress, Gunther and Hodge, Bob (1979) *Language as Ideology*. London: Routledge.

Kress, Gunther and Threadgold, Terry (1988) 'Towards a social theory of genre', *Southern Review*, 21: 215–43.

Kress, Gunther and van Leeuwen, Theo (1996) *Reading Images. The Grammar of Visual Design*. London: Routledge.

Kreutz, Henrik (1988) 'Die Integration von empirischer Forschung, theoretischer Analyse und praktischem Handeln', in Henrik Kreutz (ed.), *Pragmatische Soziologie*. Opladen: Leske and Budrich, pp. 11–32.

Krippendorff, Klaus (1969) 'Models of messages: three prototypes', in G. Gerbner, O. Holsti, K. Krippendorff, W.J. Paisley and P.J. Stone (eds), *The Analysis of Communication Content. Development in Scientific Theories and Computer Techniques*. New York: Wiley, pp. 69–106.

Krippendorff, Klaus (1980) *Content Analysis. An Introduction to its Methodology*. Beverly Hills, CA: Sage.

Kriz, Jürgen and Lisch, Ralf (1988) *Methodenlexikon*. München: Psychologie-Verlags-Union.

Krohn, Wolfgang and Küppers, Günter (1989) *Die Selbstorganisation der Wissenschaft*. Frankfurt: Suhrkamp.

Kromrey, Helmut (1994) 'Strategien des Informationsmanagements in der Sozialforschung', *Angewandte Sozialforschung*, 18: 163–83.

Labov, William and Waletzky, Joshua (1967) 'Narrative analysis: oral versions of personal experience', in J. Helm (ed.), *Essays on the Verbal and Visual Arts*. Proceedings of the 1966 Annual Spring Meeting of the American Ethnological Society. Seattle: University of Washington Press for the American Ethnological Society, pp. 12–44.

Lalouschek, Johanna, Menz, Florian and Wodak, Ruth (1990) *Alltag in der Ambulanz. Gespräche zwischen Ärzten, Schwestern und Patienten*. Tübingen: Narr.

Lamnek, Siegfried (1988) *Qualitative Sozialforschung*, Vol. 1: Methodologie. München: Psychologie-Verlags-Union.

Lamnek, Siegfried (1989) *Qualitative Sozialforschung*, Vol. 2: Methoden und Techniken. München: Psychologie-Verlags-Union.

Lasswell, Harold D. (1941) *Describing the Contents of Communication. Experimental Division for the Study of Wartime Communication*. Vol. 9. Washington, DC: Library of Congress.

Lasswell, Harold D. (1946) 'Describing the contents of communication', in B.L. Smith, H.D. Lasswell and R.D. Casey (eds), *Propaganda, Communication and Public Opinion*. Princeton, NJ: Princeton University Press, pp. 74–94.

Lazarsfeld, Paul, Berelson, Bernhard and Gaudet, Hazel (1955) *The People's Choice. How the Voter Makes up his Mind in a Presidential Campaign*, 2nd edn. New York: Columbia University Press.

Lee, Penny (1996) *The Whorf Theory Complex. A Critical Reconstruction*. Amsterdam: Benjamins.

Lee, Raymond M. and Fielding, Nigel (1996) 'Qualitative data analysis: representations of a technology: a comment on Coffey, Holbrook and Atkinson', *Sociological Research Online*, 1(4). http://www.socreonline.org.uk/socreonline

Leithäuser, Thomas, Volmerg, Birgit, Salje, Gunther, Volmerg, Ute and Wutka, Berhard (1977) *Entwurf zu einer Empirie des Alltagsbewußtseins*. Frankfurt: Suhrkamp.

Lemke, Jay L. (1995) *Textual Politics. Discourse and Social Dynamics*. London: Taylor & Francis.

Lepenies, Wolf (ed.) (1981) *Geschichte der Soziologie: Studien zur kognitiven, sozialen und historischen Identität einer Disziplin*. Frankfurt: Suhrkamp.

Levinson, Stephen C. (1983) *Pragmatics*. Cambridge: Cambridge University Press.

Lewin, Kurt (1951) *Field Theory in Social Science*. New York: Harper & Brothers.

Lindzey, Gardner and Aronson, Elliot (eds) (1968) *The Handbook of Social Psychology*, 2nd edn. Vol. 2: Research Methods. Reading: Addison-Wesley.

Lindzey, Gardner and Aronson, Elliot (eds) (1985) *The Handbook of Social Psychology*, 3rd edn. Vol. 2: Research Methods. Reading: Addison-Wesley.

Lisch, Ralf and Kriz, Jürgen (1978) *Grundlagen und Modelle der Inhaltsanalyse*. Reinbek: Rowohlt.

Lobel, Sharon A. (1989) 'Inhaltsanalysen von Tiefeninterviews', in J. F. Schneider (ed.), *Inhaltsanalyse alltagssprachlicher Beschreibungen sozialer Interaktionen*. Beiträge zur SYMLOG-Kodierung von Texten. Saarbrücken-Scheidt: Dadder, pp. 67–87.

Lucy, John (1992) *Grammatical Categories and Cognition. A Case Study of the Linguistic Relativity Hypothesis*. Cambridge: Cambridge University Press.

Luhmann, Niklas (1981) *Soziologische Aufklärung*, Vol. 3. Opladen: Westdeutscher Verlag.

Luhmann, Niklas (1984) *Soziale Systeme*. Frankfurt: Suhrkamp.

Luhmann, Niklas (1990a) *Die Wissenschaft der Gesellschaft*. Frankfurt: Suhrkamp.

Luhmann, Niklas (1990b) *Soziologische Aufklärung*, Vol. 5: Konstruktivistische Perspektiven. Opladen: Westdeutscher Verlag.

Luhmann, Niklas (1995) 'Was ist Kommunikation?', in N. Luhmann, *Soziologische Aufklärung*, Vol. 6. Opladen: Westdeutscher Verlag, pp. 113–24.

Lutz, Benedikt and Wodak, Ruth (1987) *Information für Informierte. Linguistische Studien zu Verständlichkeit und Verstehen von Hörfunknachrichten*. Wien: Akademie der Wissenschaften.

Lyons, John (ed.) (1970) *New Horizons in Linguistics*. Harmondsworth: Penguin.

Maag, Gisela (1989) 'Zur Erfassung von Werten in der Umfrageforschung', *Zeitschrift für Soziologie*, 18: 313–23.

Maas, Utz (1984) '*Als der Geist der Gemeinschaft eine Sprache fand'. Sprache im Nationalsozialismus. Versuch einer historischen Argumentationsanalyse*. Opladen: Westdeutscher Verlag.

Maas, Utz (1988) 'Probleme und Traditionen der Diskursanalyse', *Zeitschrift für Phonetik, Sprachwissenschaft und Kommunikationsforschung*, 41 (6): 717–29.

Mach, Ernst (1968) [1905] *Erkenntnis und Irrtum. Skizzen zur Psychologie der Forschung*. Darmstadt: Wissenschaftliche Buchgesellschaft [zuerst Leipzig].

Macheiner, Judith (1991) *Das grammatische Varieté oder die Kunst und das Vergnügen, deutsche Sätze zu bilden*. Frankfurt: Eichborn.

Maingueneau, Dominique (1987) *Nouvelles tendances en Analyse du Discours*. Paris: Hachette.

Maisel, Richard and Persell, Caroline Hodges (1996) *How Sampling Works*. Thousand Oaks, CA: Pine Forge.

Malinowski, Bronislaw (1966) [1935] *Coral Gardens and their Magic*, Vol. 2: The Language of Magic and Gardening. London: Bloomington [New York: American].

Malmkjaer, Kirsten (ed.) (1991a) *The Linguistics Encyclopedia*. London: Routledge.

Malmkjaer, Kirsten (1991b) 'Discourse and conversational analysis', in K. Malmkjaer (ed.), *The Linguistics Encyclopedia*. London: Routledge, pp. 100–10.

Malmkjaer, Kirsten (1991c) 'Systemic grammar', in K. Malmkjaer (ed.), *The Linguistics Encyclopedia*. London: Routledge, pp. 447–52.

Manning, Peter K. and Cullum-Swan, Betsy (1994) 'Narrative, content, and semiotic analysis', in N.K. Denzin and Y.S. Lincoln (eds), *Handbook of Qualitative Research*. Thousand Oak, CA: Sage, pp. 463–77.

Mathes, Rainer (1992) 'Hermeneutisch-klassifikatorische Inhaltsanalyse von Leitfadengesprächen. Über das Verhältnis von quantitativen und qualitativen Verfahren der Textanalyse und die Möglichkeit ihrer Kombination', in J.H.P. Hoffmeyer-Zlotnik (ed.), *Analyse verbaler Daten*. Opladen: Westdeutscher Verlag, pp. 402–24.

Matouschek, Bernd and Wodak, Ruth (1995/96) 'Diskurssoziolinguistik. Theorien, Methoden und Fallanalysen der diskurs-historischen Methode am Beispiel von Ausgrenzungsdiskursen', in *Wiener Linguistische Gazette*, 55–6, pp. 34–71.

Matouschek, Bernd, Wodak, Ruth and Januschek, Franz (1995) *Notwendige Maßnahmen gegen Fremde?: Genese und Formen von rassistischen Diskursen der Differenz*. Wien: Passagen.

Matthiesen, Ulf (1994) 'Standbein-Spielbein. Deutungsmusteranalysen im Spannungsfeld zwischen objektiver Hermeneutik und Sozialphänomenologie', in D. Garz (ed.), *Die Welt als Text*. Frankfurt: Suhrkamp, pp. 73–113.

Mayring, Philip (1988) *Qualitative Inhaltsanalyse. Grundlagen und Techniken*. Weinheim: Deutscher Studienverlag.

Mayring, Philip (1991) 'Qualitative Inhaltsanalyse', in U. Flick, E. von. Kardorff, H. Keupp, L. von. Rosenstiel and S. Wolff (eds), *Handbuch Qualitative Sozialforschung*. München: Psychologie-Verlags-Union, pp. 209–13.

McClelland, David C., Atkinson, John W., Clark, Russell A. and Lowell, Edgar L. (1953) *The Achievement Motive*. New York: Appleton Century Crofts.

Mead, George H. (1938a) *The Philosophy of the Act*. Chicago, IL: University of Chicago Press.

Mead, George H. (1938b) *Mind, Self, and Society*. Chicago, IL: University of Chicago Press.

Meinefeld, Werner (1997) 'Ex-ante Hypothesen in der Qualitativen Sozialforschung: zwischen "fehl am Platz" und "unverzichtbar"', *Zeitschrift für Sozialforschung*, 26: 22–34.

Menz, Florian (1991) *Der geheime Dialog: medizinische Ausbildung und institutional-isierte Verschleierungen in der Arzt-Patient-Kommunikation; eine diskursanalytische Studie*. Frankfurt: Lang.

Merten, Klaus (1983) *Inhaltsanalyse. Einführung in Theorie, Methode und Praxis*. Opladen: Westdeutscher Verlag.

Meulemann, Heiner and Elting-Camus, Agnes (eds) (1993) *Lebensverhältnisse und soziale Konflikte im neuen Europa, Sektionen, Arbeits- und Ad hoc-Gruppen.* 26. Deutscher Soziologentag. Opladen: Westdeutscher Verlag.

Mey, Jacob (1985) *Whose Language?* Philadelphia, PA: Benjamins.

Mey, Jacob (1993) *Pragmatics: An Introduction.* Oxford: Blackwell.

Ming-Yulh, Tsay (1995) 'The impact of the concept of post-industrial society and information-society: a citation analysis study', *Scientometrics, 33:* 329–50.

Moi, Toril (ed.) (1986) *The Kristeva Reader.* New York: Columbia University Press.

Moreno, Jacob L. (1953) *Who Shall Survive? Foundation of Sociometry, Group Psychotherapy and Sociodrama.* New York: Beacon House.

Morris, Charles (1938) *Foundations of a Theory of Signs.* Chicago, IL: University of Chicago Press.

Morris, Charles (1946) *Signs, Language and Behavior.* New York: Prentice Hall.

Motsch, Werner (ed.) (1987) *Satz, Text, sprachliche Handlung.* Berlin: Akad. Verlag.

Muhr, Thomas (1991) 'ATLAS/ti – a prototype for the support of text interpretation', *Qualitative Sociology,* 14 (4): 349–71.

Muhr, Thomas (1994) 'ATLAS/ti: Ein Werkzeug für die Textinterpretation', in Andreas Böhm, Andreas Mengel and Thomas Muhr (eds), *Texte verstehen. Konzepte, Methoden, Werkzeuge. Schriften zur Informationswissenschaft,* Konstanz: Universitätsverlag, pp. 317–24.

Mullins, Nicholas C. (1973) Theory and Theory Groups in Contemporary American Sociology. New York: HarperCollins.

Mullins, Nicholas C. (1981) 'Ethnomethodologie. Das Spezialgebiet, das aus der Kälte kam', in Wolf Lepenies (ed.), *Geschichte der Soziologie: Studien zur kognitiven, sozialen und historischen Identität einer Disziplin.* Frankfurt: Suhrkamp. pp. 97–136.

Oevermann, Ulrich (1983) 'Zur Sache. Die Bedeutung von Adornos methodologischem Selbstverständnis für die Begründung einer materialen soziologischen Strukturanalyse', in Ludwig von Friedeburg and Jürgen Habermas (eds), *Adorno Konferenz 1983.* Frankfurt: Suhrkamp, pp. 234–89.

Oevermann, Ulrich (1993) 'Die objektive Hermeneutik als unverzichtbare methodologische Grundlage für die Analyse von Subjektivität. Zugleich eine Kritik der Tiefenhermeneutik', in Thomas Jung and Stefan Müller-Doohm (eds), *'Wirklichkeit' im Deutungsprozeß. Verstehen in den Kultur- und Sozialwissenschaften.* Frankfurt: Suhrkamp, pp. 106–189.

Oevermann, Ulrich (1996) 'Becketts "Endspiel" als Prüfstein hermeneutischer Methodologie. Eine Interpretation mit den Verfahren der objektiven Hermeneutik (Oder: Ein objektiv-hermeneutisches Exerzitium)', in Hans-Dieter König (ed.), *Neue Versuche, Becketts Endspiel zu verstehen. Sozialwissenschaftliches Interpretieren nach Adorno.* Frankfurt: Suhrkamp, pp. 93–249.

Oevermann, Ulrich, Allert, Tilman, Konau, Elisabeth and Krambeck, Jürgen (1979) 'Die Methodologie einer "objektiven Hermeneutik" und ihre allgemeine forschungslogische Bedeutung in den Sozialwissenschaften', in Hans-Georg Soeffner (ed.), *Interpretative Verfahren in den Sozial- und Textwissenschaften.* Stuttgart: Metzler, pp. 352–434.

Oevermann Ulrich, Allert, Tilman, Konau, Elisabeth and Krambeck, Jürgen (1983) 'Die Methodologie der objektiven Hermeneutik', in Peter Zedler and Heinz Moser (eds), *Aspekte qualitativer Sozialforschung. Studien zu Aktionsforschung, empirischer Hermeneutik und reflexiver Sozialtechnologie.* Opladen: Westdeutscher Verlag, pp. 95–123.

Orlik, Peter (1987) 'Ein semantischer Atlas zur Codierung alltagssprachlicher Beschreibungen nach dem SYMLOG-Raummodell', *International Journal of Small Group Research, 3:* 88–111.

Orlik, Peter and Schario, Reinhild (1989) 'Die Analyse sozialer Interaktionsfelder in der Romanliteratur', in Johannes F. Schneider (ed.), *Inhaltsanalyse alltagssprachlicher Beschreibungen sozialer Interaktionen. Beiträge zur SYMLOG-Kodierung von Texten.* Saarbrücken-Scheidt: Dadder, pp. 19–51.

Osgood, Charles E. (1959) 'The representational model and relevant research methods', in Ithiel de Sola Pool (ed.), *Trends in Content Analysis.* Urbana: University of Illinois Press, pp. 33–88.

Osgood, Charles E., Saporta, Sol and Nunnally, Jum (1954) *Evaluation Assertive Analysis.* Chicago, IL: University of Chicago Press.

Parsons, Talcott (1951a) *The Social System.* Glencoe, IL: The Free Press.

Parsons, Talcott (1951b) *Toward a General Theory of Action.* Cambridge, MA: Harvard University Press.

Peirce, Charles S. (1958–67) *Collected Papers Vol. 1–8.* Cambridge, MA: Harvard Harvard University Press.

Pennycook, Alistair (1994) 'Incommensurable discourses?', *Applied Linguistics*, 15 (2): 115–37.

Petöfi, János S. (1971) 'Probleme der kotextuellen Analyse von Texten', in Jens Ihwe (ed.), *Literaturwissenschaft und Linguistik. Ergebnisse und Perspektiven.* Bad Homburg v. d. H.: Gehlen, pp. 173–212.

Phillipsen, Gerry (1992) *Speaking Culturally.* New York: State University Press.

Pittenger, Robert E., Hockett, Charles F. and Danehy, John J. (1960) *The First Five Minutes. A Sample of Microscopic Interview Analysis.* Ithaca, NY: Martineau.

Projektteam 'Sprache und Vorurteil' (1989) *'Wir sind alle unschuldige Täter!' Studien zum antisemitischen Diskurs im Nachkriegsösterreich.* 2 Vol., Endbericht, unpublished.

Projektteam (1996) 'Identitátswandel Österrichs im reränderten Europa', Endbericht, unpublished.

Propp, Vladimir I. (1958) [1928] *Morphology of the Folktale.* The Hague: Mouton.

Psathas, George (ed.) (1979) *Everyday Language. Studies in Ethnomethodology.* New York: Irvington.

Redder, Angelika (ed.) (1983) *Kommunikation in Institutionen.* Osnabrücker Beiträge zur Sprachtheorie, 24.

Redder, Angelika (1984) *Modalverben im Unterrichtsdiskurs. Zur Pragmatik der Modalverben am Beispiel eines institutionellen Diskurses.* Tübingen: Niemeyer.

Redder, Angelika (1990) *Grammatiktheorie und sprachliches Handeln: 'denn' und 'da'.* Tübingen: Niemeyer.

Redder, Angelika (1994) '"Bergungsunternehmen" – Prozeduren des Malfeldes beim Erzählen', in Gisela Brünner and Gabriele Graefen (eds), *Texte und Diskurse.* Opladen: Westdeutscher Verlag, pp. 238–64.

Rehbein, Jochen (1977) *Komplexes Handeln. Elemente zur Handlungstheorie der Sprache.* Stuttgart: Metzler.

Rehbein, Jochen (1984) 'Beschreiben, Berichten und Erzählen', in Konrad Ehlich (ed.), *Erzählen in der Schule.* Tübingen: Narr, pp. 7–41.

Rehbein, Jochen (1988) 'Ausgewählte Aspekte der Pragmatik', in Ulrich Ammon, Norbert Dittmar and Klaus Mattheier (eds), *Sociolinguistics. An International Handbook of the Science of Language and Society. Soziolinguistik*, Vol. 2. Berlin and New York: de Gruyter, pp. 1181–95.

Rehbein, Jochen (ed.) (1997) *Funktionale Pragmatik im Spektrum.* Opladen: Westdeutscher Verlag.

Reichertz, Jo (1994) 'Von Gipfeln und Tälern. Bemerkungen zu einigen Gefahren, die den objektiven Hermeneuten erwarten', in Detlef Garz and Klaus Kraimer (eds), *Die Welt als Text.* Frankfurt: Suhrkamp, pp. 125–52.

Reichertz, Jo (1995) 'Die objektive Hermeneutik – Darstellung und Kritik', in Eckhard König and Peter Zedler (eds), *Bilanz qualitativer Forschung*, Vol. II: Methoden. Weinheim: Deutscher Studienverlag, pp. 379–423.

Reichertz, Jo and Schröer, Norbert (1994) 'Erheben, Auswerten, Darstellen. Konturen einer hermeneutischen Wissenssoziologie', in Norbert Schröer (ed.), *Interpretative Sozialforschung*. Opladen: Westdeutscher Verlag, pp. 56–84.

Reisigl, Martin (1999) *Wie man eine Nation herbeiredet*. Dissertation Universitaet Wien.

Reisigl, Martin and Wodak, Ruth (1999) '"Austria first": a discourse-historical analysis of the Austrian "Anti-Foreigner-Petition" in 1993', in Martin Reisigl and Ruth Wodak (eds), *The Semiotics of Racism*. Vienna: Passagenverlag.

Renkema, Jan (1993) *Discourse Studies. An Introductory Textbook*. Amsterdam: Benjamins.

Richards, Tom and Richards, Lyn (1991) 'The NUDIST qualitative data analysis system', *Qualitative Sociology*, 14 (4): 307–24.

Ricoeur, Paul (1992) *Oneself as Another*. Chicago, IL: University of Chicago Press.

Ritsert, Jürgen (1972) *Inhaltsanalyse und Ideologiekritik. Ein Versuch über kritische Sozialforschung*. Frankfurt: Athenäum.

Sacks, Harvey (1971) 'Das Erzählen von Geschichten innerhalb von Unterhaltungen', in R Kjolseth and F. Sack (eds) *Zur Soziologie der sprache*. KZfS 1971, sonderheft 15, pp. 307–14.

Sacks, Harvey (1972a) 'An initial investigation of the usability of conversational data for doing sociology', in David Sudnow (ed.), *Studies in Social Interaction*. New York: Free Press, pp. 31–73.

Sacks, Harvey (1972b) 'On the analysability of stories by children', in John J. Gumperz and Dell Hymes (eds), *Directions in Sociolinguistics. The Ethnography of Communication*. New York: Holt, Rinehart and Winston, pp. 325–45.

Sacks, Harvey (1974) 'On the Analysability of Stories by Children', in R. Turner (ed.), *Ethnomethodolgy*: Harmondsworth: Penguin. pp. 216–32.

Sacks, Harvey (1984) 'Notes on methodology', in J. Maxwell Atkinson and John C. Heritage (eds), *Structures of Social Action. Studies in Conversation Analysis*. Cambridge: Cambridge University Press, pp. 21–7.

Sacks, Harvey (1985) 'The interference-making machine: notes on observability', in Teun A. van Dijk (ed.), *Handbook of Discourse Analysis*, Vol. 3: Discourse and Dialogue. London: Academic Press, pp. 13–23.

Sacks, Harvey (1992a, 1992b), *Lectures on Conversation*. 2 Vols, Gail Jefferson (ed.). Cambridge: Blackwell.

Sacks, Harvey and Schegloff, Emanuel A. (1979) 'Two preferences in the organization of reference to persons in conversation and their interaction', in George Psathas (ed.), *Everyday Language. Studies in Ethnomethodology*. New York: Irvington, pp. 15–21.

Sacks, Harvey, Schegloff, Emanuel A. and Jefferson, Gail (1978) 'A simplest systematics for the organization of turn taking for conversation', in Jim Schenkein (ed.), *Studies in the Organization of Conversational Interaction*. New York: Academic Press, pp. 7–55.

Sandig, Barbara and Rothkegel, Annely (eds) (1984) *Text–Textsorten–Semantik: linguistische Modelle und maschinelle Verfahren*. Hamburg: Buske.

Saville-Troike, Muriel (1987) 'The ethnography of speaking', in Ulrich Ammon, N. Dittmar and K.J. Mattheier (eds), *Sociolinguistics. An International Handbook of Science of Language*, Vol .1. Berlin and New York: de Gruyter, pp. 660–71.

Saville-Troike, Muriel (1989) *The Ethnography of Communication. An Introduction*, 2nd edn. Oxford: Blackwell.

Schegloff, Emanuel A. (1987) 'Between micro and macro: contexts and other connections', in Jeffrey Alexander (ed.), *The Micro-Macro Link*. Berkeley: University of California Press, pp.207–34.

Schegloff, Emanuel A. (1992) 'On talk and its institutional occasions', in Paul Drew and John Heritage, *Talk at Work: Interaction in Institutional Settings*. Cambridge: Cambridge University Press, pp. 101–34.

Schegloff, Emanuel A. (1998) 'Text and context paper', *Discourse & Society* 3: 4–37.

Schegloff, Emanuel A. and Sacks, Harvey (1973) 'Opening up closings', *Semiotica*, 8: 289–327.

Schegloff, Emanuel A., Jefferson, Gail and Sacks, Harvey (1977) 'The preference for self-correction in the organization of repair in conversation', *Language*, 53: 361–82.

Schenkein, Jim (ed.) (1978a) *Studies in the Organization of Conversational Interaction*. New York: Academic Press.

Schenkein, Jim (1978b) 'Sketch of an analytic mentality for the study of conversational interaction', in Jim Schenkein (ed.), *Studies in the Organization of Conversational Interaction*. New York: Academic Press, pp. 1–6.

Schiffrin, Deborah (1994) *Approaches to Discourse*. Oxford: Blackwell.

Schlobinski, Peter (1996) *Empirische Sprachwissenschaft*. Opladen: Westdeutscher Verlag.

Schmidt, Siegfried, J. (1992) 'Über die Rolle von Selbstorganisation beim Sprachverstehen', in Wolfgang Krohn und Günter Küppers (eds), *Emergenz: Die Entstehung von Ordnung, Organisation und Bedeutung*. Frankfurt: Suhrkamp, pp 293–333.

Schneider, Johannes F. (ed.) (1989) *Inhaltsanalyse alltagssprachlicher Beschreibungen sozialer Interaktionen. Beiträge zur SYMLOG-Kodierung von Texten*. Saarbrücken-Scheidt: Dadder.

Schoepflin, Urs (1993) '*Bibliometrische Analysen der Entwicklung einer Disziplin: Zur Geschichte der Soziologie*', in Heiner Meulemann and Agnes Elting-Camus (eds), *Lebensverhältnisse und soziale Konflikte im neuen Europa*, 26. Deutscher Soziologentag, Sektionen, Arbeits- und Ad hoc-Gruppen. Opladen: Westdeutscher Verlag, pp. 566–7.

Schramm, Wilbur (1954) *The Process and Effects of Mass Communication*. Urbana: University of Illinois Press.

Schröder, Peter and Steger, Hugo (eds) (1981), *Dialogforschung*. Jahrbuch 1980 des Instituts für Deutsche Sprache. Düsseldorf: Schwann.

Schröer, Norbert (eds) (1994) *Interpretative Sozialforschung*. Opladen: Westdeutscher Verlag.

Schuster, Gudrun (1994) 'Die objektive Hermeneutik nach Oevermann', in Arbeitskreis Qualitative Sozialforschung (eds), *Verführung zum qualitativen Forschen*. Wien: WUV-Universitätsverlag, pp. 101–15.

Schütz, Alfred (1932) *That's not what I meant,* New York: Morrow.

Searle, John R. (1969) *Speech Acts. An Essay in the Philosophy of Language*. Cambridge: Cambridge University Press.

Searle, John R. (1982) [1979] *Ausdruck und Bedeutung. Untersuchungen zur Sprechakttheorie*. Frankfurt: Suhrkamp. [*Expression and Meaning. Studies in the Theory of Speech Acts*. Cambridge: University Press.]

Shannon, Claude E. and Weaver, Warren (1949) *The Mathematical Theory of Communication*. Urbana: University of Illinois Press.

Shi-xu (1996) *Cultural Representations. Understanding Chinese and Dutch Discourse about the Other*. Universität Amsterdam: Dissertation.

Silbermann, Alphons (1974) 'Systematische Inhaltsanalyse', in René König (ed.),

Handbuch der empirischen Sozialforschung, Vol. 4: Komplexe Forschungsansätze. Stuttgart: Enke, pp. 253–339.

Silverman, David (1993) *Interpreting Qualitative Data. Methods for Analysing Talk, Text and Interaction.* London: Sage.

Silverman, David (ed.) (1997) *Qualitative Research*, London: Sage.

Sirkin, R. Mark (1995) *Statistics for the Social Sciences*, London: Sage.

Smith, Bruce L., Lasswell, Harold D. and Casey, Ralph D. (eds) (1946) *Propaganda, Communication and Public Opinion.* Princeton, NJ: Princeton University Press.

Soeffner, Hans-Georg (eds) (1979) *Interpretative Verfahren in den Sozial- und Textwissenschaften.* Stuttgart: Metzler.

Spencer Brown, George (1979) [1969] *Laws of Form.* New York: Dutton.

Sperber, Dan and Wilson, Deidre (1986) *Relevance, Communication, and Cognition.* Oxford: Blackwell.

SSCI® Social Sciences Citation Index® (1994) SSCI User Guide, ISI® CD Editions, Version 3.05 Upgrade, 12/94.

Stock, Wolfgang G. (1995) 'Wissenschaftsevaluation mittels Datenbanken–methodisch einwandfrei?', *Spektrum der Wissenschaft*, Nov.: 118–21.

Straehle, Carolyn, Wodak, Ruth, Weiss, Gilbert, Muntigl, Peter and Sedlak, Maria (1999) 'Struggle as metaphor in European Union discourses on unemployment', *Discourse and Society*, 10 (1): 67–100.

Strauss, Anselm (1987) *Qualitative Analysis for Social Scientists.* Cambridge: Cambridge University Press

Strauss, Anselm and Corbin, Juliet (1990) *Basics of Qualitative Research.* Newbury Park, CA: Sage.

Strauss, Anselm and Corbin, Juliet (1994) 'Grounded theory methodology: an overview', in Norman K. Denzin and Yvonna S. Lincoln (eds), *Handbook of Qualitative Research.* Thousand Oak, CA: Sage, pp. 273–85.

Strauss, Anselm and Corbin, Juliet M. (eds) (1997) *Grounded Theory in Practice.* Thousand Oak, CA: Sage.

Streeck, Jürgen (1983) 'Konversationsanalyse: Ein Reparaturversuch', *Zeitschrift für Sprachwissenschaft,* 2: 72–104.

Streeck, Jürgen (1987) 'Ethnomethodologie', in Ulrich Ammon, Norbert Dittmar and Klaus Mattheier (eds), *Sociolinguistics. An International Handbook of the Science of Language and Society.* Soziolinguistik. Ein internationales Handbuch zur Wissenschaft von Sprache und Gesellschaft: Vol. 1. Berlin de Gruyter, pp. 672–9.

Sturm, Gabriele (1989) 'Strukturanalyse persönlicher Konstruktsysteme von Erstgebärenden', in Johannes F. Schneider (ed.), *Inhaltsanalyse alltagssprachlicher Beschreibungen sozialer Interaktionen. Beiträge zur SYMLOG-Kodierung von Texten.* Saarbrücken-Scheidt: Dadder, pp. 89–108.

Sudman, Seymor (1976) *Applied Sampling.* New York: Academic Press.

Sudnow, David (ed.) (1972) *Studies in Social Interaction.* New York: The Free Press.

Swales, John M. (1991) *Genre Analysis. English in Academic and Research Settings.* Cambridge: Cambridge University Press.

Tannen, Deborah (1986) 'That's Not What I Meant! New York: Morrow.

Tellis, Winston (1997a) 'Introduction to case study', *The Qualitative Report*, 3 (2) [http://www.nova.edu/ssss/QR/QR3–2/tellis1.html] August 1999.

Tellis, Winston (1997b) 'Application of a case study methodology', *The Qualitative Report*, 3 (3) [http://www.nova.edu/ssss/QR/QR3–3/tellis2.html] August 1999.

Thorngate, Warren (1976) '"In general" vs. "it depends": some comments on the Gergen-Schlenker debate', *Personality and Social Psychology Bulletin*, 2: 404–10.

Titscher, Stefan (1995a) 'Das Normogramm', *Zeitschrift für Soziologie*, 24: 115–36.

Titscher, Stefan (1995b) 'Kommunikation als Führungsinstrument', in Alfred Kieser, Gerhard Reber and Rudolf Wunderer (eds), *Handwörterbuch der Führung*, 2nd edn. Stuttgart: Poeschel, pp. 1309–18.

Titzmann, Michael (1977) *Strukturale Textanalyse*. München: Fink.

Turner, Roy (ed.) (1974) *Ethnomethodology*. Harmondsworth: Penguin.

van Dijk, Teun A. (1977) *Text and Context. Explorations in the Semantics and Pragmatics of Discourse*. London: Longman.

van Dijk, Teun A. (1980) *Textwissenschaft. Eine interdisziplinäre Einführung*. München: DTV.

van Dijk, Teun A. (1984) *Prejudice in Discourse*. Amsterdam: Benjamins.

van Dijk, Teun A. (ed.) (1985a) *Handbook of Discourse Analysis*, Vol. 1: Disciplines of Discourse. London: Academic Press.

van Dijk, Teun A. (ed.) (1985b) *Handbook of Discourse Analysis*, Vol. 2: Dimensions of Discourse. London: Academic Press.

van Dijk, Teun A. (ed.) (1985c) *Handbook of Discourse Analysis*, Vol. 3: Discourse and Dialogue. London: Academic Press.

van Dijk, Teun A. (ed.) (1990a) *Discourse Analysis in the 90s*. Special issue of TEXT.

van Dijk, Teun A. (1990b) 'Social cognition and discourse', in Howard Giles and William P. Robinson (eds), *Handbook of Language and Social Psychology*. New York: Wiley, pp. 163–86.

van Dijk, Teun A. (1993) 'Editor's foreword to Critical Discourse Analysis', *Discourse & Society*, 4 (2): 131–2.

van Dijk, Teun A. (ed.) (1997) *Discourse and Interaction*. London: Sage.

van Leeuwen, Theo (1993) 'Genre and fields in critical discourse analysis: a synopsis', *Discourse & Society* 4 (2): 193–223.

van Leeuwen, Theo and Wodak, Ruth (1999) 'Legitimizing Immigration Control: A discourse-historical analysis', *Discourse Studies*, 1(1): 83–118.

van Raan, Antony F.J. (1994) 'Assessment of research performance with bibliometric methods', in Heinrich Best (ed.), *Informations- und Wissenverarbeitung in den Sozialwissenschaften*. Opladen: Westdeutscher Verlag, pp. 499–524.

Vass, Elisa (1992) *Diskursanalyse als interdisziplinäres Forschungsgebiet*. Universität Wien: Diplomarbeit.

Verschueren, Jef, Östman, Jan-Ola and Blommaert, Jan (eds) (1995) *Handbook of Pragmatics. Manual*. Amsterdam: Benjamins.

Vogt, Rudolf (ed.) (1987a) *Über die Schwierigkeit des Verständigens beim Reden: Beiträge zu einer Linguistik des Diskurses*. Opladen: Westdeutscher Verlag.

Vogt, Rudolf (1987b) 'Zwei Modelle zur Analyse von Diskursen', in Rudolf Vogt (ed.), *Über die Schwierigkeit des Verständigens beim Reden: Beiträge zu einer Linguistik des Diskurses*. Opladen: Westdeutscher Verlag, pp. 3–34.

Volosinov, Valentin N. (1975) [1929] *Marxismus und Sprachphilosophie*. Grundlegende Probleme der soziologischen Methode in der Sprachwissenschaft. Frankfurt: Ullstein.

von Aleman, H. and Ortlieb, P. (1975) 'Die Einzelfallstudie', in J. van Koolwijk and M. Wieken-Mayser (eds), *Techniken der empirischen Sozialforschung*, Vol. 2. München: Oldenbourg, pp. 157–77.

von Friedeburg, Ludwig and Habermas, Jürgen (eds) (1983) *Adorno Konferenz 1983*. Frankfurt: Suhrkamp.

Waugh, Linda R. (1982) 'Marked and unmarked: a choice between unequals in semiotic structure', *Semiotica*, 38 (3): 299–318.

Weber, Robert Philip (1990) *Basic Content Analysis*. 2nd ed. Newbury Park: Sage.

Weick, Karl (1979) *The Social Psychology of Organizing*, 2nd edn. Reading: Addison Wesley.

Weiner, Bernhard (1986) *An Attributional Theory of Motivation and Emotion.* New York: Springer.

Weiss, Gilbert and Wodak, Ruth (1999a) 'Debating Europe: Globalization rhetoric and European Union employment policies', in Irene Bellier (ed.), *European Identities.* Boulder, CO: Westview Press.

Weiss, Gilbert and Wodak, Ruth (1999b) *The EU Committee Regime and the Problem of Public Space. Strategies of Depoliticizing Unemployment and Ideologizing Employment Policies.* (forthcoming).

Weitzman, Eben A. and Miles, Mathew B. (1995) *Computer Programs for Qualitative Data Analysis.* Thousand Oaks: Sage.

Werner, Oswald and Bernard, H. Russell (1994) 'Ethnographic sampling', *Cultural Anthropology Methods* (CAM), 6 (2): June. [http://www.lawrence.edu/fac/bradl-eyc/ossie.html] August 1999.

Wersig, Gernot (1968) *Inhaltsanalyse. Einführung in ihre Systematik und Literatur. Schriftenreihe zur Publizistikwissenschaft* vol. 5. Berlin: Volker Spiess.

Widdowson, Henry G. (1995) 'Discourse analysis: a critical view', *Language and Literature,* 4 (3): 157–72.

Wiedemann, Peter (1991) 'Gegenstandbezogene Theoriebildung', in Uwe Flick, Ernst von Kardorff, Heiner Keupp, Lutz v. Rostenstiel and Stephan Wolff (eds), *Handbuch Qualitative Sozialforschung.* München: Psychologie-Verlags-Union, pp. 440–5.

Wilke, Stefanie (1992) *Die erste Begegnung. Eine konversations- und inhaltsanalytische Untersuchung der Interaktion im psychoanalytischen Erstgespräch.* Heidelberg: Asanger.

Willems, Herbert (1996) 'Goffman's qualitative Sozialforschung. Ein Vergleich mit Konversationsanalyse und Struktularer Hermeneutik', *Zeitschrift für Soziologie,* 25: 438–55.

Willis, Paul (1977) *Learning to Labour.* Columbia, NY: Columbia University Press.

Winterhager, Matthias (1994) 'Bibliometrische Basisdaten zur Entwicklung der Sozialwissenschaften in Deutschland', in Heinrich Best (ed.), *Informations- und Wissenverarbeitung in den Sozialwissenschaften.* Opladen: Westdeutscher Verlag, pp. 539–52.

Wittgenstein, Ludwig (1984) Werkausgabe Vol. 1: *Tractatus logico-philosophicus,* Tagebücher 1914–1916, Philosophische Untersuchungen. Frankfurt: Suhrkamp.

Wodak, Ruth (1981) *Das Wort in der Gruppe: linguistische Studien zur therapeutischen Kommunikation.* Wien: Verlag der Österreichischen Akademie der Wissenschaften.

Wodak, Ruth (1984) *Hilflose Nähe? Mütter und Töchter erzählen. Eine psycho- und soziolinguistische Untersuchung.* Wien: Deuticke.

Wodak, Ruth (1986) *Language Behavior in Therapy Groups.* Los Angeles: University of California Press.

Wodak, Ruth (1989) *Language, Power and Ideology.* Amsterdam: Benjamins.

Wodak, Ruth (1995) 'Critical linguistics and critical discourse analysis', in Jef Verschueren, Jan-Ola Östman and Jan Blommaert (eds), *Handbook of Pragmatics. Manual.* Amsterdam: Benjamins, pp. 204–10.

Wodak, Ruth (1996) *Disorders of Discourse.* London: Longman.

Wodak, Ruth and Benke, Gertraud (1997) 'Gender as a sociolinguistic variable: new perspectives on variation studies', in Florian Coulmas (ed.), *The Handbook of Sociolinguistics.* Oxford: Blackwell, pp. 127–50.

Wodak, Ruth and Matouschek, Bernd (1993) '"We are dealing with people whose origins one can clearly tell just by looking": critical discourse analysis and the study of neo'racism in contemporary Austria', *Discourse & Society,* 2 (4): 225–48.

Wodak, Ruth and Menz, Florian (eds) (1990) *Sprache in der Politik–Politik in der Sprache. Analysen zum öffentlichen Sprachgebrauch.* Klagenfurt: Drava.

Wodak, Ruth and Reisigl, Martin (1999) *Discourse and Discrimination. The Rhetorics of Racism and Antisemitism.* London: Routledge.

Wodak, Ruth and Schulz, Muriel (1986) *The Language of Love and Guilt. Mother–Daughter Relationships from a Cross-Cultural Perspective.* Amsterdam: Benjamins.

Wodak, Ruth and Vetter, Eva (1999) 'Competing professions in times of change: the discursive construction of professional identities in TV talk-shows', in R. Wodak and Chr. Ludwig (eds), *Challenges in a Changing World. Issues in Critical Discourse Analysis.* Wien: Passagen.

Wodak, Ruth, De Cillia, Rudolf, Blüml, Karl and Andraschko, Elisabeth (1989) *Sprache und Macht–Sprache und Politik.* Wien: Bundesverlag.

Wodak, Ruth, Nowak, Peter, Pelikan, Johanna, Gruber, Helmut, de Cillia, Rudolf and Mitten, Richard (1990) *'Wir sind alle unschuldige Täter!' Diskurshistorische Studien zum Nachkriegsantisemitismus.* Frankfurt: Suhrkamp.

Wodak, Ruth, Menz, Florian, Mitten, Richard and Stern, Frank (1994) *Die Sprachen der Vergangenheiten. Öffentliches Gedenken in österreichischen und deutschen Medien.* Frankfurt: Suhrkamp.

Wodak, Ruth, de Cillia, Rudolf, Reisigl, Martin, Liebhart, Karin, Kargl, Maria and Hofstaetter, Klaus (1998) *Zur diskursiven Konstruktion nationaler Identitaet,* Frankfurt: Suhrkamp (translated as Wodak, R., De Cillia, R., Reisigl, M. and Liebhart, K. (1999) *The Discursive Construction of National Identity.* Edinburgh: EUP).

Wunderlich, Dieter (ed.) (1972) *Linguistische Pragmatik.* Frankfurt: Athenäum.

Wunderlich, Dieter (1978) [1976] *Studien zur Sprechakttheorie,* 2nd edn. Frankfurt: Suhrkamp.

Yin, Robert K. (1993) *Applications of Case Study Research.* Newbury Park, CA: Sage.

Yin, Robert K. (1984) *Case Study Research: Design and Methods.* Beverly Hills, CA and London: Sage.

Zedler, Peter and Moser, Peter (eds) (1983) *Aspekte qualitativer Sozialforschung. Studien zu Aktionsforschung, empirischer Hermeneutik und reflexiver Sozialtechnologie.* Opladen: Westdeutscher Verlag.

INDEX

Page numbers in *italics* refer to figures, *g* denotes a glossary definition.